Rivulets of the Absolute

Rivulets of the Absolute
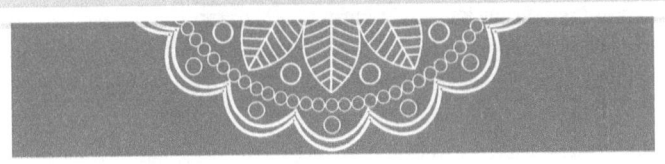

Copyrighted Material

Rivulets of the Absolute

Copyright © 2016 by Siddha Varma Healing, LLC. All Rights Reserved.

No part of this publication may be reproduced, stored in a retrieval system or transmitted, in any form or by any means—electronic, mechanical, photocopying, recording or otherwise—without prior written permission from the publisher, except for the inclusion of brief quotations in a review.

For information about this title or to order other books and/or electronic media, contact the publisher:
Siddha Varma Healing, LLC
vitalforcehealing@gmail.com
varmahealing.com

ISBN: 978-0-9971663-0-9 (print)
       978-0-9971663-1-6 (eBook)

Printed in the United States of America
Cover and Interior design: 1106 Design

The remedies as well as all spiritual practices detailed are not intended for self application or self practice, without proper initiation.

To the GURU,
who is truly this book's author,
scribe of my life, and
redeemer of my spirit.

"Our very presence is reflected everywhere and in everything. And everywhere and everything resonates in us. Springing from Itself and falling back on Itself; Creation, Sustenance, and Destruction end. There is no self at all."

—Siddha Healer Pal Pandian

Contents

Dedication	v
Blessings From the Master	xi
Preface	xv
Introduction	1
1. Appointment With Life	13
Bhagavan Sri Ramana Maharshi	21
Shocking Encounter	31
"A Siddha Healer"	33
The Tamil Siddhas	37
The Guru Relationship	40
2. The World of the Tamil Siddhas	51
Ancient Times	56
Siddha Chronicles	62
3. Mind, Body, and Spirit Health and Disease:	71
The Siddha Tradition's Perspective	74
Anatomy: Macrocosm and Microcosm	80

The Three Primary Qualities (Gunas) 84
The Five Elements (Mahabhutas) 85
Microcosm: Humoral Pathology 86
Vata-Pitta-Kapha 87
Anatomy of the Sages 93
Personality 93
The Five Sheaths 94

4. Learning the Art of Siddha Science 101
Varma—Vital Force 102
A Secret Science 104
Levels of Varma 107
Tridosha—A Diagnostic View 109
Energy: The Five Major Airs 113
The Precedence of Vasi 121
Vasi—God Within 125

5. The Nucleus of Siddha Tradition—Vasi 129
Essence of Healing Wisdom 134
Master-Student Relationship 135
My Master and I 138
Preparation for the Road Ahead 144
Adangal: A Paradoxical Practice 146

6. Siddha Tantra 151
Living in Darkness 151
The Door Opens 156
The Dark Underground 161
Two Paths of Tantra 165
Sri Chakra Upasana 167
Goddess Valai 170

7. Shadows of the Psyche 185
Rotten Things 185

Deities and Knots	187
Taking My Leave	188
The Healing Center	190
Unraveling the Knotted Mind	198
Daring the Turbulent Waters	206
8. The Abyss	211
Shadow Work Continues	219
9. Blossoming of the Tradition	227
Siddha Vasi – The Pinnacle of Yoga	230
The Quest of the Ancients	232
Striving Forth	237
Ancient Pollination	241
10. Nectar of the Absolute	251
Stepping Beyond Limitations	251
Amritha Kalai	254
Underlying Matrix	262
Nuances of Amritha Kalai	266
11. The Web of Life	269
The Feminine Psyche	277
The Inner Masculine	283
The Emergent Union	286
Dreaming of Navatri	289
12. Vasi: The Unique Path of the Siddhas	299
Vasi Yogam	304
The Fountainhead	306
Broken Identity	309
Reverberation	310
The Mother of Vital Forces	315

13. The Water of Life	*319*
Primal Matter	*319*
The Essence of Eternity	*324*
A Golden Glimpse	*326*
14. The Bitter Truth	*333*
Is This It?	*342*
The Spin of Oblivion	*346*
Locked in a Dream	*350*
Falling to the "Great Sleep"	*354*
The Path of the Awakened	*355*
Appendix	*361*
Siddha Tradition at Present	*361*
Guru Lineage	*363*
Family Lineage	*364*
Academic Setting	*366*
The Solution	*370*
Healer Pal and His Lineage	*372*
A Final Note	*376*
Glossary	*379*
Bibliography	*387*
Acknowledgments	*391*
About the Author	*395*

Blessings From the Master

Nowadays, not only is it hard to find a Master, but it is also hard to find a disciple. Even in Eastern countries, proper receptacles are scarce due to the modern-day lifestyle. This mechanical and acquisition-oriented approach shows itself in the many new-age trends. Steve is a rare disciple, gifted with humble receptivity and a genuine learning spirit. Ancient Tamil Siddha tradition is not commonly available even in its region of origin, as it demands a courageous mind, free of prejudice. Why would a courageous mind be required? In my Siddha lineage, we do not offer any theory before or alongside the practices we teach. The purpose of this is that the practitioner should arrive at the theory by way of his own insightful experiences during the journey of the practice. Of course, the mind is always afraid of treading in the dark, for the dark is an unknown path—as if one were traveling without a map. One should be aware of his own proprioceptive language and learn to rely upon the inner guru. This is our way.

Steve's surrendering heart and his trust in me have allowed him to make this journey steadfastly. The vital principle of the Siddha system that differentiates it from other spiritual paths is the quality of feeling the divine in day-to-day life, what my lineage refers to as fusion of the Absolute in the Temporal. Most other spiritual paths teach how to dissolve into the Source, whereas the Siddhas speak of bringing the Breath of the Absolute into the Temporal. This is symbolized by the dancing Siva, Lord Natarajar, rather than the static depiction of Lord Siva in a meditative posture. For this the Siddhas have created many platforms, such as tantra, alchemy, martial arts, healing, and Vasi yogam.

Vasi yogam is the unique aspect of the Siddha tradition. Vasi is the breath of Existence, and Vasi yogam is about learning how that breath is in the temporal level and how it is in the unmanifested Absolute.

Even in Tamil Nadu, many Siddha teachers teach pranayama or kriya yoga, attempting to place them under the banner of Vasi yogam. However, even now, the authenticity of the teachings of Vasi yogam remain only within the oral lineage. All available yoga practices cultivate a motive for becoming, but the authentic Vasi yogam begins with the breath of Being-ness.

There is a popular saying in Tamil Nadu: "If your heart were a rose, then your thoughts would be fragrant." Steve's writings fulfill this saying. And I am proud to say that he is the first disciple of the oral lineage who has carried these Siddha teachings beyond India by bringing them to the United States. I am even more glad to say that, in all the years through all of the various hardships, he has not wavered even once.

The Siddhas' blessings be ever with him.

Arunachala Siva
Pal Pandian

Preface

The first time that we fall in love, usually as a young teenager, we all feel its novelty. Consumed in the uniqueness of first love, we think of little else. We focus attention solely on the object of our affection. This same thrill of attentive, devoted passion enabled this book to come about. That it was awakened and sustained in me by my teacher is a testament to the grace of the guru.

When Siddha Healer Pal Pandian asked me to write this book and detail the tradition of the Tamil Siddhas, I had no idea how to begin. Looking back, it now seems rather funny. Even then, I knew that for all humankind's traditions that span medicine, healing, yoga, internal alchemy, external alchemy, astrology, martial arts, tantric knowledge, gnana yoga (the path of wisdom), and so forth, their common source and origin lies within the tradition of the Siddhas. Why the hesitancy, when all I had to do was start at the beginning? The reason lay not in the content but rather in how to communicate this most ancient wisdom. Furthermore, the wisdom never, with one notable exception, had been written about with authority. The task of putting written form to an oral tradition that contained all of the fundamental secrets of existence overwhelmed me.

Only after I had completed or, more accurately, attempted a large portion of the writing, did Pal gently offer his guidance.

"It's fine, what you have written. But I cannot feel you in the words. Please simply write what you have experienced. What you have come to know for yourself. A little theory, of course, will be necessary to explain our various aspects. But still, it should only be what you know and in your own words."

Up to that point, I had been trying very hard to keep myself out of the writing, feeling that my experiences would be of little value to other people. However, from that point onward, the writing flowed with ease and gave me such joy that every day I was astounded to find its undiminished quality.

Western societies have developed a strong hunger for the practices of the East, especially yoga and meditation. When we gain what is thought of as success in the West, in those countries that are rich in possessions, our feeling of dissatisfaction propels some of us to seek something more. This alone shows that whatever is gained externally will never be enough to fully satisfy us. From this, we learn the beautifully valuable lesson that what is truly sought can only be found within. In order to achieve the goal of the internal journey, one must be led by the most accurate map. This ensures that the quickest route is traversed.

Although the Siddhas represent the least known and most mysterious ancient tradition in all of India, They first discovered and mastered all of the various healing and spiritual methods. Throughout history, all who have practiced yoga, meditation, tantra, mantra, healing, and so forth have embarked on paths laid out by the Tamil Siddhas thousands of years earlier. Yet Their lineage and contributions are largely unknown. This is due to Their reflexive and deeply abiding humility. Nevertheless, the time has come for Their contributions to humanity to become better known by the world. I hope that the chapters that follow play a role in accomplishing that goal.

The path of the Tamil Siddhas is polymorphous. It is a multi-faceted journey that ends in gnana, or enlightenment. Similarly, each individual has many dimensions. A policeman on the job appears in a certain light. Conversely, he has many other shades of existence: father, son, husband, friend, and so on. Each role that we play in our lives requires unique aspects of our being. Attempting to determine ourselves based on only one aspect is both unwise and futile. It is similar to judging a movie based on a single frame. What is actually a flow of millions of frames is condensed to a single frame. In no way does it represent the movie. It has lost its wholeness. The Siddha masters are They who feel the inner being of each aspect of existence in its natural connection to the All. This book is written and will unfold itself only in the same manner. Should a sole aspect be singled out to the exclusion of the rest, its actual meaning will be lost. This writing is the journey of my life's quest, and so reading it in a sequential manner is recommended. Each chapter may appear as individual, but at the same time each contains the attributes of the entire book. Each chapter hides and holds the quintessence of all of the others. It cannot be otherwise. They who gave birth to all healing and spiritual paths have never attempted to separate them in any way. Stretching from antiquity to the present day and beyond, the Tamil Siddha tradition offers humanity the opportunity to know and live our integration in the Cosmos.

Introduction

His medicinal teacher's final request before leaving the planet was that he continue to serve humanity. The instruction was to continue to heal all those who sought him and to never accept payment. Tens of thousands have streamed to him from all corners of the globe to drink the nectar of divine healing, whether by herbal concoctions, tantric talismans, his healing touch, or even his glance of grace. Himself a student of electronics and communication in India, a land renowned for producing scholars, he forewent all possibilities of building a career and certainly all notions of worldly security. His healing spirit is infectious yet was born of incredibly devoted practice. At one point, he was directed to attend to all who came to him in the slum areas of Madurai, India. As many as three hundred people per day would await his compassionate healing. This he performed with his usual grace and humility and without any concern for financial or personal gain. He has lived like this for more than twenty years, guided and nourished solely by the divine inspiration of unparalleled compassion and profound love for his guru. He has lived by relying solely on divine grace. He is Siddha Healer Pal Pandian of Tiruvannamalai, India. Hailing from the most ancient of all traditions, the Tamil Siddhas, he found me and took me into the deeply mysterious worlds of the most secret and rare of all of India's hidden treasures.

Just as when viewed from space all drops of water and grains of sand are known to be one source, called Earth, all of humanity's legends and traditions can be traced to a single origin. Hiding within all of the traditions of every culture that has ever existed are common themes that endure as reminders of our roots. That we are intimately intertwined with one another and with all existence is their incessant call. The heroes of our legends frequently display the range of humanity's emotions, motives, and trials. All the while, they possess what are usually thought of as supernatural powers, such as flying, supernormal strength, clairvoyance, and so forth. These archetypes, or models, have persisted in order to remind us of the hidden realms that contain humanity's latent potential. Buried deep within each one of us is our inseparable connection to everything else. This touchstone is our own undeniable origin. All feelings and experiences of disconnect that we encounter in life, whether felt as a slight strain or deep distress, exist to call us back to our original nature.

Introduction

These sojourns into disconnected living exist on both the personal and societal levels. They tend to appear as conflict. When humanity is filled with too much conflict, we are apt to pause. Only then do we reflect on how we have become so lost, so out of tune with the unceasing rhythms of Nature[1] and one another. We often see societal reflection like this occur after a war. Looking back at our former foes, who now may be our allies, we wonder what could have led to such animosity. Even in personal relationships, one often looks back, at least near one's own death, and feels that all the negativity was such a waste of energy, of life—of ourselves. Having become spellbound by the modern approach of mechanical living, divorced from Nature, we spend our lives in a singular mode of acquiring. Then we wonder why we are never satisfied.

> *The world is too much with us; late and soon,*
> *Getting and spending, we lay waste our powers;*
> *Little we see in Nature that is ours;*
> *We have given our hearts away; a sordid boon!...*

(William Wordsworth, "The World Is Too Much with Us," in *Great Short Poems,* ed. Paul Negri [Mineola, NY: Dover, 2000])

---

[1] Our greater surroundings, normally confined to the natural setting of our immediate environment, are juxtaposed with Nature. Throughout this book, the word *Nature* is capitalized, for it denotes all of existence, having issued from the Mother aspect of the divine (Shakti, the Goddess). Often portrayed in the Western world as Mother Nature, She is that which is not created yet creates.

When we, as a society, exerted dominance in our relationship with Nature and lauded the analytical and scientific over the innately felt and known, we lost our primal senses of wonder and respect. The degree of respect that we feel for our greater surroundings is always reflected in how we relate with others and with ourselves. These are lessons that our common legends and myths have ached to remind us of throughout time. Once we hoist anchor from our origins within, we must sail the salty, stormy fortunes that we have laid out for ourselves. Accustomed to a collective society, an individual must have unusual courage and rebelliousness in order to set his or her own course and attempt to cross the ocean to the infinite. Such an individual must risk all in order to regain themselves.

Every one of us invariably has those moments when we ache to break ranks with the sailing fleet of humanity and seek the shores that call us to our origins. Perhaps we remember ourselves as little children and recall our lost innocence and vigor. The loss of that wonder and feeling of aliveness, which remain like a forgotten scent in the deep alleys of our mind, haunts us. Yearning for a fresh vision of ourselves, others, and our lives, we too often are willing to succumb to the pack mentality and surrender our deepest feelings only to trudge onward with the collective. This book is an attempt to aid those few who, against all convention and the greater number of their brethren, refuse to be tempted to stay the course any longer. First we sense, then we feel, and finally we come to know in our very bones that we are much more than that to which the sheep in the herd confine themselves.

This book begins with a brief introduction to the basics of my life, and when writing it I was unconvinced that it would have any place in a work dedicated to the details of the Tamil Siddha masters. When I was instructed to include more first-person narrative, it became obvious that the basics of my life are a natural place for the reader to begin, because knowing a little about the author, his circumstances, and his motivations is helpful.

After providing the particulars about the author, this book delves into the Tamil Siddhas. This section was the most difficult to write. Theirs is not only an oral tradition but also one of extreme secrecy, and it contains countless varieties of what the common-minded call "miracles." The challenge was not one of ignorance or disbelief, for I had already been privy to numerous miracles and shown the inner workings of many realms of the Siddhas. Rather, the task that I faced was how to present such things so that a broader audience would not be inclined to dismiss them out of hand, considering them fanciful or thinking that I was simply boasting about accomplishments in which I am a mere spectator. As usual, Pal's simple words of instruction guided me to write just what I have experienced and come to know personally. This exact manner easily flowed into chapter 6: "Siddha Tantra," because that spiritual path into which he initiated me was previously unknown to me. Yet once begun, my experiences did not merely speak to me. They shouted in an undeniably clear tone.

From there, the chapters deal with the Siddha masters' broad range of healing methods and the basics of health, disease, and treatment. A good deal of time is spent detailing the Siddhas' understanding of the human body (and mind) in terms of not just physical anatomy but also the body's subtle, or unseen nature. This deep wisdom born from Their insight and enlightened state is best illustrated by the knowledge of how life is formed in the womb, in all of its divine detail.

The final section of this book is a brief exposition of the more esoteric arts of the Tamil Siddhas. Beginning with Their yoga practice, called Vasi yoga, which is the most powerful and direct of spiritual initiations, it moves to the most mysterious of scientific practices, alchemy. Chapter 14: "The Bitter Truth" is particularly noteworthy, because Pal asked if I would be willing to include it. That chapter provides a direct, succinct look into what is meant by seeking the return to one's origins and what the purpose of it is. The appendix to the book encapsulates the current situation and what one can expect to find of these ancient masters. The focus is primarily on Their most well-known, accessible art—Siddha medicine.

The many forms of meditation, the general misunderstanding of the word *yoga,* and the inaccurate practice of yoga today stand as prime examples of the necessity for this book. Words like *karma* have only recently come into vogue in the West, yet they have existed for thousands of years. This long-time usage has resulted in a general yet deeply distorted misunderstanding of many vital tenets. The notion of reincarnation is a prime example. Past-life regression has been utilized even in clinical settings and is, of itself, a fine practice. However, there exist some overriding principles that have long been unknown. In this very vein, legend says that a great sage of South India was sitting with a few of his disciples when one of them broached this very subject:

Several of the devotees were discussing among themselves the revelation that one man among them, who was sixty-three years of age, had recently learned that in his previous life he lived as a peasant boy in a nearby village and died at the age of six. When they told their master about this, the sage, who usually was silent on such subjects, merely stated that, yes, it was true. He continued on to state that the very boy who the older man was in his previous life was living right now in that very village and was three years old!

When we approach ancient wisdom with our linear, analytical, time-obsessed methods, we are doomed to unimaginable error. This is true of most attempts to utilize meditation, yoga, or tantra in today's societies. To say that there is a lack of authenticity due to a monumental lack of true insight, understanding, and wisdom is a grand understatement. Yes, the old man had lived his "previous" life as a small village boy and met a tragic end at six years of age. Yes, that boy was alive and three years old in that village at the same time as he existed at sixty-three years old in that very room. Yet what is time and space to the infinite of which all is composed? Furthermore, how are we to evolve in any manner if we stubbornly continue to approach God with our self-confining notions, of which time, space, and causality are the very foundations? Ignorance, which is most succinctly grounded in innocence, is the most cherished quality that we can seek to embody. Knowing that we do not know is sufficient to open us to our lost sense of childish wonder, vitality, and innocence.

> *A man's ignorance sometimes is not only useful, but beautiful—while his knowledge, so called, is oftentimes worse than useless, besides being ugly. Which is the best man to deal with—he who knows nothing about a subject, and, what is extremely rare, knows that he knows nothing, or he who really knows something about it, but thinks that he knows all?*
>
> (Henry David Thoreau, "Walking," *Atlantic Monthly* [June 1862])

Introduction

The title of this book (*Rivulets of the Absolute*) is an obvious play on words, pointing to the small streams of refreshment allowed to flow to the reader from the oceanic wisdom of the Tamil Siddha masters. Because rivulets seem the opposite of the Absolute, the title cautions the reader that this book will not reveal itself in a purely intellectual way. It is not intended to simply provide information, nor is it a how-to manual. Approaching it with the idea of gaining more information to fit within what one already knows will prove futile, and the chapters will appear nonsensical. The actual flow is reflective of how the darkly mysterious realms of the Tamil Siddhas opened up for me. Much of its deepest qualities lie within a more spontaneous adventure.

Within the chapters are tenets that have long been kept secret and unknown to any other tradition. They are touched upon here at the request of Siddha Healer Pal Pandian. The words chosen stem solely from my own experience of mysteries such as Vasi, alchemy, Amritha Kalai healing, and Siddha Tantra. While all other yogic, healing, and spiritual methods are based on the discoveries of the Siddha masters, the most vital aspects of Siddha have been kept hidden throughout time. Paradoxically, that which is most vital is, in turn, that which is most basic. The only other authoritative writing about the Tamil Siddhas is Healer Pal's book, *Siddhas: Masters of the Basics*. Again, we see the play on words, contrasting masters and basics. He chose these two titles purposely, as a reflection of their related nature. In truth, this book serves as an introduction to the much more voluminous, detailed one that he has authored.

Decoding the ancient manuscripts of the Tamil Siddhas is possible only for one who has been admitted into the deepest realms of their mysterious and graceful clan. Containing the countless healing applications and spiritual practices of antiquity, these mysteries invariably include details of humanity's history. The ones quoted here come solely from Healer Pal.

Over the years, I have never ceased to be amazed at how the wisdom hidden within the purposely ambiguous writings lay the foundations for all subsequent spiritual, religious, and scientific traditions throughout the world. Bits and pieces of the Tamil Siddhas' divine insight have been allowed to spread in order to aid the development of society throughout the ages. All the while, the masters themselves have remained hidden and allowed humanity to utilize these scraps of grace in their own way. Yet in our own modern, mechanical age, the time has come for the Tamil Siddha masters to step forth from the shadows of the ancient past. The purpose is not to seek the limelight but instead to breathe vitality, potency, and authenticity into those traditions that have always existed, for the sole purpose of serving the inhabitants of our now frenzied yet still beautiful planet.

Humanity and her needs are multifaceted. All aspects of our being require proper nourishment. This nourishment should be capable of reaching us in all stages of our evolution. To be served most properly, an equally grand and polymorphous platform is necessary. The immense variety of dimensions of the Tamil Siddhas is brought forth in this book. The path of the Tamil Siddhas has reached within the recesses of my individual being and holds me now, for I walk my path within Her. It has colored all the various stages of life. The Siddhas' tradition is ancient, yet we can see its meaning in the wholeness of our experience, in all of our present life circumstances. This holding, this walking is possible only when the tradition Herself is alive, sees your entirety, and recognizes you from the "deepest before." From here, She picks you up in Her arms, and the journey begins. My own journey began long before I knew anything of such matters. My trials were preparation for the earnest adventure that was to follow. Thus, the stage was set in my early years.

CHAPTER 1

Appointment With Life

The defining moment in life came when I was twelve years old. It was not something I had asked for. Perhaps because of this, I was entirely unprepared. As I was standing in the kitchen, with no noticeable thoughts, roasting a marshmallow over an open flame, it came to me in a flash: "We are all going to die." That was it. That single, simple thought emerged from nowhere. The problem was that it stood completely alone, solid and terribly real in my awareness.

It seems funny now to recall the twelve-year-old me involved in a philosophical struggle. I was never a very good student. My parents would not allow me to attend kindergarten, because they thought that I lacked the necessary maturity. When the next year came and I was required to attend first grade, their reasoning was obvious. I did not just fail, but rather I failed spectacularly. Not even close to passing. Because it was the 1960s, and I was the last of six children in the family, my parents did not interfere much. In today's world, the diagnosis of mild autism most likely would have been given. Somehow, I managed to escape first grade the second time around, but I have always wondered why my siblings never teased me about my early struggles at school.

The two themes that predominated in my early years—flying and dreaming—may explain the academic failures. For one, I was convinced that I could fly. Every night as I lay in bed, I would lift up and fly over our house, neighborhood, and the entire city. The wind and some unseen power would slowly lift and carry me. What really stood out was that, when I was awake, I knew what the roofs of the houses, community buildings, and the rest of the city looked like from above. Whenever the wind blew, I waited for it to lift and carry me away. Whether awake or asleep, I had no doubt that I could fly.

Awake or asleep? I asked myself that question daily. There was simply no way for me to tell the difference between the waking state and the dreaming state. The two overlapped so much that most of the time I was unsure which was which. To other people, such as my parents and teachers, I often appeared dull. Drifting off into daydreams, I was not bothered with results. Feeling that whatever I was experiencing was a dream, I was unconcerned with the outcomes of my actions or those of people around me.

I recall some of the consequences of my confusion. Standing at the top of the stairs in our house, wearing a towel around my neck as a cape, I waited for the breeze to carry me down to the bottom of the stairs. Once, I actually tumbled down the stairs. The tears that sprang to my eyes then were not so much from pain but rather from disbelief and confusion at the inability to float and fly. I would like to take a moment now to apologize to all of my classmates who I unexpectedly punched or pinched. After I figured out that pinching myself while dreaming felt as real as it did doing it while awake, I pinched my classmates, thinking that their response would give me a better clue. However, I was not always cruel or stumbling around like a zombie. After recognizing my classmates' painful responses, I attempted to entertain them and regain their trust, usually by regaling them with comedic routines from the previous night's *Red Skelton Show,* mimicking Red's loony seagull character in particular. While we waited for our turn to play tether ball, I fancied myself the hilarious friend. Then again, five-year-old boys will laugh at anything.

As I have already taken the opportunity to apologize to my classmates for the odd behavior, my parents also deserve some attention. Although they had been strict in raising my five older siblings, I was fortunate. They interfered and demanded very little of me. The most likely reason for that, of course, is that I showed little promise of being normal. Whatever the reason, I am forever grateful to them for the way in which our lives mingled. Being spared the Catholic schools that my five older siblings attended is a fine example of the more relaxed and liberal upbringing that I received. Yet we did attend church every week. When I was very young, my father held me during the service, and so I naturally drifted in and out of sleep. Gazing at the statues of Jesus as I did so seemed to have a strong, lasting influence on me. Even from the earliest age, I felt the most powerful, intimate, natural relationship with Jesus. The relationship was so real to me that I developed an extremely independent approach to all things religious. This approach has persisted throughout my life. Priests, the Bible, and exhortations of guilt and reward were both comical and meaningless to me.

I am not sure what it is about my twelfth year. Of course, I was entering puberty, and the carefree childhood of wandering barefoot in the woods was slipping away. Yet the experience that I had during the simple act of staring at a flame while roasting a marshmallow should have tipped me off that life was about to begin taking some unexpected turns. About the time I was slapped with the concrete fact of mortality, I had another uncomfortable experience. While riding my bike in aimless circles, I was suddenly struck by the most intense pain. My lower back locked. I do not recall how I made it home from that bike ride. Despite having gone through all of the usual broken bones, bleeding lips, and scars of boyhood, I had never before imagined such pain. Even breathing brought horrible distress. I swear to this day that blinking or moving my eyes brought spasms of pain. While I was the owner of a grand imagination, I have no doubt that what really stood out for me was not only the physical pain. I also suffered intense mental pain, mainly confusion. It even spilled over to my emotions. I wondered, What is this? I knew that it was not an illness or accident. All I wanted to do was play. Instead, those two seminal experiences at the age of twelve defined my life. For the next thirty years, both my body and mind would be plagued by those experiences. The pain in my lower back and the concrete awareness of the fleeting nature of all things mingled with each other and stalked me. All avenues of escape were temporary. If the physical pain subsided, the mental pain asserted itself. These two seemingly unrelated events, one of the psyche and the other of the physical body, blended to become my personal crisis.

Nothing means anything. The faintest echo of that thought remained within. Knowing that everything and everyone turns to dust cast a pall of meaninglessness over all things human. Relationships, accomplishments, and adventures all rang as hollow. No matter what occurred for any of us, it would be merely temporary. For some inexplicable yet horribly pertinent reason, this thought threw me into deep dejection. Keeping it to myself always seemed best. I searched for distractions so that I would not examine it more deeply. I followed the usual routines in college, relationships, and jobs, all the while, aping the normal courses of society, and feeling like a great pretender, a bad impersonator of myself. I found some solace in the writings of great English poets and Russian novelists. Those authors were tortured souls, for sure, but their clawing for beauty and the truth of existence thrilled me. Driven by inner strife, their expressions provided momentary glimpses of their innate aspirations.

When my daughter was still quite young, my marriage to her mother ended. That was not surprising, as I held little ambition for life. The existential crisis that had begun in childhood, while hidden, continued to haunt me from the darkness of the subconscious. Whatever was attained would not last. Therefore, nothing that I achieved would ever bring satisfaction. Without knowing why or how to proceed, I began to seek answers in earnest. I did not even know what I was searching for with any clarity. I was aware, however, that in some strange way, the search enabled me to begin to feel alive again. Searching in the dark for an unknown, unseen goal seemed much more natural than stumbling through life and vainly trying to accumulate money, power, and accolades. Life had already taught me that I would forever be unfulfilled by ordinary achievements. What I had achieved, acquired, and accomplished up to that point had done absolutely nothing to soothe the internal torment. I thought, What does it all mean? Why am I here? What is the purpose, the meaning, of life, of my life, of the world? Yet I knew with absolute clarity that the answers would never be found in social or scientific forums. The crisis was within my own being. Only I could feel its existential nature. I reached the conclusion that

I must strike out into the unknown if I were to have any hope of reaching resolution.

Having been raised in the Christian tradition, I naturally began my search by studying the Bible and its various versions for potential hidden meaning. Briefly, I read the religious texts of Judaism, Islam, and Hinduism. Scouring those traditions, I searched for that which would resonate with my already known, yet somehow forgotten, connection with the Absolute. The words in those books were beautiful. I never doubted the experiences of the saints, prophets, and seers of any religion. Nevertheless, something in their approach to God bothered me. It left me feeling even more destitute and excluded from existence. My intimacy with the divine seemed contradictory to what the religionists spoke and preached. Because my bond with God had developed naturally when I was very young, I was incapable of intellectualizing it.

At the lowest point in the search, spending time in nature reminded me of my timeless bond with God. The affirmation came from the wind. The rustling of leaves or the invisible movement of the wind over water inevitably drew my attention to more subtle realms, which naturally calmed the aching, tense mind. When I was in this more sensitive state, the feeling of the breeze on my body brought forth my earliest memories. Again, as during my childhood, barely earthbound, I experienced the same scene as I had effortlessly throughout my life: an emerald-green forest containing a flowing brook, beside which stretches a large fir tree, beneath which sits Jesus, my head on His lap and His hand stroking my head in the most loving, comforting, accepting manner imaginable.

I would never be satisfied feeling any distance from God. Thus, I continued, beginning with the book titled *A Course in Miracles*, Abraham-Hicks law of attraction, yoga postures, chakra meditations, and countless breathing, or *pranayama*, methods. From there, I tried meditation courses, joining an ashram, numerous new-age endeavors, and Sri Yogananda's *kriya yoga*, among many others. I walked every one of those paths with my usual intense, exhaustive approach, looking for answers. In each practice, a typical pattern occurred. At the beginning, I would experience immediate results. This was particularly true of all pranayama and yogic traditions. What should have taken months or even years of patience would inexplicably happen immediately. I never understood what was occurring. Keeping to myself, I had no one to consult. Thus, these experiences never seemed odd to me. Over time, however, the powerfully felt results would disappear, and I again would feel adrift and desperate.

The grand avenue finally opened when I found myself having a powerful attraction to the great Indian sage Bhagavan Sri Ramana Maharshi, whose ashram lies at the foot of the holy hill named Arunachala. There the cure for both my psychological and physical crises awaited.

Bhagavan Ramana Maharshi

Bhagavan Sri Ramana Maharshi

Bhagavan Ramana Maharshi is widely recognized throughout India as the greatest sage of the twentieth century. He resided at the foot of Arunachala from 1896 to 1950. At the tender age of sixteen, He spontaneously achieved the highest state of enlightenment. This singularly rare occurrence was brought about by a sudden, inexplicable death experience. There was no reason for it to occur, for He was healthy and robust. The experience was forced upon Him by sheer fate. As it overcame Him, He felt no panic. Instead, in that very moment, He calmly set out to solve the mystery of death itself. He allowed himself to fall completely into the shock and fear of the crisis with no inclination to consult doctors, family, or friends. He felt that He had to solve the problem himself, then and there.

When He inquired deeply as to "what is it that dies," it was revealed to Him that death is for the body alone and that the true being is untouched by death. In that moment, His identity was totally consumed in the unchanging, deathless Supreme Consciousness of Being. When many years later, He was asked about the experience, Bhagavan emphasized that it was in no way intellectual and that it happened in a flash. In a moment, the schoolboy was completely and permanently transformed into a sage. There was neither quest nor striving nor conscious preparation. Years later, He described the realization as follows:

> *Though all the senses were benumbed, the aham sphurana (Self-awareness) was clearly evident. This Self-awareness never decays. It is unrelated to anything. It is Self-luminous. Even if this body is burnt, it will not be affected. Hence, I realized on that very day so clearly that that was "I."*
>
> (Suri Nagamma, *Letters from Sri Ramanasramam*
> [Tiruvannamalai, India: Sri Ramanasramam, 2006], 3)

A short time afterward, He stole away from home to make his way to His beloved Arunachala. Upon entering the inner sanctum of the great Arunachalaswara temple, He embraced the Siva Lingam statue, which means *agni*, or fire, and said, "Father, I have come at thy bidding. Thy will be done."

Arunachaleswara temple at the foothills of holy Arunachala

His life was unique in that He never claimed to be a teacher or that He gave initiation to anyone. He made no distinctions among people with regard to class, color, creed, or religion. Stating that self-inquiry, or *atma vichara*, was the surest path to self-realization, Bhagavan preferred to teach through His silent Presence. Whether a person was devoutly religious or an atheist made no difference to Him. He encouraged all to find the changeless Source through their own introspective effort. Of course, we all are aware of the mind only because of its ever-changing nature and the constant, often disturbing, flow of thoughts. If, however, turned inward in the quest of its origin, this awareness of "I" disappears in its Source. The previously felt "I" consciousness is relative, fleeting, and finite. Identified with the body as "I," this consciousness will die. But the Source, or God, is infinite and eternal. Self-inquiry is the quest for the Self, or Source, by following, rather than answering, the primordial question "Who am I?" When asked if one should practice self-inquiry by repeating the question "Who am I?" Bhagavan gave the following reply:

> *No, it is not repeating or meditating on "Who am I?" It is to dive deep into yourself and seek the place from which the "I" thought arises in you and to hold on to it firmly to the exclusion of any other thought. Continuous and persistent attempt will lead you to the Self.*

(M.M. Menon, "M.M. Menon Was from Palghat Kerala," In Laxmi Narain, *Face to Face with Sri Ramana Maharshi,* [Hyderabad, India: Sri Ramana Kendram, 2005], 274)

Because He lived as a renunciate and spoke infrequently, many are tempted to ignore the profoundly tender and compassionate radiance that He showered on those who sought his company. Bhagavan was no idle statue. For many years, He arose at 3 a.m. and began the preparations for breakfast by cutting vegetables and grinding rice and lentils. Although He never touched money, because He had no need for it, He kept to a punctual routine and was scrupulous about not wasting anything. He created hand-bound notebooks from the scraps of paper that others would throw away. He saved the normally unusable parts of vegetables and fruits and made them into tasty chutneys. He never spoke ill of anyone, even criminals and miscreants. When others complained to Him that He was not censuring some of the devotees for their conduct, He replied as follows:

> *Who is to correct them? Is it not the Lord alone who has the authority to correct everyone? All we can do is to correct ourselves. That itself is correcting others.*

(Natesa Mudaliar [Sadhu Natanananda], "Sadhu Natanananda (Natesa Mudaliar) Was a Scholar Who Authored Many Books on Sri Ramana," In Laxmi Narain, *Face to Face with Sri Ramana Maharshi*, [Hyderabad, India: Sri Ramana Kendram, 2005], 130)

His love and deep affection toward animals was well documented, and, based on those accounts, one can only marvel at His ability to communicate with the animal kingdom. The animals returned His communication in equal parts wisdom, naturalness, and love. Indeed, animals of all sorts went to Him to settle quarrels among themselves and their quarrels with humans in the area. Birds, dogs, cows, monkeys, squirrels, tigers, other animals, insects, and even plants were revered by Him as equal manifestations of the Supreme Consciousness. The animals knew that He was their friend and protector and sought His company and blessings on countless occasions, as in the following example:

> *Once a monkey with her baby stood at the window by the side of Bhagavan's sofa. As he was reading something, he did not notice her. After a while, the monkey screeched, and the attendants tried to drive her away, but she would not go.*
>
> *Bhagavan then looked up and said, "Wait! She has come here to show us her baby. Don't people bring their children to show Bhagavan? For her, her child is equally dear. Look how tender the child is." So saying Bhagavan turned towards her and said in an endearing tone, "Hello! So you have brought your child? That is good! Come in. I will see that nobody harms you." Bhagavan then urged her to come in. The mother monkey came with the baby and gave her child to Bhagavan. After fondling the baby, Bhagavan gave the baby back to its mother. He gave some fruits to the mother and sent her away. The monkey was full of contentment and joy.*
>
> (*Bhagavan Ramana: The Friend of All* [Tiruvannamali, India: Sri Ramanasramam, 2008], 91)

Bhagavan's silent Presence was enough to answer the questions of those with any degree of ripeness and sincerity. Freed of the burden of constantly revolving thoughts, this very Presence penetrated deeply into the hearts of His devotees. Wolter Keers, a Dutch teacher, described his own experience of sitting with the Maharshi as follows:

> *There was a radiant power and energy in Bhagavan's presence that effortlessly swept through the mind and matter. . . . The light radiating from Bhagavan filled my being, sweeping away all my darkness in one stroke. Effort seemed redundant when his presence alone was enough to evaporate the usual mental flow of thoughts, ideas, and problems.*
>
> (Walter A. Keers, "Wolter A. Keers Was a Dutch Teacher and Writer Who Lectured on Yoga and Advaita in Europe," In Laxmi Narain, *Face to Face with Sri Ramana Maharshi*, [Hyderabad, India: Sri Ramana Kendram, 2005], 198)

Although He transformed and gave liberation to many, Bhagavan never allowed any show of deference to be afforded Him. Whether food, medicine, or anything else, if it was good for Him, then it should be good enough for everyone. Countless incidents demonstrating His extreme humility abound. Never did He allow himself to be a burden of any kind on anyone else. He shared incredibly tender human interactions that are often

Rivulets of the Absolute

overlooked. Robert Adams, a nineteen-year-old American, described his arrival at Bhagavan's ashram:

> *The Maharshi guided me to a little shack that I might use while I was staying there. He came inside with me. I bet you think we spoke about profound subjects. On the contrary, he was a natural man. He was the Self of the universe. He asked how my trip was, where I was from and what made me come there. Then he said I should rest. . . . I was awakened at about five in the evening by Ramana himself, who had brought food for me. Can you imagine that?*

(Robert Adams, "The Cow Lakshmi," In Laxmi Narain, *Face to Face with Sri Ramana Maharshi,* [Hyderabad, India: Sri Ramana Kendram, 2005], 358–359)

Old Hall

There are many wonderful books on the life, and thus the teachings, of this most wonderful sage. The profoundly deep, healing quality of stillness is still felt today in His ashram, where the power of his silent Presence continues. Indeed, people from around the world flock to the town to imbibe of the nectar of the company of Bhagavan and Arunachala. I did so shortly after a friend gave me a magazine whose cover was a picture of Bhagavan. A few glances at that picture over the next few days were all it took to prompt me to examine it more closely. Sometime later, I saw my first picture of Arunachala. The mountain was beautiful and, in my mind, the word "Arunachala" appeared. Later I heard the actual pronunciation of the name and realized, to my delight, that the silent voice in my head had spoken it properly. At that moment, I knew that I must go to India to commune with both Bhagavan and Arunachala.

Up to that point, I had been seeking the elusive state of enlightenment while mainly ignoring the mundane aspects of life. Looking for ultimate transcendence from the paradox of life, I had failed to chart a life course that I could live in a daily manner in order to bring fulfillment to myself and those around me. In time, I would meet my teacher, Siddha Healer Pal Pandian, who would ever so patiently and lovingly initiate, teach, and guide me in the various paths of Siddha wisdom. From him, I would learn that such an exclusive approach as I had followed to what we call spirituality not only is inauthentic to the crisis but also would be unsuccessful. In his profound compassion and wisdom, as my journey began under his watchful care, Healer Pal gave me the following words to guide me:

> *Like a seed, we, too, have the potential to grow and come to fruition if we can find the environment and conditions to nurture us. Just as a papaya seed requires conditions different from a rice seed, each of us is born with unique qualities and capabilities that require specific conditions and climate. Very few are lucky enough to identify and find the right soil, conditions, and nurturing to transform this potential into a reality. A majority, like a seed on concrete pavement, barely manage to go beyond the survival issues. However, if we follow the inner voice and sustain the urge for unfoldment, we can surely fulfill our life's purpose.*

Prior to meeting my teacher, however, I first had to undergo years of seeking in various paths, including meditation, yoga, austerities, and others. I took my first trip to India in 1999. During this visit, a mysterious meeting took place, which, like a small plant that, lovingly embedded in the ground, would grow to eventually bear fruit and flower in the form and substance of meeting my Teacher, the ever perfect mirror, guide, and dearest form of Friend.

Shocking Encounter

In his younger days, Yogi Ram Suratkumar, a *jnani*, or Fully enlightened being, known as the Divine Beggar of Tiruvannamalai, had been in the presence of Bhagavan. When I arrived in India in 1999, He was in his last days of his physical body. Two companions and I went to His ashram to pay our respects and receive his *darshan*, or divine sight. Returning from the ashram to our quarters, we passed a field where many *swamis* and *sadhus* had gathered. Saints, seekers, and many others had flooded the small town for the divine yogi's final hours. Trailing behind my friends, I gazed over the field and saw dozens of dignified men wearing orange robes. My eyes locked with the eyes of another man, one who was sitting in the dust against a wall at the back of the field. As I gazed into his eyes, I was dumbstruck. My mind went completely blank save for an overwhelming desire to walk toward him and meet him. His appearance was completely different from that of the orange-garbed men. He was wearing a robe that I could only assume once had been white. As I drew near him, I noticed that the robe was filthy, with brown and gray stains, his hair was disheveled, filled with dirt, and his beard was unkempt. His eyes! Yes, his eyes shone with a madness and yet a brilliance that I had never encountered. A smile covered his entire face and, as he directed his gaze to me, his head swayed in a wild and utterly mad manner. In that instant, I could not move a muscle. I could only stare and smile back at him. I did not know what to do. Wanting to express the profound sense of love and respect that was welling up inside me, I finally was able to reach into my pocket, withdraw some rupees, and extend them to him. I wanted to give him all of the money I was carrying, but I did not do so as I felt it would be insulting to him in some strange way. He graciously accepted the rupees. He held his hands in Namaste to me, and I returned the gesture. In that moment, I knew two things with certainty: He did not care in the least for the money but accepted it only to please or, rather, to bless me in the act of giving, and I wanted more than anything to fall at his feet. Having been in India for only a few days, and on my first trip there, I felt awkward, such a clumsy Westerner and even a bit shy to make the customary sign of respect. I stood there frozen, my hands clasped, mind utterly still, and heart swelling with intense feelings of devotion. Suddenly, my mind restarted, and I felt that I must leave him and find my companions. As I left, I realized that while I had walked toward this unique being and stood with him, I had been unconscious of my surroundings, including all of the other people. From the moment I had locked eyes with him until my mind restarted, it was as if we were the only two people there, as if nothing else existed. I realized that no one else had noticed him or me while I was with him. I remembered this strange meeting for years to come. I recalled it with a feeling of some regret in that I yearned to have the opportunity to show my profound respect by honoring his presence in the proper fashion. It was only some years later that I recognized what had occurred—I had come face to face with a Siddha.

> *He is Dharma, birthless, kinless,*
> *Resides in the wild, lives by alms,*
> *He, seeing anybody who renounced,*
> *Sunders their bonds of birth,*
> *—you have seen a Divine Madman.*

(Siddha Thirumular, "Thirumanthiram," Verse 1616, In Pal Pandian, *Siddhas: Masters of the Basics* [Chennai, India: Pal Pandian, 2008])

"A Siddha Healer"

After the first several years of traveling to India, I broke away from all groups, encounters, and teachers. I had found several repeating patterns. Many of the people who flocked to the group meetings were very different from me. Most had little responsibility in life. Because they did not have the deep roots in society that are provided only by being a parent, having a solid career, and following a robust daily routine, their questions and company seemed trivial to me. Likewise, many of the teachers simply pronounced maxims, such as "We are all one" and "You are already what you are seeking." I had already heard them countless times. Staring into the students' eyes and holding their gaze seemed to be the extent of their teaching. I had learned that feeling the energy of a person or place provided only a temporary experience. Anything fleeting like that would never suffice, because the crisis had lurked inside me since childhood. That lurking crisis was actually my saving grace, because it gifted me a feeling of intolerance with any path or pursuit that did not fully resolve the ultimate dilemma: death. It granted me the innate wisdom to recognize that even if these folks were doing good work, they could not provide what I was seeking.

After I broke away from the group approach, I spent time in meditation at the ashram of Bhagavan Ramana Maharshi, on the slopes and in the caves of Arunachala, and performing giri valam or pradakshina (circumambulation) of Arunachala. Keeping to myself, I spent time in silence. When I did interact, it was with the local inhabitants. In this way, the time was always refreshing and replenishing. I distinctly remember one day when I was walking down Arunachala, alone and silent as was my usual routine. When I reached the town, a young man ran up to me, said that he knew my name, and asked whether I remembered him. After some time, I recalled that he was a rickshaw driver from my very first trip to India.

We exchanged pleasantries and asked about each other's family, and then he said, "You must meet my guru. . . . I will take you to see him in few days."

I asked him who his guru was.

He simply replied, "A Siddha doctor."

Although I had fondly remembered meeting the radiant madman during my first trip to India, the world of the Siddhas had remained unknown to me. Having never heard the words "Siddha" and "doctor" used together, I was quite confused. But the rickshaw driver was an agreeable chap and truly enthusiastic that I should meet his teacher. Although I was not actually seeking a guru, I was perhaps not entirely averse to the idea. He agreed to pick me up in his rickshaw in a few days.

As promised, in a few days he picked me up. As we approached a small, humble house in the middle of a field, I noticed that it was surrounded by countless wild plants and herbs and enjoyed a spectacular view of Arunachala. When I stepped inside the house, I saw many pots and containers strewn about and was greeted warmly by Siddha Healer Pal Pandian. We sat on the floor facing each other. At the beginning of our meeting, there was little speaking, but eventually we spoke of various matters yet none that I could recall afterward. However, I do remember being extremely happy and at ease simply sitting with him in his small house. My driver friend had instructed me to feel free to ask Pal any questions that I wanted. Because I was aware that this was the purpose of my visit and Pal had been kind enough to make himself available, I searched for something meaningful to ask. Yet my mind was blank. I managed to come up with some lame question about health issues. Later that I day, I wondered why I did not speak of my back pain. In recollection, I realized that my body had been completely relaxed while I was with Pal. That was the reason that the question did not occur to me. We met for just over a half hour.

What struck me most were Pal's incessant yet completely natural smile and the gentle laughter which was interspersed between his sentences. He gazed at me only briefly and spent most of the time looking down at the floor, but I never felt his attention shift away from me for even a moment. Before taking my leave, I asked who his guru was. My friend quickly interceded, telling me that Pal would not reveal such a thing or that perhaps his guru did not have a name. I was unsure of which might be the case. Again, I had been a clumsy Westerner! Although asked innocently, I later became aware of how rude the question had been. It would be two years before I met Pal again and would be granted the gift of his divine friendship, guidance, and loving support. As we left his little house, I still had no better understanding of what a Siddha truly is. Yet I was convinced, beyond any doubt, that I had indeed been sitting face to face with one.

Sometime during the following two years, my friend mailed me a copy of Pal's new book, *Siddhas: Masters of the Basics*. As I read it, I was equally fascinated and mystified. I did learn that the Siddhas were not simply ancient yogis who meditated in caves and forests. Because they had developed entire arts and sciences that reached into all aspects of humanity's needs, their systems for healing and spiritual evolution resonated deeply within me.

That this book was the first authoritative writing by a member of the Tamil Siddha clan did not escape my notice.

The Tamil Siddhas

The 18 Tamil Siddhas—Lord Murugan is in the center

From the time my spiritual quest began, I had heard the term *Siddha* and its definition as a perfected being. The word *siddhi*, as I understood it, referred to the supernatural power possessed by a Siddha. In Tamil, the language of southeastern India, the root word of Siddha is *chit*, or consciousness, therefore Chittar, or Siddha, is one who abides as pure consciousness. This denotes one who is perfected. This perfected state encompasses all worldly and spiritual realms.

Existing since time immemorial, Siddhas are the wellspring and the masters of all forms of yoga, *tantra*, martial arts, science, alchemy, astrology, medicine, and healing. All of prehistoric India was the land of the *Dravidians*. South India is unique, because there the ancient spiritual scientists, or yogis, of ancient Tamil Nadu encoded their sacred works in both esoteric poetry and oral tradition. These yogis are known as the *Tamil Siddhas*.

The hallmark of the Siddhas is the combination of extreme secrecy and profound humility. It is impossible to separate these two attributes. They keep secrecy in order to ensure the purity of their wisdom. Humility? I had never encountered this quality until I met my teacher. I had thought that humility was the deflection of praise or a way of acting, but I found much more in its truest expression.

Over the years, I had searched for details about the Siddhas in books and by speaking with numerous people from throughout India. By the time I received Pal's book, I had discovered that finding accurate information about the Siddhas was nearly impossible. As I pored through the pages of his book, I found direct, clearly communicated Siddha wisdom. It was unlike anything that I had ever heard or read, from any source. The quality of the words was uniquely capable of reaching into my being. Whether their medicinal system or their spiritual truths, learning about them thrilled me to my very core. Paradoxes that had long plagued me were confronted directly. I came to understand so much of what I had encountered in my spiritual quest, so much of what I had observed and experienced, in a new light.

When outsiders speak about or write about the Siddhas from beyond their lineage legends, superstitions, and even prejudices abound. The Siddhas themselves have done nothing to challenge or refute such things. Direct confrontation, notoriety, and praise have never been of interest to them. Indeed, they have long been referred to as the *Reluctant Masters*. They have always been notoriously difficult for the common-minded masses to find and relate to. Their preference is to simply abide, live, and share the truth of Existence. They do not teach, because they have never needed to do so or wanted be viewed as teachers. Their very Being exudes Truth.

This lack of sermonizing, preaching, teaching, and trying to gain followers has maintained Siddha wisdom's purity and authenticity. The difference between the Siddhas and other traditions is that the Siddhas have remained practical, committed, and creatively engaged with nature and all existence. Therefore, they are easily overlooked. Being overlooked, in turn, enhances their natural secrecy and lack of notoriety. The result is that their cherished wisdom has remained unchanged and their humility, that elusive trait, has continued its unhindered flow. Because their approach is unique, misunderstanding naturally occurs.

Although greatly misunderstood throughout the ages due to their intermingled tenets of humbleness and secrecy, their radiant life-giving Presence remains to this day. All that today's world knows of tantra, yoga, alchemy, medicine, and healing has come from the Siddhas. Yet the world remains ignorant of the origin of these arts. Sharing yet laying no claim to these arts (thus, allowing others to carry the burden), the Tamil Siddhas embody humility beyond common understanding. Their secrecy and humility are the reasons that it took me so long to find accurate information about them. What I finally found astounded me. Most surprising was that all of the spiritual paths that I had attempted, *all of them* are descendants from Siddha. My search for primal, authentic, complete, and shockingly powerful spiritual wisdom had finally found its mark.

The Guru Relationship

When I was able to return to India after having read Pal's book, the long flight left a single, strong impression on me: acute soreness in my back. Noticing this, my rickshaw-driving friend insisted that I have a Varma nerve massage. This massage does not in any way resemble the relaxing type of session we ordinarily associate with the word "massage." It is perhaps better called nervous system manipulation or invigoration. The session lasted perhaps an hour and a half, and I was not overly impressed with the technique. It appeared simple, devoid of fancy hand movements and the like. Some aspects of it were rather uncomfortable for me. My driver friend, who has a slightly more sensitive constitution than I do, expressed a greater discomfort when his time came. From the time the session ended until I fell into my usual deep sleep that night, I had absolutely no back pain. Waking the next morning free of pain, I was literally shocked throughout the day by an amazing revelation. My mood had changed. Until that moment, I had no idea how living in chronic pain affected mental and emotional states. But the lightness that I felt would be short lived, because the following evening I was uncharacteristically incapable of falling asleep.

I spent the night not only without sleeping but also experiencing deeply dark moods and feelings of intense dread. When the morning broke, I became aware that my body had begun to swell and was highly sensitive, with an acute sensation of burning. The symptoms progressed to the point that the pain was so extreme that I felt as if my skin would burst into flames or I would explode. Soon I was visited by Pal. It was then that I learned that the young man who had given the Varma treatment was, in fact, one of Pal's students. Pal's presence was soothing, and his obvious concern was so very tender. While he was visiting me, the pain diminished greatly, and I was no longer concerned with any physical or mental derangements. When I explained my situation, his first question was posed lovingly: "But why did you not call me earlier?"

The reaction that I experienced was due to latent physical and mental impurities in the nervous system. The purification process that I endured was simply necessary. When I asked what had happened to me, Pal explained in simple terms. In those early days, he would answer my questions, but he rarely offered any extra words. If I wished to know more, it seemed that it was my duty to dig further.

"The nervous system is the meeting place between the physical and non-physical bodies," Pal explained.

"Why should it be so polluted, Sir?" I prodded.

"Since it links the two bodies, at least on the physical level, it will tend to hold unresolved tendencies, thoughts and, of course, impurities of diet, too."

"Wow. OK. And these medicines, Sir, will they heal the nervous system fully?"

"Of course." He laughed. "It will take some time, so you will have to take certain medicines home with you. Over the next few months, it will return to balance, and you will be fine."

"Is there anything else I can do to help with the healing, Sir?"

"Yes. Please pay attention to four things: your attitude to life, daily routine, diet, and any medicines I provide. In this order of importance. Of course, the first two you easily address by coming here," he said, waving his hand toward Arunachala, "but you must keep your diet pure. This is of great benefit."

He gave me homemade Siddha medicine that not only soothed the symptoms but also provided authentic health to the nervous system and mental state. During the time that he attended to my ailments, he asked further questions about my health. I spoke to him about the dizziness and fatigue, and he assured me that these had been the beginning of the nervous system derangements manifesting as physical diseases. In time, the nervous system derangement surely would have solidified as perhaps multiple sclerosis or some other chronic disease. Next, I related to him that I had been diagnosed with benign prostatic hyperplasia (BPH) and was taking medication for it. He said not a word. With wide eyes, he gazed intently at my lower body for some time and then looked up at me and said, "It will be fine."

From that moment onward, I never again took the BPH medication and have remained completely free of all signs of BPH ever since.

The days passed, and my body regained its strength. At the same time, I gained a much more solid sense of being grounded and relaxed with myself. In those weeks, Pal visited me almost daily, and as our relationship grew, his manner of interacting with and healing me evolved to finer and more astonishing heights. These healing sessions took on an esoteric feeling. He first sat opposite me, asked my full birth name, and had me place my hands on his. Instantly, he entered a semi-trance state, with his eyes alternately closed and gazing at the area above my head. Occasionally, he very gently touched my back or various areas of my head with soft motions. At other times, he blew gently on the crown of my skull or into my face. During these sessions, I naturally fell into a deep semiconscious state. My eyes closed, and my entire body and mind spontaneously relaxed. I had never felt such softness in the waking state. I treasured these healing sessions for the incredibly expansive and wonderfully relaxed state they provided. The feeling of release and newly discovered sense of freedom that I experienced in the days that followed astounded me. After each session, as I moved through the days and nights, I became increasingly aware of a heightened awareness, mental sharpness, and emotional or psychic grounding that I had never known before. Even my eyes saw people, trees, animals, and all movements in a new, brighter perspective. But one aspect of my psychic makeup was most affected and, in turn, provided the most immediate effects.

For years I had been on an exclusive search, of what I had assumed was a spiritual manner, and had subjected myself to various teachings, teachers, and austerities. The most notable experience while I practiced these various austerities was my utter lack of interest and ability to form and maintain relationships with the opposite gender. On the surface, I was convinced that I was consciously practicing celibacy in order to reach some higher spiritual state. That, however, was a psychic derangement. During one healing session, Pal did something extremely subtle that produced the most astonishing results. I was never aware of what exactly he had performed, because it quickly placed me in the wonderfully relaxed state of semiconscious bliss. When I returned to ordinary awareness, I was shocked beyond my wildest imagination. Instantly and without the slightest doubt, I was aware that whatever had previously prevented me from relating to the opposite gender in an uplifting, intimate, loving manner had been completely eradicated! I even felt the elimination of the blockage physically, as a rush of pure energy or light emanating from the base of my body, flowing through every cell, and pouring out of my head. Every particle of my physical body was vibrating. These sensations were so powerful, but what was even more noticeable was my sight. It was as if, for the very first time, I could see everything in the room, as if a long-time blindness had been removed. After each of the previous healing sessions with Pal, my eyes and mind possessed a softer view of nature and humanity, but this was far beyond that. A dark veil had been removed from my being, body, and mind. Bursting into tears of relief, release, and sheer joy, I attempted to convey my profound gratitude and respect. When I had gained a semblance of composure, I asked Pal what had occurred, or rather, what had been affecting me in such a way. He stated that an entity had taken root in me. Out of infinite, abounding compassion, he had released me from the entity's grip. From that day forward, I saw all beings—of both genders and indeed all of nature—in a new, increasingly clear, compassionate manner.

Of all that passed during that trip, the most surprising had yet to occur. Shortly before it was time for me to depart, I felt a strong urge to ask Pal if he would teach me this healing art called *Siddha Varma healing*. The urge was surprising to me, because I had never felt any inclination to join the healing profession. Even more relevant was that no Westerner had ever been instructed in the Siddhas' healing realm. I had no idea of the enormity of what I had innocently asked for, but somehow I felt that he would consent. The certainty sprang simply from the new yet intense bond that I felt with him coupled with my most sincere gratitude for the healing that he had blessed upon me. My joy when he gladly replied that I should return the following year to begin the healing journey only added to the already felt sense of lightness, invigoration, and soaring spirit.

Throughout the next year, the healing continued, and my relationship with Pal deepened. He was available to me at any hour of any day. Calling and emailing him regularly, I pestered him with countless questions. Absorbed in learning all that I could about the Siddhas and their traditions, I constantly asked for clarifications of material from his book and other sources. Whenever I felt emotional distress, grace was present. One day while experiencing profound grief while lying on my side, I silently called out to Pal. Instantly, the mountain Arunachala appeared before my eyes. A jolt hit my forehead so powerfully that it pushed my head backward. Coursing into the middle of my skull, the jolt traveled down my spine, finally coming to rest in the base of my body. The strong emotion waned. Awe and gratitude took its place, and I simply sat up and resumed the work that I had to do. Based on such intimate encounters, I opened up to Pal and showed my vulnerability. In turn, he cared for every aspect of my health and life circumstances. This he communicated with a degree of sensitivity, wisdom, and love that words cannot convey.

Whenever I speak with him or am with him, it is as if I am with my own truest self. Nothing is unknown to Pal. No matter the circumstances, every interaction we have is as if there is one person rather than two people. The most startling aspect of it all is that this absence of "other" feels entirely natural. It is also the most refreshing, life-renewing experience of which I could ever dream. Never could I have imagined being so completely accepted and totally approved of without any conditions. Devoid of judgement and demands, his attentive and beautifully divine influence on me and my life course had only begun to bloom. From this flow of divine love, the natural response kindled in me was and continues to be utter amazement and a yearning to find some offering worthy of such gifts. Never could I have imagined a person who possesses this degree of extreme humility, gentleness, patience, and overflowing spirit of kindness. Although the guru-disciple relationship may be a mystery to the Western mind, my experience is of the most profoundly deep, rich, intimately beautiful, and mysterious love affairs that this world can offer. Looking back at my life before I met Pal, this unique expression of divine grace, I wonder how I even lived. Here words truly fail me. This book is my best attempt to set down on paper what I have been fortunate enough to learn.

> *My love for you has driven me insane*
> *I wander aimlessly the ruins of my life,*
> *my old self a stranger to me*
> *Because of your love I have broken with my past*
> *My longing for you keeps me in this moment*
> *My yearning for you gives me courage*
> *I look for you in my innermost being.*

(Molana Jalal-e-Din Mohammad Molavi Rumi, *Rumi's Love Poems,* ed. Maria-Magdalena Blidarus [2010])

The Siddhas worship all of creation, all of existence, as divine—meaning that each particle has its own inherent intelligence—and deifies it as such. Nature, Existence, all of creation is known as the Mother Goddess, and is referred to in the feminine form, as She and Her, similar to the way in which the Western world refers to God as He and Him. Long before Hinduism, the ancient Dravidian culture (referred to by historians as the *Uma* cult) worshipped the divine as this feminine.

CHAPTER 2

The World of the Tamil Siddhas

Their holy heart trembles not,
Neither comes death, nor suffering, nor night, nor day,
Nor fruits of karma to experience,
Those who, attachment dropped, subsided with themselves.

(Siddha Thirumular, "Thirumanthiram," Verse 1624, In Pal Pandian, *Siddhas: Masters of the Basics* [Chennai, India: Pal Pandian, 2008])

Upon landing in the United States, I quickly realized that I was not the same man who had left for India some months earlier. The physical transformation was nothing short of astounding. Gone were the dizzy spells, intermittent numbness in the extremities, solar plexus pain upon awakening each day, and again, all signs of BPH. I had shed the excess body weight and regained enthusiasm for a healthy, plant-based diet. The most noticeable effects other than these immediate physical results were my feeling of being extremely grounded in my life and a profound sense of physical, mental, and emotional well-being and even vibrancy.

The ability to more easily digest life's events is characterized as being better able to flow with the ever-changing rhythm of our days and nights. Indeed, all parts of our lives—work, family, friends, lovers, money, food, and so forth—are affected. That is exactly what I felt when I returned: happy to wake each day and encounter what might come with enthusiasm and a much greater feeling of appreciation. I was able to form loving relationships naturally and with a sense of relaxed ease. Gone were the notions that I must refrain from ordinary pursuits in order to achieve an elevated state of consciousness. Pal's advice to pay attention to four things in their order of importance (attitude to life, daily routine, diet, and Siddha medicines) proved both simple and profoundly effective. Because so many wonderful things were unfolding for me, I yearned to learn more about the Tamil Siddhas. I read Pal's book daily. The aspects that were too esoteric were the basis for the emails with which I bombarded him. The incessant questions. He replied to all of my communications, but what I would not understand until many years later was that his answers spoke solely to what I was capable of grasping at that time. I also spent much time reading and learning about the Tamil Siddhas Themselves: Their histories and the many systems of healing which They created. By his touch and invitation for instruction, Pal had brought me into the realms of the Siddha masters.

For me, the greatest passion in life had always been the spiritual quest. Having already traveled the roads of restraining passion, long meditation, prayer, yoga postures, and the like, I had come to some conclusions based on my experiences. Chief among these conclusions was that each path contains some virtue and is useful in some way. Another was that I hungered for that which is complete in nature and utterly unspoiled by time. What I sought was authenticity. Living without attaining full enlightenment had become intolerable. If I were not guided on the most sure and quick path by a true master, my life's quest would remain unfulfilled. It would have to be the most direct path. Stepping into the world of the Siddhas is much like exploring another dimension, one that defies everything we know. There I found that the line between the possible and the impossible, the logical and the illogical, was blurred. Thus, only the distillation of supreme wisdom would suffice as a guide in that world. By sheer monumental grace, my life course was flowing in the direction of the ocean of such unconventional wisdom.

The Siddha lineage is the first and most ancient of the lineages of prehistoric India that flourished well before the Vedic age. Many of the later traditions, such as Buddhism and Hinduism, refer to Siddhas. However, it was in the land of the Dravidians, those prehistoric inhabitants of India, where the original masters, the Tamil Siddhas, originated. Although there has always been an emphasis on eighteen Siddhas, it is widely known that there were many more than eighteen. Yet these eighteen are the primal ones who reached the states of human potential in relation to divinity, began the oral tradition, and eventually encoded the methods, in scripture form, on palm leaves. Many of Their followers attained Siddhahood, thus creating the lineage.

Attempting to date the origin of the Siddhas is as futile as attempting to understand the chronology of the happenings prior to the Big Bang and existence of the physical universe. We know that what we consider history is predated by much more human civilization than that of which we have direct evidence. The ambiguity of the Siddhas' origin is also unavoidable because Their lifestyles were so contradictory to the typical ways of civilization. Forsaking all social behavior, They existed deep in the forests and in remote caves. Preferring not to be found by the common masses, They dived deeply into Their penances, perfected Themselves and, out of compassion, shared Their healing and spiritual sciences with humanity through a few trusted disciples.

The Siddha tradition is reputed to have originated from Lord Siva (God, in our Western context), who revealed it to Goddess Uma (Parvati or Shakti), His consort.

Thus revealed Sadasivam to Devi.
The Goddess passed it on to Nandhi.
Nandhi exposed it to Dhanvanthri.
Dhanvanthri taught it to Ashwini.
Agasthiyar received the knowledge from Him,
To be passed on to Pulasthiyar.
Pulasthiyar conveyed it to Theraiyar.

(Yugimuni Siddhar, "Yugi Chintamani," Verse 800, In Pal Pandian, *Siddhas: Masters of the Basics* [Chennai, India: Pal Pandian, 2008])

The Siddhas are the originators of all of the various spiritual paths throughout time and, just as important, ancient medicine and genuine healing arts. Thus, the Siddha tradition is, in truth, the mother tradition of all present-day spiritual pursuits, healing, and medicine.

Although finding proof of the Siddhas at the fountainhead of mystical wisdom, in terms of data, is always comforting, experience is far more real and meaningful. To this end, you need only continue reading this book in order to discover my experience of the Tamil Siddhas' wisdom in the realms of tantra, yoga, alchemy, medicine, and healing. The chapters that follow detail my search in these arts, with an emphasis on firsthand experience. But before we delve into specific aspects of the

Siddhas, some history is necessary in order to provide context as to when and where this mystery-shrouded clan originated.

Ancient Times

I have found that, when attempting to distill the truth about a subject, the best place to begin is with current notions that have long been accepted as fact. From a sound understanding of those accepted beliefs, one can question them and then search out other possibilities. This broader perspective then provides much more information. It is an ideal platform from which to begin afresh. This process is necessary if we wish to be open to the possibility of alternative realities. Without considering fresh information (based on additional data), we would remain prejudiced and confined to existing theories. From such a stagnant vantage point, learning anything new would not be possible.

Before the British rule of India, Western scholars believed their own ancestors' stories and biblical accounts that they were the first and most civilized in antiquity. However, the excavation in the 1920s of an ancient site challenged these notions. Termed the Indus Valley Civilization, and spanning present-day northwest India, southern Pakistan, and northeast Afghanistan, its cities of Harappa and Mohenjo-Daro forced Western scholars to reconsider previous ideas. (The countries of present-day India, Pakistan, Bangladesh, and Nepal, are all included in what is called the land of the Dravidians, or Tamilians, because those areas were inhabited by a common race). The archaeologists found enormous cities that had extremely advanced infrastructure. A Bronze Age civilization that dated back to at least 3300 BC, its sanitation system, water system, and city design would not be matched until the much later Roman Empire. The Indus Valley Civilization's language, which the archaeologists discovered on the monuments and tablets in the excavation, still has not been deciphered. Art, law, philosophy, and advanced farming techniques all flourished there, millennia before they were practiced elsewhere. The engineering required for a clean and well-functioning metropolis (containing a population numbering in the millions), surrounded by well-irrigated, bountiful agricultural lands, had not been witnessed before. Most relevant, however, are the conclusions drawn by those Western archeologists. They concluded that Sanskrit was the original language of India, which necessitated ignoring all previous civilizations, including the very one they were excavating. The immediate effect was to marginalize large segments of the population of the Indian subcontinent, particularly in the southern states of Tamil Nadu and Kerala. Those areas that had much more ancient roots that had encompassed the entire Indian subcontinent would be ignored. These conclusions have remained largely unchallenged and treated as fact. They have had broad influence on our perceptions of India and Indian traditions to the present day.

Most that we think of as quintessentially Indian is based on these assumptions, which seem to have been enforced in order to support colonial rule. By shifting the emphasis from the ancient Tamil to Sanskrit, academics transferred importance from the original language to the first Indo-European language. Because the invaders (Aryans) seemed to have appeared from distant lands, the implication was that they civilized the wild and primitive lands of the Indian subcontinent. Following the invasion, Hinduism and the caste system began. The earliest scriptures of Hinduism are the *Vedas*, of which the *Rig Veda*, dating to 1500 BC, is the most ancient. In fact, the *Rig Veda* is among the oldest Sanskrit writing. I have always found it confusing that the same British academics who claimed the antiquity of Sanskrit were simultaneously standing on and excavating an enormous metropolitan area that contained large tablets and buildings with writing that they dated as more than 2,000 years older than Sanskrit! The chief reason behind these odd inconsistencies lies in how colonial powers always found ways to support their rule over foreign lands. Separating the native people from one other and from their traditions proved a useful tool. In lands that contained varied tribal populations, such separation was a simple matter of endorsing and giving privilege to one segment. That segment would then aid the colonial power in subjecting and ruling the masses. This approach made the British rule of India easier and appeared to legitimize Britain's position of power.

When I looked more closely at the methods used by historians and scholars to label civilizations, I was both astonished and dismayed. The narrow-mindedness of using just a few basic yardsticks to define a society as civilized defies common sense. Too much time in book learning and a lack of life wisdom can do that to us, I suppose. Intoxicated by our academic environments and seeking the platitudes of our colleagues who are immersed in the same confined world, we can lose our most cherished quality: spontaneity. To be spontaneous in thought is by no means impetuous but rather involves that which abides in us when we are children: the trait of finding out things for ourselves, birthing them from our own discovery without prior ideas of what we will find. This is true spontaneity. This is the very reason that little children can learn languages very easily. They are unusually open, their minds uncluttered by what they think they already know. Lacking such open space in their minds, scholars hold on to the unwavering notion that the combination of a written language and urban dwellings is sufficient to prove that the society was civilized and that the lack of these two items is sufficient to deem a society uncivilized. To me, such criteria are insufficient. Based on these criteria, ancient societies' contributions to humanity largely have been overlooked, because those societies have been considered primitive. From this arrogant perspective, the modern age, with its many languages and urban settings, has divorced itself from its very roots.

Recently, I saw a BBC documentary that proved that not all scholars are bound to their historical brethren. Titled *The Story of India* and hosted by Michael Wood, the series began by recounting how humans first arrived at the Indian subcontinent. The commonly held belief is that humans first left Africa about 70,000 to 80,000 years ago. It may well have been much earlier than that.

Nonetheless, the first migration out of Africa had long been considered a move north to Europe. However, scientific data presented in the documentary supports a different case.

Scientists from the Madurai Kamaraj University in Tamil Nadu took samples of DNA from residents of the surrounding villages. In inhabitants whose ancestors have lived in the area for countless generations, they found a particular genetic marker. This marker, known as M130, is understood to be a genetic marker of the humans who first left Africa. The same M130 marker was found in all of the inhabitants of a particular isolated village. As the scientists further examined the data points, they arrived at the conclusion that the first migration out of Africa went around the Arabian Sea and down into South India. From there, the rest of the world was subsequently populated. Even today the people of India call their homeland Mother India. India may be the mother of all of us. According to the documentary, all non-Africans can trace their lineage to these first migrations into South India.

Later in the documentary, the host and crew were allowed to film an ancient fire ritual. Only recently have scholars—or any outsiders—been allowed to view and study that ritual. In the ritual, linguists found a form of chanting that defies anything they have ever learned or studied. Most of the mantra contains sounds that resemble no human language or speech. Never having been written down, it is tens of thousands of years old. It predates any human language that is commonly accepted to have developed 10,000 to 15,000 years ago. In fact, entire portions of the mantra closely resemble animal sounds, particularly those of birds. This is a prime example of how humans would have communicated, passing on information orally, without any need for a written language.

The inevitable decline of the Indus Valley Civilization is often attributed to an influx of invaders. Called Aryans (whose literal translation is invaders), these people are thought to have originated in central Asia and eastern Persia. This theory of an Aryan invasion has itself come under scrutiny, because some people in North India prefer the idea that the remnants of Alexander the Great's army accounted for the changes, especially the caste system. Whatever the truth may be, it is generally held that the Aryans brought lighter skin color to the population of the Indian subcontinent. The other notable change they introduced was societal stratification, or the caste system, which would have a tremendous effect in India throughout history.

Prior to any invasion and predating the rise of the Indus Valley Civilization, an even more ancient people, with its own culture and language, populated the Indian subcontinent. Having evolved from those first migrants from Africa, the people and their culture can accurately be described as the most original of Indian civilizations. This is supported by the genetic data. The echoes of these ancestors can be found today in the ebony-skinned inhabitants of the villages and cities of Tamil Nadu in South India. Their spiritual, medicinal, and healing saints, still revered by the simple people of Tamil Nadu, are the Siddhas.

Siddha Chronicles

Long before the rise of the Indus Valley Civilization and with the later continental developments of Sanskrit, Hinduism, and the caste system, the Indian subcontinent was the domain of the Dravidians. Historians' findings coupled with Tamil literary works such as *Tholkapiam* and *Thiruvasagam* reveal the antiquity and boundless wisdom that spread throughout these lands. From these and other works came the three Tamil academies *(sangams)*, which propagated the sixty-four Arts of Tamilians. These arts encompassed all aspects of living and imparted knowledge in areas such as cooking, architecture, war, magic, languages, arithmetic, and poetry. In addition, healing, medicine, martial arts, astrology, alchemy, and spiritual practices are known to have been included in the arts. Gatherings were attended and led by the Siddhas with the support of the kings. The refinement of society and its individuals was the aim of these gatherings of wise beings. The first academy, located in the old city of Madurai in the Tamilian continent of Lemuria, was composed of 49 districts consisting of 549 members and existed from 9990 BC to 5550 BC. The code book used at this initial academy was *Agathiyam*, which was founded by the primal Siddha Agasthiyar. The second academy, in the city of Kavadapuram, existed from 5550 BC to 1850 BC and ended due to an enormous flood that submerged many parts of the kingdom. King Mudu Thirumaran escaped with many others in sailing vessels and settled in the present-day southern India city of Madurai, where the third academy lasted for approximately 1,850 years.

Whatever the later historical facts of India may be, it is certain that the changes from outside brought more than just the caste system. The changes also created the religion of Hinduism. Hinduism represented an enormous change from the earlier practice of worshipping the goddess aspect of the divine and celebrating intimacy with nature. Hinduism replaced these practices with a punishing separation of classes and an age of countless rituals. This was the beginning of the Vedic age. This is the very culture that the British advertised as being the original and ancient culture of India. It is also what people throughout the world, even now, think of and practice as ancient Indian wisdom and culture. However, that view is inaccurate. In order to prove its inaccuracy, we need only look at how the Siddhas, whose traditions and language of Tamil long preceded the Vedic age, responded to such influences.

The Siddhas openly mocked the emphasis on religious ceremonies and ritual worship:

> *It is a waste to make floral offerings;*
> *And to chant mantras to an idol,*
> *When God is within you;*
> *It's like a vessel, which doesn't realize, What is there in it?*

(Siddha Siva Vakkiyar, "Siva Vakkiyar Padangal,"
Verse 521, In Pal Pandian, *Siddhas: Masters of the Basics*
[Chennai, India: Pal Pandian, 2008])

In stark contrast to the religious orthodoxy that held a stranglehold on power, the Siddhas urged spiritual aspirants to strive for an intense, direct, and personal confrontation with God. Exhorting the people to shed their delusions, pretensions, empty rituals, and barren morality, the masters laid forth an abrasive, uncompromising path. Obviously, this approach did not sit well with the power structure. Another direct confrontation of the Siddhas with the elite was the Siddhas' open derision of the caste system. Ascribing the lowest caste to the rank of untouchable was never acceptable to Them. Furthermore, the Siddhas were marked as nonconformists and rebels due to Their manner of speech. The orthodox Hindus used an extremely formal way of communicating based on precise usage of Sanskrit. To use words in a different fashion was considered not only unrefined but also unclean. Yet the Siddhas paid no mind to social customs and precedence. The Siddhas' use of the language of the common people, coupled with deeply veiled meanings, only further confused those in authority. Much like that social and religious rebel Jesus, the Siddhas shunned formalities and so antagonized the orthodoxy:

> *In the clash of caste, we will kindle the fire,*
> *In the open market we will plant our staff,*
> *On the cross road of the street, we will play and dance,*
> *In the undesirable house, we will make friendships,*
> *Strolling, loitering, we will sleep,*
> *Felicitous women we will enjoy,*
> *All the five primal Brahma are ignorant.*
> *O Snake, Dance, saying this.*

(Pampatti Siddhar, "Songs of Pampatti Siddhar," Verse 3, In Pal Pandian, *Siddhas: Masters of the Basics*, [Chennai, India: Pal Pandian, 2008])

Direct language, such as the above quote by Pampatti Siddhar, would have been extremely shocking and confrontational to those in power. Furthermore, the Siddhas saying that They would enjoy the company of felicitous women would appear to others as a very uncouth statement. In actuality, Pampatti Siddhar was stating that no one is unclean, unfit, or below anyone else. By no means did He mean that They cavorted with women. He did, however, mean to shock those in power. The fact that they could not see the hidden meaning in such words showed their outright prejudice and ignorance.

Themselves hailing from all levels of society, including the highest (Brahmins), wealthy merchants, warriors, and even some from the lowest level of society, the Siddhas made no such distinctions. Status and power have never mattered to Them; They have only ever valued maturity of spirit. In a society that had become overwhelmed by an elitist and ritual-based mentality, the Siddhas became viewed as rebels who represented a threat to the elites. Thus began a long history of misrepresentation of both the Siddhas and Their methods. Throughout time, They have been labeled and maligned as heretical, false, and impure. The exception is that the common and simple-minded people of Tamil Nadu continued to revere Them, sing Their praises, and seek the comfort of Their wisdom and healing.

Throughout thousands of years of keeping to a strictly oral tradition and imparting their fullest knowledge only through the Guru-Sishya (teacher-student) relationship, the Siddhas remained veiled from the mainstream. Over time, the most trusted disciples were instructed to record the vast storehouse of Siddha knowledge by writing poetic verses on palm-leaf manuscripts. Encompassing all aspects of Siddha divine insight, including medicine, healing, astrology, alchemy, yoga, tantra, and spiritual essence, the manuscripts contain the vast array of human potential. In the manuscripts lie Their works on the origin of metallurgy and its various uses, the archetypal healing deities, the mysterious power spots, and medicinal preparations. All of this knowledge flowed from Their invaluable yogic insights that emerged from the mystery of the life-giving and life-taking rhythms of nature.

Even the language of the Siddhas is unconventional, which is another reason for the mystery that surrounds Them. Written in what has become known as the *twilight language*, the Siddha poems are characterized by a dark, ambiguous style and contain endless symbolism, metaphors, analogies, and double meanings. The grammatical usage is known only to the masters themselves. To this very day, They remain the only ones capable of truly understanding and deciphering the full meaning and import of the manuscripts. In Tamil there is an old saying that sums up this situation: "Only a tiger can lick another tiger."

Virtually all that I read about the Siddhas and their unorthodox ways seemed to make sense but in a non-cerebral way. I was no longer surprised by Their secrecy and humility, because Pal naturally exuded these qualities. In fact, in his presence, secrecy and humility did not seem like different attributes. Secrecy appeared not as material being withheld for selfish or arrogant reasons, such as other people being unworthy, but rather as folded into humility. Pal was always ready to give, yet he had nothing to prove or establish. During that first year, while I was being treated by him, I would often be surprised by him appearing suddenly, seemingly out of nowhere. While sitting at a chai stand, strolling the alleys on my return from the mountain, or simply picking up fruit at a roadside stand, I would look up and see him there. I was convinced that he had not been there a moment earlier and that I was witnessing his siddhis, or supernatural power. Upon deeper reflection, however, I decided that the most likely explanation was Pal's complete lack of ego-centered living. He leaves no footprints where he strides, because he possesses no goals of his own. Simply flowing with existence in this way casts an unmistakable spell on those of us who remain fixated on our mortal fancies. This natural flowing with existence is true humility. It seems secretive only to the rest of us.

Having read of the Siddhas' history and independent nature, I wondered what my first year of instruction by Pal in Varma would be like. I had taken literally much of what I had read about the Siddhas. Should I take a pen and paper for note taking? Would the education be transmitted orally? Frankly, I had no idea what would take place or how. What I did possess was tons of enthusiasm and determination. Maybe determination is not the best word, but it is the word I would have used to describe my mindset at that time. Much later, I recognized it as pure trust born from fate, from destiny being fulfilled. Those were the qualities with which I boarded the plane for the long flight to India that year. Although I was aware of little else, the purpose of the trip was crystal clear for me.

CHAPTER 3

Mind, Body, and Spirit

My journey of healing instruction would wind its way over the course of ten years. In truth, it is never ending, because the levels of Siddha Varma healing are vast. Yet from the beginning, what I ached most for was introduction into the spiritual realms of the masters. That would, however, have to wait. While I was with Pal during those early years, whenever I attempted to broach spiritual subjects, he consistently replied using the framework of the healing realm. Many years later, his possible reasons for this approach became more clear. The derangements of the body and mind first had to be balanced. Otherwise, the tremendous influx of energy could not be integrated. Indeed, the vicious cycle of energy influx and energy dissipation is witnessed daily in society.

We constantly spend our life force, mental, emotional, and physical, in countless interactions that are of no actual use for our daily life. Embarking on true spiritual paths, of which Siddha healing is one, provides a tremendous amount of energy. It is essential that one be capable of receiving it and grounding it in a graceful way. Years later, Pal explained it to me.

"It is very important that you never hold on to the energy from healing sessions," Pal said. "If we attempt to keep, to hold on to, what comes to us, it can cause many problems."

"Even great masters are known to feed the poor on festival days, to attend or lead poojas [ritual worship]. Why would They do these things? Although They are beyond the need for approaching the divine with such rituals, They know that They must give back. There is so much power that is accumulated. By giving in this way, it does not stagnate within Them. And that is Life, Nature. She will always demand that we participate with Her."

Although ignorant of how Varma healing instruction would unfold, I had come to understand some of the basics of what I was about to step into. The exhaustive research and incessant pestering had taught me many things. But far more important, relevant, and alive for me was my own experience. My body had changed dramatically. Long-held subconscious impressions had been erased. I was left with an incredibly fresh feeling of aliveness. This helped my mind to be very sharp. Coupled with natural enthusiasm, it assisted me in understanding the Siddhas and their many paths.

When I had first stepped into Pal's small house some years earlier, I had immediately noticed the many containers strewn about. There were metal pots and open fire pits outside and glass and plastic containers inside; they contained an endless variety of herbs, oils, pastes, and powders. When he had come to me during my healing crisis the previous year, I had directly experienced the various aspects of both Siddha medicine and Siddha Varma healing. Although they are distinct disciplines, in the hands of a master healer, their overlapping natures blur the lines of demarcation. A true Siddha healer encompasses the arts of medicine, healing, and alchemy within his or her very being. For me, however, the difference between Siddha medicine and Siddha Varma healing would be clear and well defined. My having no background in natural medicines would not present any difficulty. Varma healing would, itself, be the sole focus of my instruction. Nevertheless, I was fascinated by the medicines that Pal and his assistants prepared. Countless varieties of herbs, minerals, and even animal products littered Dwarka Mayi, his healing center. There, in a small private room, my journey into this ancient healing art began.

The medicinal system of the Siddhas has long been openly shared, and so its practice is widespread. On the other hand, Siddha Varma, the therapeutic and energetic healing dimension, has not. It is a science in its wisdom yet resembles an art in its practice. Despite this difference, Siddha medicine and Siddha Varma rest upon the same definitive logic and science. Before I could receive any instruction, I had to deeply understand the foundations of how the Siddhas view health, disease, anatomy, pathology, and so forth. Exploring these areas of the Siddha tradition as a whole gave me an appreciation for the uniquely deep possibilities of Siddha Varma healing.

Health and Disease: The Siddha Tradition's Perspective

The word *health* in English is based on the Anglo-Saxon word *hale*, which means whole. To be healthy is to be whole. Furthermore, the English word *holy* is also based on the same root word. It would appear that humanity has long understood that wholeness gives meaning to life. This wholeness, or integrity of being, is itself health. According to the Siddhas, health is described as a "spontaneous, dynamic, nurturing pulsation at every moment.... a flowing river of natural existence." Having been granted at the moment of conception, our very being is created and grounded by this naturally occurring flow. Thus, health is our most basic memory and true birthright. In truth, life and health are not simply linked. They are, in fact, both one. The inherent possibility of tuning into natural law by living in an existential way is life's gift to us.

This law of nature is ingrained within each of us. It is revealed within the body as its own natural understanding and memory of balance. The body knows its own health. It also contains its own healing potential in the form of the most ideal pharmacy ever created. The body, like all of nature, is filled with this pulsating intelligence that simply requires our sensitive and humble recognition. Those who come to understand this flow of nature, of which the body and mind are composed, live their lives devoid of societal stress, both physical and mental. From this wonderfully felt sensitivity, they move through life with ever-expanding strength, grounding, courage, and wisdom. They naturally fulfill their purpose. As their lives unfold, humility and gratitude blooms as their predominate reactions and responses to life's inconsistent circumstances. This is the most natural feeling of being intricately woven into one's greater surroundings. By releasing our demands and obsessive tendencies, we begin to awaken. It is a "falling back" into the rhythmic flow of existence. From Her (Nature's, Creation's, or Manifestation's) essence, our bodies are formed. We are surrounded by all we need in order to grow and sustain ourselves. She has filled our planet with the very items that will remind the body and mind of their balance when illness arises. Balance is relaxation in the arms of Nature.

This view of what constitutes health and what manifests as disease certainly differs from our modern view. What our Anglo-Saxon ancestors seemed to understand, that to be healthy is to be whole, modern medicinal systems have yet to grasp. Lacking a viewpoint of what is whole, the current allopathic approach is instead based on the purely scientific model of the body being nothing more than a machine. In other words, modern medical systems are reductionist models that assume the person to be a mere biological lump of flesh. From this viewpoint, when disease occurs, we are provided with pharmaceuticals, which are nothing more than induced chemical agents, and surgery. Should we have issues with our minds or emotions, the arsenal of today's medical professionals is similarly limited. Where this system has indeed achieved wonderful heights is the arena of care of trauma and wounds. Yet for the illnesses that afflict human beings' minds and bodies at alarming rates, the focus of modern medicine is severely limited. However, a person is not simply a body but much more. The proper scope of treatment would necessarily include the body, mind, and spirit. In other words, treatment must include the physical being, the energy of the being, and the consciousness of the being.

What is even more stark in contrast to modern medicine is how the Siddhas understand the human body. From this understanding, all without modern gadgets, they came to learn how to prevent and cure all forms of disease. This living knowledge evolved from their own direct experience and the resultant yogic insights. At the core of this understanding is the intimate relationship between the individual and the cosmos.

In contrast to our reductionist and mechanistic worldview today, the Siddhas understood and declared that a grand unity permeates existence. This unity is not ordinarily seen by us, because it requires vision that is not clouded by appearances and the opinions of others.

Mind, Body, and Spirit

> *Whatever is in the macrocosm is in the microcosm,*
> *Whatever is in the microcosm is in the macrocosm,*
> *Macrocosm and microcosm are one*
> *When you look in right understanding.*

(Siddha Sattaimuni, In Pal Pandian, *Siddhas: Masters of the Basics,* [Chennai, India: Pal Pandian, 2008])

In order to have this deep insight, it is necessary to, as Siddha Sattaimuni states, "look in right understanding." That a human being is a part of nature is a step toward such an understanding. Beyond that, it is known that She, Nature, organizes every particle of livingness in every human being. Plainly put, the Siddhas insist that what exists in the cosmos also exists in exact replica in the human body. The human form contains within it the universe's reflection. This knowledge holds enormous potential. The universe is intelligent in design and capable of regenerating itself in an ever-present state of balance and harmony. The cosmos is constantly in the process of creation, movement, and destruction. This flux of infinite parts is ingrained as the cosmos' very nature. However, only when viewed from a holistic perspective is this grand intelligence of harmony revealed. Ordinarily, the human mind's inherent tendency to separate and analyze causes us to view the cosmos as broken into parts. From that perspective, one is tempted to see countless individual components undergoing infinite types of drama and trauma. The same holds true with the body. If the body is seen as multiple parts, pieces, and ever-smaller components, its true identity remains elusive. Intricately woven into the fabric of existence, each one of us is far more than the sum of body parts. If one is tempted to see the universe as a random, cruel, disjointed mix of separate pieces, one need only view the stars on a clear night and with an open, relaxed mind. This is a simple cure for stress and anxiety, because the universe's wonderful balance and harmony is evident in the night sky.

All the while, within us is the mirror image of the oceanic rhythm, the animating pulsation of the cosmos. It manifests as the river flow of natural existence and endlessly flowing, always changing, always moving phenomena. This life pulse aspires to live. The Siddhas call this primordial pulsation of all life *Vasi* (living). When this river flow of life hits a blockage, it sounds an alarm. These blockages are called *viyadhi,* which is literally translated as deviations from nature, meaning disease. Because life (health) is movement, intelligent and rhythmic, what we have come to call disease is discordant flow, or blockages, in the harmonious pulse of life. This is the alarm that Nature gives us to enable us to finally understand our personal boundaries. Nature does this in order to remind us to protect ourselves from influences, external demands, and obsessive activities that do not really support growth in our lives: we call these disease. The indication of disease shows how we have misconceived our

Mind, Body, and Spirit

inspiration for life. When we grow insensitive to ourselves and our life flow, a misalignment or deviation is created within us. When the misalignment gains sufficient force, or identity, it expresses itself as disease in the mind or body. The chronic diseases on which the healthcare industry thrives arise from this misalignment. Hypertension, arthritis, allergies, diabetes, autoimmune disorders, asthma, and back pain are prime examples of our life force encountering blockages. These conditions have manifested from resistance in the natural flow of life force. When the primordial pulsation of life alters from its natural, healthy flow and experiences blockages, it begs to be liberated. Once liberated, the pulsation of life resumes in its originally designed pattern of unhindered flow, which is reflected as vibrant well-being.

Based on the Siddhas' own quests and resultant experiences of wholeness, Their systems of healing have blended all aspects of mind, body, and spirit. Included is Their understanding that each of us possesses within ourselves the mirror image of all creation. By recognizing that the forces that create, sustain, and destroy the cosmos are present within the body, They developed the healing systems of Siddha Varma, Siddha medicine, and spiritual practices.

The unique understanding of health, disease, and the beautiful intertwining of a person with the cosmos provided me with the foundation for Pal to gradually give more in-depth instruction. He was quick to point out that, of course, the masters also knew and incorporated in their healing systems what we today call anatomy. Bones, tissues, blood, organs, and hormones were also well understood and taken into account by the Siddha masters. The grand difference between Them and practitioners of modern medicine lies in Their knowledge that humans, and indeed all things material, stretch far beyond the physical. As such, They never confined the body to being a mere biological structure. This is what is meant by *holistic healing*. The whole is what can be understood to contain health. This I understood. What I did not yet understand was how this is shown in us, and in an effort to understand this, I asked questions. Pal's replies helped me to see, in greater detail, the cosmos mirrored in the body. He both explained and showed what the Siddhas have long known about how all things material are created. The Siddhas' healing and spiritual realms are based on this very understanding of the subtle forces giving rise to the physical.

Anatomy: Macrocosm and Microcosm

> *Who can know the greatness of our Lord?*
> *Who can know His length and breadth?*
> *An infinite nameless flame is He,*
> *Whose unknowable roots, I venture to speak.*

(Siddha Thirumular, "Thirumanthiram," Verse 95, In Pal Pandian, *Siddhas: Masters of the Basics* [Chennai, India: Pal Pandian, 2008])

All that exists has appeared in *That*, the boundless totality in which the cosmos is born, grows, and dies. Whether It is called God, Self, Consciousness, Sivam, or *Bhramam* makes no difference. *It* is the homogenous perpetuity that pervades, sustains, and vitalizes all Existence. Impossible to truly describe yet the Source of all, undisturbed, pure Consciousness gives rise to creation. Siddha Healer Pal has described this process as follows:

> *From the Source is derived an altered state, from which is derived another, and yet another, and again and so on… until the process of evolution comes to rest at the point where no more creation or evolution is needed—from here on, there is only manifestation! This is so, because the state of evolution has reached the state of perfect cosmic unrest, a state that allows unlimited manifestation of form.*

The profound beauty of existence is represented here by Pal's description of it as "perfect cosmic unrest."

In Taoism, this unrest is called *primordial chaos*, that nebulous state of the universe before heaven and earth separated from each other. From and within the plenum, there arose this altered state of cosmic unrest. This is the causative principle for the creation of the cosmos. The first cosmic vibration emanates as the most primal of distinctions, called the *Primordial Two*.

Although They are called *Siva Tattwa* and *Sakthi Tattwa,* They can be thought of more easily as God and Goddess or cosmic masculine and feminine. Yet, They are at no point separate, for They are interdependent and present in all aspects of creation at all times. The idea of the Primordial Two can seem paradoxical and certainly did to me when I first encountered it, but Pal's explanation helped me to grasp it.

"Have you ever seen the statues or paintings of Lord Siva with a half-male and a half-female body?" he asked.

When I nodded my reply, he continued.

"Here it is shown that They are not two, but They are represented this way to help our minds understand. Siva, called Purusha, is the cosmic spirit and is depicted as masculine. Sakthi, called Prakrithi, is the cosmic substance and is the universal archetype of feminine. But remember, They are not two. What is very important is that neither is created. They have always existed, but it is the first cosmic vibration in which They are expressed. You can understand it like this: Purusha or Siva is that which is not created and does not create. Prakrithi, or Sakthi, is also that which is not created, but She does create. Neither is created or caused in any way. They are primordial divinity. Can you now see why the Siddhas, and all of the most ancient societies, worshipped the feminine, the Goddess, as Their creator?"

"Yes, that is beautiful, Sir. Really lovely. Cosmic spirit and substance. I never heard of this until now. And I can see how this is also understood as primordial masculine and feminine. That They are not created but that Sakthi, the cosmic substance, does create somehow makes sense. I have no idea how or why, but I can see this now. Perhaps it is because I have heard that long ago, before recorded history, all societies were matriarchal and worshiped the divine feminine, the Goddess, and then it all changed and became the patriarchal structure we are accustomed to."

"Yes, that is so, but it is important to remember that Purusha and Prakrithi are never separate and always exist together, everywhere. Being inseparable, these Two are the foundation from which all other derived or altered states evolve. From the Primordial Two, there arose three attributes, the *Gunas*, and from these three came the five elements. Once the five elements were created, all creation came to a halt. There was no more creation, because everything both macrocosmic and microcosmic is made of these five elements."

The three primal attributes, the Gunas, and the five elements of which Pal spoke completed, in a very succinct way, the process of how everything has come into existence. Briefly and with simple language, he had just explained how the Siddhas learned about the creation of the universe. It would take some time for me to fully grasp the significance of the five elements. That the entire universe is nothing more than the infinite combinations and interplay of these five substances seems a simple notion. The relevance that our bodies and food are combinations of these substances would eventually open for me doors of vast healing potential. At the time, however, it was enough for me to grasp that, once the five elements had been created, all creation halted, because a state of perfect cosmic unrest had been achieved. From that point onward, there was no further creation; there was only manifestation.

> *They saw twenty-five, who destroyed their birth,*
> *How Purusha entered the body corporeal, none else know,*
> *That which sought the woman's birth pit, the bipolar,*
> *In form, twain rushed and fell.*

(Siddha Thirumular, "Thirumanthiram," Verse 454, In Pal Pandian, *Siddhas: Masters of the Basics* [Chennai, India: Pal Pandian, 2008])

The Three Primary Qualities (Gunas)

The cosmic spirit, Siva, is the non-active animating principle; the cosmic substance, Sakthi, is the original material from which all further evolution comes forth. From Sakthi, all is created; to Sakthi, all returns. Three basic attributes, Gunas, are inherent to its very nature, and each has particular correlating functions:

- *Sattwa Guna:* illumination as equilibrium
- *Rajas Guna:* activity or excitement as movement
- *Tamas Guna:* inertia or darkness as restraint

Mind, Body, and Spirit

Originally existing in a state of perfect balance and harmony, these three forces remain as such. Only by the slightest imbalance among them do they interact with each other. They always chase one other in an attempt to stay in balance. This active play, or dance, among them is necessary and is, itself, cosmic unrest, or chaos.

In its most basic form, the process begins with Rajas Guna, the active Guna, attempting to manifest Sattwa Guna as light, followed by the Tamasic Guna restraining such activity. Thus the play of energy among the three Gunas solidifies consciousness into form. Although this is a simplified form and further variations ensue, it includes the basic tenets necessary for the creation of the next and final evolutionary stage of cosmic spirit and substance: the five elements.

The Five Elements (Mahabhutas)

From the state of cosmic unrest created by the interplay of the three forces (Gunas) that inherently exist in the Sakthi (cosmic substance), emerge the five elements (*Mahabhutas*):

- *Ether:* extremely subtle space or vacuity
- *Air:* gas and motion
- *Fire:* radiance and luminosity
- *Water:* fluidity
- *Earth:* solidity

These elements are not in any way to be confused with the elements of modern chemistry; these are the primordial elements (*Bhutas*) of which the universe consists. They evolve in successive states, one from the other, beginning with ether, the space element, and ending with earth, the element of solidity. In this way, creation is completed, and only manifestation remains. Most relevant is that everything in the universe is composed of these five elements. Human anatomy and physiology, causal factors of disease, food for the sustenance of the body, and materials for the treatment and healing of diseases all fall within the five elemental categories. All manifested things, including the human body and the human mind, have derived from the original balance of the Source, having traveled through the state of cosmic unrest to take a manifested form via the five elements.

Microcosm: Humoral Pathology

In the human body, the five elements manifest through the three biological humors (functions), which are called *doshas* and known collectively as the *tridosha*. Health is nothing more than the perfect balance of these three doshas (humors), and all disease is a result of their imbalance. The five elements combine in pairs to form the three doshas: *vata* (air), *pitta* (fire), and *kapha* (earth). They are pairs in that vata is a combination of the ether and air elements, pitta is a combination of the air and fire elements, and kapha is a combination of the water and earth elements. Each person has one of the doshas as his or her predominant nature, or constitution, and so is a vata, pitta, or kapha type.

In both the cosmos and the human form, all five elements always coexist yet adopt varying roles in order to accentuate the quality most summoned for any particular expression. The Siddha masters cryptically spoke of the secret ways of nature. They stated that none of the five elements are ever absent in the cosmos—anywhere or anytime. In exactly the same way, each individual expresses, from the time of birth, one of the three doshas (vata, pitta, or kapha) as predominate, although his or her basic constitution includes all three doshas. At various times of a person's life, one dosha will dominate the other doshas. This variation among the doshas depends on time of day, diet, age or phase of life, season of the year, climate, and other factors.

Vata-Pitta-Kapha

The three doshas, or combinations of the five primal elements, enable existence to take human form and govern not only our physical nature but also our emotional and mental natures. Furthermore, each of the doshas has inherent qualities:

- Vata: movement and propulsion
- Pitta: heat and conversion
- Kapha: form and stability

These three basic functions intermingle to influence all human form and expression, from the simple to the complex. However, each person is usually marked, based on his or her particular nature, by one dosha in a unique manner. According to Pal, this mark is "Nature's gift to us." This predominant constitution of each person's physical and mental makeup is called the *prakrithi*. Its literal meaning is "the first-born nature or form." After our birth, our prakrithi does not change, but the influence of incompatible climates, long-held habits, lifestyles, diet, and so forth, do cause apparent alterations, or derangements, to our natural constitutions. This inherent constitution with which we are each born is formed as a combination of our parents' prakrithi, which are formed by the intermingling of their own individual states of body, mind, lifestyle, and so forth during union and the resultant conception. Each person usually has one of the following as his or her dominant constitution:

- Vata people are airy in terms of physical characteristics, with thin frames, low body weight, and sensitivity to cold, wind, and dryness. Psychologically, vata people are active, creative, secure, inspired, and flexible when in balance. When imbalanced, they are anxious, dull, insecure, depressed, and unstable.
- Pitta people are fiery in terms of physical characteristics, with moderate frames, moderate body weight, strong

appetites, good circulation, and warm extremities. They are sensitive to heat and light and, when balanced, they are decisive, ambitious, knowledgeable, intelligent, and motivated. When suffering from derangement, they are confused, envious, complaining, irritable, and angry.
- Kapha people are watery in their natures and generally have stocky frames, sturdy builds, and good tissue development. They dislike movement and easily put on weight. Psychologically, they are emotional, caring, stable, conservative types, but, when imbalanced, they can become sluggish, possessive, insensitive, attached, and stubborn.

When I had become familiar with the expressions of each dosha, I found that I could easily recognize, through behavior, speech, and gait which dosha was a person's predominant nature. When I attended business meetings or seminars, I often entertained myself by observing both the natural reactions of myself and the individuals around me. As a mixed pitta-vata type, I could easily relate to both pitta and vata people and, of course, kapha individuals really stood out for me, since that attribute is the one I most rarely embody. A classic example occurred when I attended a seminar.

The woman presenting the seminar attempted to give compelling reasons for each of us to continue with the instructional series by signing up for additional courses. When she felt confident that she had provided all of the reasons we should sign up, she asked all of us in attendance, "OK, so who wants to sign up for level two?" Immediately, the vata-dominant individuals who were interested raised their hands; they needed little time for reflection. They are often up for new and different experiences, because they need the simulation. Next, the pitta-dominant folks in attendance asked a few questions for clarification and then volunteered. Slower than vata people in terms of making changes, those of pitta nature do become decisive when they understand the purpose and feel the need. Meanwhile, the kapha individuals had been sitting back and observing it all. After quietly pondering over the various points that the presenter had made, they would invariably respond, "Let me think it over for a while, and then I'll decide."

That vata people are quick to seek new and varied experiences is natural, because the word *vata* translates as "air," with its main characteristic being movement. Thus, when walking, vata people exhibit a lot of body movement, and their feet make light or airy contact with the ground. As for pitta people, *pitta* means "fire," with its main characteristic being to break down or metabolize. In order to embrace anything, they need to find its purpose. Only then will they participate. Pitta people's gaits reflect this need for purpose: They tend to walk in a military fashion, like marching, swinging arms with head facing up and forward. They seem to always know where they are going. The earth and its solidity are reflected in kapha individuals. Grounded and solid in both frame and function, they inherently feel the need to have all of the information before making decisions. Their walking pace is consistent but not quick, and their feet have the tendency to fully meet the ground.

Although most of us have one of the three doshas as our dominant constitution, some may display a combination of two doshas as equally dominant, such as my pitta-vata nature. The ancient Siddhas described ten types of prakrithi for all people; these ten types are composed of the three doshas and their combinations. When the tridosha is balanced, the person enjoys health; when imbalanced, the person's health fades, and the imbalance eventually manifests as physical, mental, or emotional illness. The appearance of any symptom of ill health is the first sign of an individual having lost some sensitivity or balance in relation to the nature of his or her constitution.

The basic constitution assigned to or possessed by an individual speaks volumes about what is natural to him or her. When Pal first explained this in detail to me, I was amazed that, by simple observation, I could easily, and with almost certainty, recognize whether a person was of a basic vata, pitta, or kapha nature. This knowledge is vital for a healer. If an individual appears to be of a mixed type, or if there is any doubt as to his or her prakrithi, it can be confirmed through pulse diagnosis. Because all disorders result from an imbalance of the doshas, their alteration can be detected through the pulse. Through pulse diagnosis, which is, in truth, an indicator of energy flowing through subtle channels in the body (the *nadis*), the Siddhas can detect imbalance. The pulse is altered long before any signs of illness appear.

Although I had been exposed to the concepts of the tridosha in my earlier travels in India, I was unaware of their actual significance. They began to really make sense to me when I learned about the five elements, how they come about, and their being the building blocks of everything. This explanation was strikingly simple compared to the anatomy and physiology classes I had taken in high school and college. Its very simplicity was instantly recognizable as true. Of course, it is simple in content, because Pal explained it simply. Because Nature's operations are the most primal, Her forces have no need to hide behind multisyllabic phrases. These forces seem simple, yet their infinite interplay gives rise to all things.

In the study of anatomy, including organs, the endocrine system, and bones, it is the varying attributes of vata, pitta, and kapha that are actually being observed. But much more is involved. We all have various feelings, predisposed likes and dislikes, habits, fixations, and a host of other uniquely ordered attributes. These areas should also be considered anatomical, because they are essential components of what constitutes each of us. Thus, the Siddhas have always viewed the spirit, mind, and physical body as a combined whole that forms a person. Because of this holistic view, Pal took the time to patiently answer my questions about true anatomy. It was essential that I grasp the composition of not only the body but also the mind and the spirit.

Anatomy of the Sages

The human being, the person, is not limited to the physical body. To understand a person is to include all aspects—physical characteristics, mental attribute, personality, inherent or genetic tendencies and traits, natural constitution, energy levels, and spirit. Authentic health would certainly necessitate the inclusion of all aspects of the individual. Otherwise, any healing measures intended to restore balance would be only partially successful. Thus, true anatomy is not limited to the physical body and its components. All aspects of the physical and the metaphysical are considered. This approach is a reflection of the cosmic interplay. Most remarkable and unique is that the anatomy of the sages is used for not only Their divine healing techniques but also for *sadhana* (spiritual practices).

Personality

The core of each individual's personality is the *Atman*, Self, God, Source, Wholeness, Creator, and so on. This Atman enlivens the body with the capacity to perceive and act and gives life to the mind to feel and to the intellect to decide. Upon springing forth from the one Source, each person is born with and develops unique ways of meeting life. The types of perception, action, feeling, and thought that manifest from the body, mind, and intellect all depend upon the person's inherent nature. These inherent natures are called *Vasanas*. Best defined as latent behavioral tendencies or karmic imprints, they are similar to Carl Jung's unconscious, collective unconscious, and collective super conscious aspects of the human psyche. Children born into the same family and circumstances have individual outlooks, expressions, and predispositions to virtually all aspects of life. If the Vasanas are noble or good in their basic nature, the expressions will also be noble and good, and vice versa. Regardless, as are our Vasanas, so, too, are our thoughts, feelings, perceptions, and actions. From this understanding of Vasanas, the concept of *sheaths* and physical bodies vs. non-physical bodies was developed. The common terms are the *physical body*, *subtle body*, and *causal body*.

THE FIVE SHEATHS

- ### FOOD SHEATH (PHYSICAL BODY)

The physical body is commonly referred to as the *food body* or *food sheath*, because it is created by the consumption of food, maintained by the consumption of food, and finally becomes food for other creatures. The generative fluid from the father and egg from the mother are, obviously, physical components of their respective bodies that develop during adulthood. From small bodies at the time of birth, our bodies grow as a result of the fuel that we consume. In this sense, the physical body is literally what we consume, as in the saying, "You are what you eat." Upon death, even if the body is cremated, the micro components of the ashes will merge, dissolve, or be consumed. The food body contains the five organs of knowing, *gnanendriyas*, which grant the powers to hear, feel, see, taste, and smell, and the five organs of action, *karmendriyas*, which grant the powers to express, procreate, excrete, grasp, and move.

- VITAL AIR SHEATH (PRANIC BODY)

The *pranic body*, or *vital air sheath*, consists of the *dasa vayu*, or ten vital airs (movements, energies, and directional flows). Of these ten vital airs, five are major (*prana*, *udana*, *samana*, *vyana*, and *apana*), and five are minor. The dasa vayu control and sustain the faculties of the physical body, and their essence flows throughout the nadis, or subtle energy channels, of which there are 72,000 in the human body. When the vital airs are in good health and balance, the physical body remains healthy; the vital airs' relative health or lack thereof is reflected in the tridosha on which humoral pathology is based. As a person ages, the vital airs gradually lose their abilities. Their influence is shown by the deterioration, in older people, of the functions they facilitate. For example, older people have difficulty seeing, digesting, walking, eliminating waste, and so forth. The vital air sheath is more subtle than the food sheath, but influences it.

- MENTAL SHEATH (MANOMAYA KOSAM)

The *mental sheath*, or *Manomaya Kosam*, is, as one would expect, composed of the mind. As the next most subtle aspect of the body, it controls both the vital air sheath and the food sheath. When the mind is well composed, the body's physiology functions efficiently. When it is not, the body's physiological functions express disorder. The mind consists of impulses, feelings, emotions, and passions and is replete with likes and dislikes. It likes to possess or attain. Another weakness of the mind is its natural tendency to slip into the past or future rather than remaining in the present.

- INTELLECTUAL SHEATH (VIGYANMAYA KOSAM)

Composed of the intellect, which is the faculty to understand, have insights, and make decisions, the intellectual sheath, or *Vigyanmaya Kosam*, judges mental and physical activities. In this manner, it exerts itself over the previous, more dense (less subtle) sheaths already listed.

- BLISS SHEATH (ANANDAMAYA KOSAM)

The Vasanas, the innate, inherent material from which one is compelled to act on unfulfilled *karma*, reside in the *bliss sheath*, or *Anandamaya Kosam*. When in the bliss sheath, we are in deep sleep, that is, dreamless sleep. The moment we enter the portal of deep, dreamless sleep, all agitation ceases. This is what is meant by the term "bliss sheath." While we are in that state, our Vasanas are unmanifested in physical terms. However, they manifest as thoughts (intellect) and desires (mind) in our dream state; these thoughts and desires are translated into actions in our waking state (pranic body and physical body). The bliss of the bliss state is relative, being a mere respite from our ceaseless need to act on our latent tendencies and unfulfilled karma, and so we are compelled to return to the dreaming and waking states. The bliss state is, in no way, the absolute bliss of self-realization.

The bodily sheaths as a group encompass what is meant by the phrase *body-mind-spirit*, which is also described as consisting of the physical body, subtle body, and causal body. What I came to understand was the composition of the individual sheaths and their interrelated nature. The physical body, a combination of the food sheath and the gross aspect of the vital air sheath, influences the physical body's actions and perceptions. The subtle aspect of the vital air sheath, the mental sheath, and the intellectual sheath comprise the subtle body, with its thoughts, feelings, emotions, and desires. The bliss sheath alone, the repository of the Vasanas, is the causal body. These latent tendencies or karmic imprints manifest for each of us as the waker, the dreamer, and the deep sleeper. Each of us identifies with and moves through each of these three states. In turn, we partake of our everyday experience, that is, of being compelled to fulfill our Vasanas. This manifests as our much cherished personality. It is this that we call living.

Consciousness is the foundation of not only the microcosm but also the macrocosm. When the consciousness functions through the combination of all physical bodies, it expresses itself as *Virat*, the cosmic waker. As Consciousness functions through the combination of all subtle bodies, it called known as *Hiranyagarbha*, the cosmic dreamer. Consciousness that functions through the combination of all causal bodies expresses itself as *Ishwara*, the cosmic deep sleeper. The macrocosm is the combination of these three cosmic expressions of Consciousness. The microcosm can be thought of as a drop of sea water and the macrocosm as the ocean. Both the drop of water and the ocean are composed of sea water. One who understands that water is both the drop and the ocean realizes the Self is one and all, the all-pervading Being. This is the Consciousness around which the microcosm and macrocosm revolve.

This inherent hierarchy relates to Siddha Varma healing in that systems that lack the knowledge, ability, and profound sensitivity to access and influence all levels of a person, all levels of a person's being, are less than holistic. Furthermore, the various layers of a being are intimately connected with the cosmos, the macrocosmic Being. The divine insight, knowledge, and methods that flow from profound compassion and unmatched sensitivity comprise the realm inhabited by the Siddhas.

The time that I spent learning about the Siddhas' concepts of anatomy, health, disease, and the wholeness of the universe was actually quite brief. In the small room at Pal's healing center, he revealed the ancient art of Siddha Varma healing in a most direct manner. When I arrived at the center each morning, the pace at which he instructed was very brisk. I returned to the healing center each evening for additional instruction. In between the morning and evening sessions, I ate lunch and reviewed what we had covered in the morning session. I admit that an unusual amount of commitment, clarity, and focus was required in order to keep up with the pace. Spontaneous enthusiasm propelled me through that period, motivating the high level of sensitivity, clarity, and persistence that the learning demanded. Those qualities were required, because Varma is such a rare and vast art. Previous knowledge is not very helpful. Actually, if we stick to our usual manner of learning, of relying on only our mental and intellectual powers, the learning does not go very deep. Stuck in our own minds, in our previously accumulated notions and ideas of how things are and should be, we close off ourselves from learning or experiencing anything new. This is particularly true of Siddha Varma healing due to its esoteric and deeply radical nature.

My enthusiasm was spontaneous in that it came from a depth of my being that was previously unknown to me. Our first meeting and all subsequent meetings felt not like accidents but rather like long-awaited events of my destiny. The obvious factor that led my heart and life to intertwine with those of Pal Pandian was the healing that he graciously bestowed upon me. Even today I cannot understand how that occurred or what actually took place within me. From the moment he released me from years of physical pain and, even more importantly, from mental, emotional, and spiritual stagnation, I was drawn into his world. Without my expending any effort, without my understanding, my life and very essence, like metal shavings, were undeniably drawn to the magnetism of his radiant Being. The connection certainly was not due to any decision that I made or any virtue that I possessed. Why he chose me I will never understand or dare to question. I was and remain effortlessly mesmerized by both him and his Dharma.

CHAPTER 4

Learning the Art of Siddha Science

The first several years of instruction concentrated on the first level of Varma, the therapeutic level known as *Systemic Vital Point Therapy (Kaibaham Seibaham)*. An enormous amount of information was provided, but it was not confined to theory. Whatever Pal taught me was immediately put into practice.

"It is by doing, by applying, that we come to understand Varma, for it is a living science" were Pal's first words to me on the subject. "It is a science and an art, because it deals with life, livingness. It is not a static thing. Life is always flowing, vibrating, and so the healer should likewise be always immersed in the river-like flow of life."

The simple things are what I often recall most vividly from those first few years under his tutelage. How he would enter the room, sit quietly in front of me for a few moments, and then look up with his always-present broad smile. The palpable, pulsating silence that prevailed just before his verbal greeting. Likewise, his most common, simple gestures warmed my soul. Daily there would be brief, yet welcome, breaks. Each time I had just gotten to the point of feeling that I could not possibly digest or retain another word, Pal would gently ask if I would like to take a short break. Thankful and with my head on the verge of explosion, I would try to casually answer that a break would be fine if he thought it best. I was suddenly able to breathe again, and his faithful assistant Shahul would bring some chai and biscuits. The warm tea and small snack did wonders to refresh me for the next round of intense learning.

The instruction only loosely resembled that of a typical classroom, save for the first year. It was always more practical and experiential. It must be done this way, because Varma is unlike any other system of healing. It is an esoteric art rather than a system to be theorized or memorized. This uniqueness is better understood from a more in-depth description of Varma healing.

Varma—Vital Force

Varma points are hidden deep within the human body and are not physical in nature, yet they are vulnerable to external influences. At the same time, from their secret and protected locations, they silently carry out activities in their subtle domain. Whether from an injury or an illness that slowly builds in the physical or mental frame, the Varma points provide the first symptoms of an imbalance. The vital junctures, the Varma points, are the origin that signals all mental and physical imbalance. Their vibrancy and healthy flow reflects well-being and glowing health.[2]

Forming an intricate network that spans a person's entire mind and body, the Varma points comprise a blueprint unique to the human form. All of the vital forces that enliven our bodies invariably merge, separate, and move onward in an intelligent, predetermined manner. Their meeting or crisscrossing at specific locations enables the waters of the various streams to merge and diverge. The capacity for natural, healthy exchange that occurs at the Varma spots condenses, expands, transmutes, revitalizes, pulls, and pushes all the life forces throughout the mind and body.

The flow of life forces is designed for the optimal functioning of the entire human organism and the healthy performance of its vital organs. The degree of fluidity and interconnectedness of these vital forces determines the quality of our health. When a triggering event occurs from outside (injury) or inside (disease), the root level of imbalance is the alteration of the intelligent working nature of the primal flow of life energies. This is the reason that merely treating the symptoms by performing surgery or medicating the mind and body without

---

[2] Varma points and Siddha Varma healing are in no way related to the meridians of the Chinese system, acupuncture or acupressure points, or Ayurvedic marma points.

correcting the hindered flow (the underlying issue) can provide only partial relief.

A Secret Science

Having heard of the secrecy of Varma, I had also heard of the Siddhas' manner of cryptic writing. Although historically the wisdom of their healing and spiritual arts was transmitted orally, at some point they were transcribed onto palm-leaf manuscripts. These manuscripts sounded mysterious to me—not only because they were transcribed in the Siddhas' twilight language but also because they were written on palm leaves. For some reason, I thought that the idea of a palm-leaf manuscript was the coolest thing. I wondered if I would ever get to see such a thing. I was happily surprised one evening when Pal entered the instruction room and placed palm leaves on the floor between us.

Pal explained that these manuscripts are in the form of poetic verse and most often are songs. This is a testament to their antiquity. Long before written languages existed, humankind kept the roots of its traditions alive orally. For retaining any large amount of information, song and poetic verse were most effective. Once writing was developed, rote memorization, which emphasizes stimulation of the left brain, became the norm. In contrast to rote memorization, the practice of singing verses has a strange and lovely quality. I think that the charming allure of the songs comes from their invaluable wisdom applicable to daily life. Much later, in the same ambiguous verse or twilight language, the Siddhas drew their stunningly beautiful diagrams of healing systems on these delicate palm leaves.

Although ancient manuscripts list varying numbers of Varma points, ranging from 8,000 (*Varma Vivisai*) to 251 *(Kumbamuni Narmabarai),* the majority of texts limit the number of Varma points to 108. The 108 are categorized as *Padu Varmas* (the 12 primary, or major, vital points) and *Thodu Varmas* (the 96 secondary points). Incidentally, *padu* means *perarivu*, or omniscience, according to the text *Pingalai Nikandu*, with the general meaning of perarivu being brain, which leads one to understand that the Padu Varmas are intricately connected to the brain. Thodu Varmas, although secondary, are no less utilized, and the meaning of the word *thodu* is touch or core link, which indicates the way in which they work. Through touch, the energy at one point resonates with the energy at another point.

Consistent with the maximum number of breaths being inhaled (twelve), the 12 units of energy are connected to the 12 Padu Varmas. Each of these 12 major and vital junctures again joins and influences 8 units of energy. Thus, each of the 12 Padu Varmas, by their overriding nature, directs 8 Thodu Varmas. These Thodu Varmas, in turn, oversee the corresponding functional physiological energies (*dasa vayus*). The 108 Varma points can be described, in simple, general terms, as the 12 Padu Varmas each influencing 8 Thodu Varmas, for a total of 96

Thodu Varmas; the 12 Padu Varmas and the 96 Thodu Varmas, which they influence, form the bodily network of 108 Varma points. These multiple points, or junctures, and their intricate systems of interaction enable all of the various life forces to flow, integrate, and sustain a healthy individual.

Examining the palm leaves, I saw the familiar Tamil writings, yet I was most fascinated by the diagrams. The ancient manuscripts contain incredibly intricate drawings. That they were written with so much obvious attention, detail, and care on these delicate palm leaves greatly impressed me. It also humbled me. What had I ever given myself to with such a level of devotion? Yet there before me was an example of supreme love whose sole intent was the benefit of all humankind. That the manuscripts

Siddha Palm Leaf Manuscripts

had been passed on for more than 15,000 years and now sat in front of me left me feeling very small indeed.

Levels of Varma

Although I was unaware of it when I began my time with Pal, Siddha Varma healing has many levels of potency. Over the years, he slowly introduced me to the higher dimensions. The student is introduced to the more esoteric realms as he or she evolves in understanding, practice, and maturity. The initial level, referred to as manual stimulation, is where I began. In Tamil, it is called *Kaibaham Seibaham*. We have given it the English translation of Systemic Vital Point Therapy. Working with the Varma points at this level entails many aspects of in-depth understanding. It begins with the blueprint of the 108 Varma points and their interconnected nature. Beyond this basic framework, Pal took me far deeper, into how they operate on subtle levels. Their twelve types of application, their seven modes of functionality, the six links (*Kona Nilai*), their depth (*Mathirai*) and pressure (*Pathi*), and their complementary nature (*ethir kalaam* or *maru kalaam*) must all be understood by an apprentice.

The dimensions that follow this basic level are the realms of esoteric healing. An opportunity to learn about those realms is incredibly rare, because finding a master is highly challenging. The few who exist rarely make themselves known. Most hide away in distant mountain caves or forests, and the ones who do live in society hide behind a veil of ordinary simplicity. Their reason for doing so is to retain purity and potency. Only Pal's compassion for suffering has motivated him to instruct students in the higher dimension. He has stated to me, in no uncertain terms, that the time has come for these potent and esoteric arts of the Siddhas to be brought into society. As shown in figure 1, beyond the level of manual stimulation are the higher dimensions, which include the realms of *Adangal* (rippling energy), *Thiravukol* (the influx of cosmic energy), and finally *Amritha Kalai* (nectar energy). Weaving

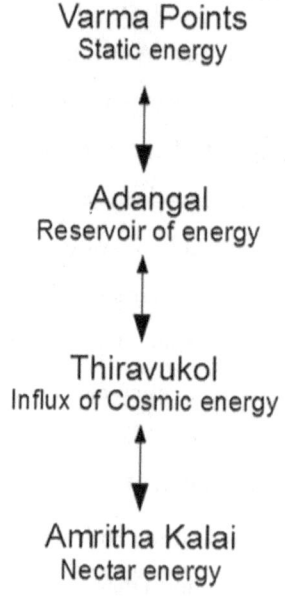

Figure 1. Potency in Siddha Varma Healing.
A ranking of the dimensions of Siddha Varma healing.

through these subtle domains demands much from a student, because it encompasses astrology, tantra, and spiritual energy.

Tridosha—A Diagnostic View

Following each day of instruction and a mid-day break, I returned each evening for additional instruction. I had no way of knowing what information would be revealed or how it would be revealed. My days were filled with direct instruction and practical application of the Varma points. The student is not usually given the location and application of the Varmas so early in the training. Unaware that the traditional approach was being ignored, I simply arrived at the appointed time each morning and evening. I recall that there were a lot of mosquitos in the room. The fan that was always blowing disoriented their flight enough that they could not land and bite. It took only a few minutes for me to realize this dilemma, after which I completely ignored the hungry little monsters.

The evening began with Pal explaining in detail the humoral pathology of the Siddhas, the tridosha of vata, pitta, and kapha. On subsequent evenings, after a general talk followed by a more specific talk, we usually went right into practical experience of the subject. On that very first evening, however, Pal guided me in pulse diagnosis, in which the tridosha plays a foundational role. Vata, pitta, and kapha each is found on the wrist and has a unique quality of speed, depth, width, height, and direction.

When the person is healthy, these attributes express themselves, each in their own way. Should illness be present, or impending, the expressions of any number of them will change. As the life energies move through the body, intersect, and are enlivened by the Varma points, they always retain their manifested reflection of the five elements. Condensed into pairs, the five primordial elements of existence express the macrocosmic creation in the human body. When in balance, we radiate health in body and mind. For this reason, pulse diagnosis is vitally important. By a sensitive reading of energy flows, a Siddha Varma healer can determine what is aligned and what is deranged, oftentimes long before any physical symptoms have manifested.

Within the range of Siddha Varma pulse diagnosis also exists the capability of registering the entire human system. Each part of the body, each organ, possesses its own unique vibrational quality. These, too, are found in the wrists and hands and so are available to be recognized as in a state of well-being or derangement. The diagnosis appears as a simple practice, at least from the perspective of an observer. However, it demands a high degree of sensitivity and lots of practice. The healer's ability to determine where the flow of life force is blocked provides him or her with the insight of how to apply Varma point stimulation to achieve healthy flow. The combination of accurate diagnosis and proper treatment is potent. A simple example can be found in the story of a young man who went to our healing center in the United States shortly after it had opened.

A thirty-year-old man, a police officer by profession, went to our Siddha healing center to seek help with an injury he had suffered recently while apprehending a suspect. Following the incident, he had experienced localized and severe abdominal pain. The doctor at the hospital gave him an exam that consisted of x-rays and such and then informed him that he had torn an abdominal muscle. The shocking news from the doctor was that it would take six to twelve months for the muscle to repair itself and that during that time he would be unable to work his job in the usual manner so would be assigned to desk duty. The young man's passion was working with his K-9 police dog, and he found this news quite depressing. We were acquainted with each other, but he had no understanding of Siddha Varma healing. He asked whether I could help with his situation, and then he went to the center, with a simple attitude and open mind, for healing sessions.

I began by applying Siddha Varma healing techniques and asking him to drink a simple tonic composed of ginger juice, lemon juice, and castor oil. Because he was in a healthy state aside from the recent injury, the healing sessions were straightforward. By separating the energy forces that comprise the physical body and allowing them to flow properly, the healing sessions directly influenced the components of the muscles. Within three weeks, his abdominal pain was gone, his range of movement and ability to function normally was restored, and he was back at work with his beloved K-9 police dog. That was four years ago, and he has had no issues since that time.

How was this healing achieved, and what is the "science" behind it? The young man's attitude served him well in that his only expectation was that Siddha Varma would—somehow, in some way—speed his recovery. Although he had no knowledge of the sessions or how they worked, he asked no questions, because he felt no need to satisfy any intellectual craving. His simple, open approach was enough for him to accept, or personalize, the healing energy of his body. As for the logic of it all, it is rather simple.

Muscles are not solid masses but rather are composed of atoms (and smaller components), which consist mostly of space and do not touch one another. In between and underlying all these components are forces, or energies, of a non-physical nature. These forces are always in motion, and this motion is not random. Their direction, speed, and vibration are of a specific and intelligent nature. These energies give rise to and sustain the physical components, such as those that were changed by the young man's injury. Once the proper flow of energies are restored, the body parts that they comprise reflect the change, in this case a torn muscle. When the subtle and vital energies are reminded of their original flow, which reflects balance and health, the physical structure also must return to alignment.

The physical does not exist independently of the unseen world of silent forces but rather is their manifestation.

The Siddhas state that the Varma healer simply aids the body and mind in remembering their natural, and inherently proper, flow of health, flexibility, and radiance. This natural flow is the primal blueprint that existed before the disease or injury. Today, a veritable buffet of "energy healing" methods exist. All of them refer to the word *energy* or one of its Eastern names. Usually they claim that the body energy with which they work is the most primal, the most important. It can all be rather confusing. By the time I went to Pal, I needed clear answers about all talk of energy, prana, chi, and so forth.

Energy: The Five Major Airs

Anyone who is familiar with or has sought what is called *alternative healing* will most likely have heard the phrase *energy healing*. Chakra healing, quantum healing, self-healing, distance healing, Reiki, and a host of other healing systems all share the concept of healing through energy. I myself had previously sought out many types of healing for my back, including chiropractic, massage therapy, physical therapy, Reiki, chakra healing, acupuncture, and prana healing. Every time, without fail, the word "energy" would be discussed at some length, and yet I noticed that the word appeared to be the extent of everyone's knowledge about the topic.

Rivulets of the Absolute

When I took the time to consider energy, I realized that the explanations I had heard were rather vague. When Pal began teaching Varma to me, I questioned him deeply about energy and energy-related terms and their actual meanings. I was unprepared for the detail he would provide. Sure, I was familiar with the terms prana, chi, and the like. But I was fascinated by exploring the body's energy in more detail and learning how and of what the body is formed.

One day while we were sitting on the floor of Dwarka Mayi, Pal's healing center, and sipping chai from the little cups served by Shahul, I decided that it was time to clear up this whole energy situation. Incense was snaking its way up from the altar where the pictures of Bhagavan Maharshi, Sai Baba of Shirdi, the Siddhas, and other masters rested. The overhead fan was blowing sweetly perfumed air about us. While we were silently enjoying our mid-morning break, a herd of goats were passing outside. The clang of the bell, swinging from the neck of the dominant male, was accompanied by the occasional "Hey!" of the shepherd keeping his flock together. Breaking the relative quiet, I asked Pal if he would please clarify some things for me.

"Sir, what are prana, *kundalini*, shakti, and all these other terms? I mean, what's the difference among them, if any, and what do they really mean? Of course, through my practice so far, I'm aware of the Varma points and their uses for Vital Force healing. But I'm also a bit confused. In the West, everyone tosses these terms around or talks about using energy for healing or even spiritual practices. What's really going on with all this?"

"Yes, everyone speaks about it, but it is both a paradox and very simple. However, at the same time, there is much more to it all. 'Energy' is a very general word. For instance, 'energy' can mean different things, like thermal, kinetic, electrical, magnetic, and so forth—all with separate meanings. To simply use the word 'energy' when speaking of an electrical device as opposed to a thermal device would be misleading. So, 'energy' is just a word, with little meaning by itself. The same applies to prana. Like chi, prana just means energy. They are functional energies—that is their role. They mean the same thing in India and China. It is that simple; they are just very general terms meaning energy. Shakti is another word for energy, and it is used when referring to spiritual practices. Kundalini, as you know, is the snake, the coiled energy at the base of the body. Surely you recall that in our first year I spoke to you about the *dasa vayu* (the ten vital airs), their meaning, and how they function in a person?"

"Certainly I do, Sir. It was our very first evening when you introduced them, at least in a general way. You spoke of the tridosha and then of the vayus."

"Correct. Then you recall that there are ten vital airs, or forces, called the dasa vayu. *Dasa* means 'ten,' and *vayu* means 'air' or 'wind.' Of these, five are major airs and five are minor airs. They are functional energies. You also asked about prana. We can say that when it is localized in the body, prana rests in the lungs. Oftentimes, as a group, the dasa vayu themselves are referred to as prana. These enable the body to function. They are responsible for the powers of knowing (gnanendriyas) and the powers of action (karmendriyas). They are vital airs, and this shows how important they are and that they should be in good form and flow in their proper fashion. They allow for air, food, and drink to come into the body, for wastes and toxins to be expelled. They also are responsible for the eyes to see, for the powers of moving and grasping, in fact, for all the things necessary for the person to live in the world. In a healthy body, they are strong and fully functional. When the life forces move about the body, they should have not only a specific movement but also a specific pulsation or quality. In this way, there is an energy that brings breath into the body and a subsequent energy that exhales, that moves the air out of the body. Each act, inhalation and exhalation, is distinct and so is enacted by the same life force but individualized, made specific at the Varma points. Also, the energy needed to enliven the liver is specific, and the energy needed by the stomach is different and unique in its own way. Each organ has its own subtle force required for it to function. This is true with all aspects of the body and mind. Over the life span, they gradually lose their vitality, so we see an old person. Their eyesight is weak, they move slowly, have trouble breathing, excreting wastes, and so forth. This shows how each of the dasa vayu has weakened."

Pal listed the five major dasa vayu in detail for me:

- *Prana:* Literally meaning "forward moving," it is the energy that receives things that enter the body as a result of eating, drinking, breathing, sensory perceptions, and mental experiences and sustains one's vital organs, especially the heart.
- *Apana:* Translated as "the air that moves away," it moves downward and outward. It is responsible for the ability to eject, or eliminate, in the form of waste, what is not needed by the body and thus is associated with the colon, kidneys, rectum, bladder, and genitals. In addition, it is the moving force in reproduction, which essentially moves new life out into the world.
- *Samana:* Meaning "balancing air," it controls the power of metabolism, or digestive fire, and the assimilation of oxygen from the air we breathe. In addition, it unifies the two opposing forces of prana and apana.
- *Udana:* Literally meaning "that which carries upward," it rules muscle function and strength in the extremities, as well as sensory function in the eyes, ears, and nose. It is the force behind all growth, the ability to stand erect, the ability to speak, and effort and enthusiasm.

- *Vyana:* Translated as "outward moving air," it pervades the whole body and is a coordinating, connecting force of the sensory perceptions. It runs through the entire network of the 72,000 nadis, the subtle energy channels, connecting the functions of nerves, veins, muscles, and joints and circulating nutrients and energy.

Pal continued instructing me about the dasa vayu. "All of these functions are carried out by the ten vital forces [or airs], and so we can say that they do so with their own inherent intelligence. The ancient masters saw all things in nature and man in this way. When They viewed any part of the heavens or earth that acted in its own manner without any help or interference from man, They called that force divine, a god or goddess. Perhaps you can now understand why there are so many deities here in India? This They used, for it was obvious to Them that anything that behaves according to its nature has its own inherent, and so intelligent, design. When They looked to influence these intelligent forces, it was obvious that They should come to understand them first. From Their divine insight, the Siddhas came to know how to interact with those forces with deep reverence for their specific designs.

"That it what Varma healing is. It is assisting the forces of the body to remember their own intelligent, inherent movement and specific qualities. All of these forces of life and living should be flowing in their ordained manner. They should also have their own specific vibrations. As they move through the body, it is the Varma points where they receive such attributes. Should this not occur properly and the Varma junctures not be able to enliven and nourish the vital life forces, illness comes. It all begins there. This is why attending to people by use of Siddha Varma healing is not just unique. It is very effective. We can help many people with this. This is my wish in giving you instruction." (See figure 2 for a diagram of Pal's explanation.)

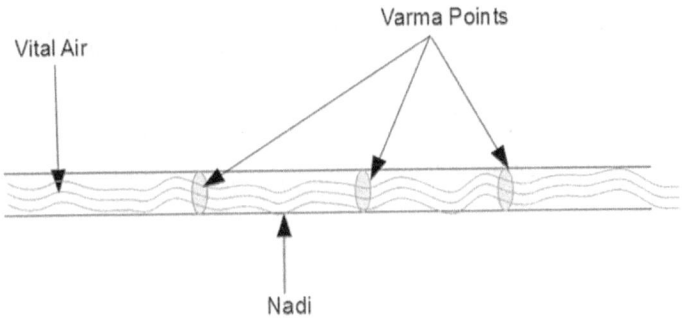

Figure 2. NADI – Vital air pathway.
A diagram of the varma points and vital air flows that comprise a Nadi.

Inspired by Pal's words, I always did my best to pay attention and learn what he imparted. Although doing so was often challenging, his naturally compassionate nature fed my spirit, enabling me to progress. Sharing not only his wisdom but also his healing spirit infused me with the aspiration to take the Siddha's healing to my home country. This was accomplished, by his request and blessing, in 2010. That was the first time Siddha Varma healing had ever been practiced outside India. I took the responsibility seriously and faithfully applied all that Pal had instructed. For instance, exact application of Siddha Varma is necessary in order to achieve good results since the vital points' functioning is so critical to health. Obviously, the requirement was for me to apply all of the knowledge he had imparted while simultaneously living with a lifestyle that enhanced my own sense of connection to the Siddha lineage. Diet, daily routine, and attitude, as well as many physical, meditative, and esoteric practices, have been necessary components for me to follow. Keeping the mind sharp and the body clean and flexible is helpful in grasping and integrating sublime and esoteric methods.

Likewise, I found understanding both modern and alternative medical terminology and diagnosis methods to be equally necessary. For instance, it is not uncommon to find Ayurvedic medicines listed as treatments for arthritis. However, there are two types of arthritis: rheumatoid arthritis and osteoarthritis. Rheumatoid arthritis is characterized by excess synovial fluid (excess kapha), and osteoarthritis occurs when the kapha has been dried up by excess vata. Knee pain, whether from arthritis, injury, or unknown causes, is often a rather simple derangement for Varma Healing to correct. A good example can be found in the story of a woman who suffered from lifelong knee pain, which she said was arthritis, yet her physicians were unsure of how to classify it.

The middle-aged woman had been plagued by pain in both knees since she was twelve years old. It is unusual for osteoarthritis to begin at such a young age, which is why her doctors were unsure of how to label it. Of kapha nature, she had some extra weight but carried it well.

Since there was no swelling or inflammation in her knees, the pain was due to an imbalance in the vata dosha. The application of Systemic Vital Point Therapy and the use of local nervous manipulation reduced her pain almost immediately.

Within three weeks, she was completely free of knee pain for the first time since childhood. Four years later, she still has no knee pain, and she walks and runs for exercise daily.

The imbalance in her body—in her doshas—caused her pain. Endured over a long period, pain changes the way we live, the way we express and experience our lives. Most importantly, *it is totally unnecessary for people to live in pain*. Siddha Varma healing enabled this woman to partake in activities that, for over thirty-five years, had seemed impossible to her, even though she yearned for them.

The Precedence of Vasi

Pal's explanation of the ten vital forces, their movement, and their specific functions gave clarity to what I had been experiencing during my healing sessions. This is what Pal terms *theory*. The fact that he introduced me into the healing dimension without theory is the opposite of the way in which we are normally instructed. By placing importance on application, Pal's manner of instruction focuses on nourishing the healing spirit within his students. Only after the student has practiced and gained a firm foundation in healing work does Pal deem the whys and hows of any importance. But our conversation was not yet finished.

"When my teacher told me of the dasa vayu, I was left with questions," Pal continued. "Two questions kept repeating for me. Why should they get separated at all? And how does that even happen? This is vitally important and reveals the most grand and secretive wisdom of our Siddhas.

"Of course, you understand now that the ten forces must separate in order to carry out their specific activities, their functions. This is because each organ and part of the human body is unique. The bladder, for instance, is watery in nature, because it is an organ of the kapha dosha [the earth]. The liver is a pitta organ, associated with fire, since it is one of metabolism. Beyond function, each organ and body part has its own unique vibration. In order to behave in their own unique way, the underlying forces that enliven the parts of the body follow this same organizing principle. Although the Varma points play a significant role, there is another hidden factor. I say it is hidden, because no other tradition of healing or spiritual system speaks of it. Only the Siddha masters have this knowledge. This factor is used in their healing and so gives depth and potency that are unique to Siddha Varma. The knowledge came from their yogic practices, and they used it for spiritual enlightenment. It is called Vasi. You know the word, but now we can speak of it in detail.

"The burning question of how the dasa vayu become separated leads us to this subject. Surely the ten forces, before being separated and specific, must have an origin. This origin is their home, the womb from which they are birthed. Since this origin exists prior to them and births them, it is most vital. But let us start at the beginning.

"At the moment of conception, when the single sperm and egg merge, there rests in this single cell a point. This point is called *bindu*, or foundation, and it is here that the cosmic energy, the *Maha Prana*, touches. This act enables the cosmic, or universal, life force to localize in the body. The immaculate energy, or fulcrum, that arises is Vasi. It is what gives life and sustains life. This is seen easily during the growth of the baby in the womb.

"During the first few weeks, the embryonic stage, there are no external factors to allow for growth. No umbilical cord to the mother and, of course, no air or nourishment taken from outside the embryo. At the same time, however, rapid cellular division occurs, and the single cell quickly replicates itself. What energy, what life force, provides this intelligence and nourishment to us from the very beginning? The embryo is beautiful. The one cell divides and multiplies without an umbilical cord, without a beating heart, and without a head having formed. We cannot say that it grows in size, but it does undergo an "unfolding" of itself. The physicist David Bohm caught this insight in his experiments. He spoke of an explicate order and an implicate order and of the universe being a whole that is connected but which we only experience as a series of unfolding and enfolding. This is what happens in the womb. If you watch a video of an early embryo, you see that it doesn't really grow. Yet it multiplies with great speed and intelligence. It enfolds itself over and over.

"Before anything external to us, we are given life and nourished from the immaculate energy that resides within us. This is life, and it is Nature's gift to us. In time, the umbilical cord forms, and our mother then begins to provide us with external nourishment. This begins the fetal stage. Eventually, upon birth, this cord is cut, we take our first breath, and we begin to take in energy in the external, or acquired, mode. However, throughout our lives, all subsequent growth and cellular division is provided by Vasi. We can think of Vasi as a battery. It is granted to us, in its fullness, at the time of conception. But, like a battery, it cannot be filled beyond its initial level. Slowly, throughout our lives, it is depleted. Once this battery of life is fully expended, Vasi leaves the body, and this we call death. Our Siddha masters discovered and unlocked the secrets of Vasi, and they used them to achieve longevity and spiritual ascension. How this insight is used in our healing is both simple and profound. It is unique to my lineage."

Vasi—God Within

With rapt attention and fascination, I listened to Pal explain in detail the vital importance of Vasi. The answer to the question of how the ten vital forces, the dasa vayu, are separated now was quite simple for me to grasp. Vasi is their womb, and it is there that prana and the other nine vayu rest in latent form. They separate from their womb only when it is necessary. The need arises when we shift from the embryonic stage to the fetal stage, when we begin to interact with the outside world. This interaction begins with our mother, via the umbilical cord. Pal then spoke in detail how this immaculate force is slowly depleted. In order to understand how the Vasi is depleted, one need look no further than the most basic function: breathing.

Virtually all yogic systems place great importance on the practice of pranayama, or breath regulation and exercises. The reason for this is known in detail by the Siddhas, for the practice holds great influence over the reservoir of life, the Vasi. The human body can inhale a maximum of twelve units, or *fingers* in yogic systems' measurement. This amount of inhalation can never be exceeded. Once inhaled, the breath energy, the prana, travels a definitive course, with eight units assigned to sustain bodily functions and the other four units assigned to the Vasi reservoir. Yet exhalation must also occur. When we are simply sitting and completely relaxed, we exhale a minimum of four units. Now we have arrived at sixteen units being used, four more than we are ever capable of bringing in simply by resting. Should the body—or even the mind—be agitated by movement, more than four units are exhaled. Thus, regardless of our level of activity, we lose energy, or life force, by the simple act of breathing. Where does this extra energy come from? It comes from our Vasi reservoir. Our most cherished and vital immaculate energy is slowly depleted just by the simple acts of inhalation and exhalation (Figure 3). The Siddha masters learned from Their divine insight how to slow or even stop this depletion. In certain

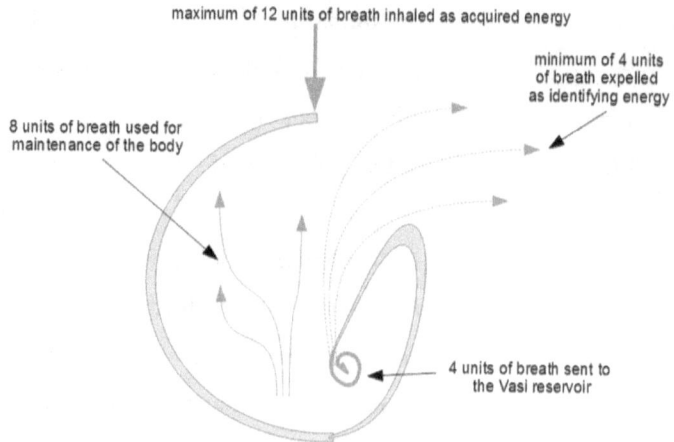

Figure 3. Energy Loop in Temporal Mode.
An illustration of breath energy via inhalation and exhalation.
Note that Vasi is depleted by the act of breathing (identifying energy).

cases, They are capable of replenishing the Vasi to its original fullness. These practices lead to Their spiritual enlightenment. From this, Their compassion has brought the understanding of Vasi to Siddha Varma healing.

By this point in Pal's instruction, Varma healing had become much more clear in my understanding. Prior to this discourse, I had little need of theory. Applying the healing techniques that Pal had taught me had been supremely effective. But now I understood and could feel what was really going on deep underneath the techniques. No longer was I confused about words like prana, chi, and life force. There are many life forces, or energies, that play animating roles in the body. I had felt their influence in our healing sessions as movements, pulsations, vibrations, and flows. Many in number and with various functions, the forces of life have a common home, a mother, a place of origin. Because Vasi gives us life in the beginning and sustains us throughout our lives, it alone is deserving of the title *life force* in its truest sense. That Siddha Varma healing influences Vasi is the reason that Pal has always referred to it as divine healing.

After our conversation, I spent much time reflecting. At one point, Pal had revealed that the Siddhas referred to Vasi in Tamil as *Siva Kalai*. At the time, I just accepted his words and made a mental note of them. Later it hit me. All that he had just spoken about to me not only explained theory but also pointed to the grand significance of what I was truly involving myself with when I gave healing sessions. Vasi is the level of existence that is influenced in the higher dimensions of Siddha Varma healing. Although I had felt this from the beginning, there was something about having a deep mental understanding now that brought profound feelings of awe, gratitude, and deeper humility. *Siva* means God. *Kalai* means specific. Siva Kalai, or Vasi, therefore means God within. It is none other than the divine nature and origin that lies within each of us.

CHAPTER 5

The Nucleus of Siddha Tradition–Vasi

Within each of us is the mirror image of the oceanic rhythm, the animating pulsation of the cosmos. It manifests as the river flow of natural existence and endless flowing phenomena and is always changing, always moving. This life pulse inspires all things to live. The Siddhas call this primordial pulsation of all life Vasi. When this river flow of life experiences a blockage, it sounds an alarm. Such a blockage is called viyadhi, which is literally translated as "deviation from one's own nature" and which we call disease. Because life is movement that is both intelligent and rhythmic, disease is characterized by discordant flow or blockages in the harmonious pulse. This is the alarm that Nature gives to enable us to finally understand our personal boundaries. To remind us to protect ourselves from influences, external demands, and obsessive activities that do not support growth in our lives. Disease is simply a blockage, or fixation, of the life-sustaining pulse that has incarnated in form of illness. It is an indication that the person has misconceived the inspiration for his or her life and has grown insensitive to himself or herself and to life, thus pushing his or her actions out of alignment with the primal inspiration.

The blockages that alter the natural flow of unseen forces become visible through injury, as in the police officer's torn muscle, or erupt as disease. Either way, attending to the afflicted Varma points can enable the intelligent flow of the dasa vayu to resume. Once the flow resumes, the physical body, after a time, returns to alignment. It must do so, because the body is not simply a biological structure but rather an integrated structure. Even science has long known that matter is not solid but rather is composed of waves, or vibrations, of infinite potential. According to physicists, when a particular state is viewed as a particle of experience, or matter, the state experienced is due to the observer. Indeed, we are free to view ourselves as lumps of flesh, as energy waves of various densities, or, as the Siddhas described millennia ago, as varying sheaths, or subtle bodies. There is great benefit in abandoning the narrow reductionist model of ourselves. Confining ourselves to mere biological lumps creates the limiting view of our bodies as nothing more than machines. In that machine view, our bodies are separate from us and exist only to serve us, to satisfy our insensitive and repetitive desires. We then only seek to exert control over the body, as we do with anything mechanical. The body is seen as something to be used and exploited without the least regard for the vast potential contained within it. Yet latent within us is all that is needed for us to grow, expand, and fulfill our purpose in a vibrantly healthy, harmonious fashion.

Medical practices and healing methods that divide the body and mind typically take a reductionist view of the person. No matter how small the parts that an oak tree is broken into, the parts are still not an acorn; however, that is much of what modern medicine offers us. Modern medicine is much like a fish searching desperately for the ocean but all the while focusing on the objects embedded in the sea floor and simply unaware that its search requires only a broader, more inclusive view. Those who tire of relying on modern medical practices that have proven ineffective seek our healing. In many cases, the disease has long been simmering in those unseen realms of the person's subconscious. Trauma, patterns, tendencies, and all manner of unresolved issues, no matter how seemingly insignificant, gather in the darkness of the mind. Eventually, they can accumulate sufficient weight and volume and so, like a cup filled with too much water, overflow, affecting the physical body.

Let us consider the example of a young woman who had suffered from endometriosis for several years.

She had symptoms of painful menstruation, fatigue, mood alterations, and pain during conjugation, but not until she had surgery for an unrelated disorder was the diagnosis confirmed. The only treatment offered by modern medicine is birth-control pills. Because she did not like taking them and they offered only partial relief, she sought assistance from Siddha Varma healing. At our first consultation, she admitted that her greatest fear was infertility. The possibility of being denied the chance to have children distressed her even more than the ongoing pain did.

We began our healing sessions by separating the stagnant vital forces, the dasa vayu, and discontinuing the birth-control pills. Unwinding the blockages in her body's life forces by attending to the related Varma points helped to relax the internal resistance that had accumulated. The uterus is a major natural intersection for the dasa vayu. Because she lived some distance away, we were able to meet only once a week, and so I suggested that she purchase some simple herbals to supplement the sessions. Over the next few months, her pain decreased slowly yet steadily. Reflecting that change, her moods became more grounded and consistent. In time, all of the symptoms were resolved, and her body and mind expressed their natural rhythms of fertility. Less than two years later, she reported that she was indeed pregnant for the first time.

An overriding life reality for a woman is her ability to bring forth new life. Whether she chooses or is destined to have children is irrelevant. The life purpose of all women touches on this aspect in some way. Issues with reproductive organs are a reflection of the woman having encountered events that clashed with her natural feminine consciousness. If she is unable to properly assimilate such an event, it eventually leaks into her reproductive organs, initially by altering the subtle aspects, the energy flows. When sufficient alteration has occurred and blockages have been formed, physical illness manifests. Endometriosis is a condition in which the tissue that usually lines the uterus grows outside the uterus. Its origin, although unknown to modern medicine, is the inherently feminine nature of the woman's consciousness being "turned inside out." In a world long dominated by a patriarchal theme that is generally aggressive and demeaning to the feminine, it is no mystery that such disorders are quite common.

The example of the young woman who suffered from endometriosis encapsulates the Siddha understanding of the wholeness of a person and that the body has its own inherent intelligence, or health, and ability to heal itself. All that is needed is the holistic insight and compassionate attendance from this healing ground. Siddha Varma healing utilizes the foundational memory inherent in all beings to restore them to their original source of balance. In this way, it attempts to heal not the body but rather the *person*. Having the ability to bear children restored to her a sense of fertility with regard to both herself and her life course. This is the untapped potential of the ancient system of Siddha Varma healing. Its purpose is best described by healer Pal as "dissolving the veil of ignorance that shadows the illumination of pure consciousness."

The Siddhas describe these veils of ignorance as none other than our physical ailments, mental blockages, and the primal ignorance of our existence. Our compassionate ancestors disclosed the sacred keys to dissolving these veils of illusion that shade our true nature. Their gift of healing aims to restore the original, pure state of all who suffer and seek true health, balance, and a vibrant approach to living. The removal of the veil enables the individual to flow in the fulfillment of his or her own inherent life purpose, or Dharma, the very reason for having been born.

Essence of Healing Wisdom

The essence of life, and therefore pure health, is formed and exists at a level far deeper and more subtle than the physical, cellular, molecular, bioelectric systems of the body, the chakras, nadis, or mental aspects of the person. Varma points are inherently non-physical in nature, and their creation begins in the embryonic stage long before any physical matter has come into existence. As such, they remain largely inaccessible to any form of healing focused on the purely physical aspects. In ancient times, this knowledge was passed from the Siddha masters to their trusted disciples and eventually encoded within a treatise known as *Varma Sastra*. It has always been a rare art taught to a select few, and today it is even rarer. Like many of the other Siddha dimensions, Varma science was kept hidden, passed along the generations only by word of mouth from master to disciple, creating a long, revered traditional lineage.

Although multiple reasons for the secrecy of this art exist, an obvious one is that its misapplication can cause great harm. It was the original form of martial art known to humankind. Called *Varma Adi*, it is a combat technique of extreme effectiveness and which has physical, subtle, and esoteric dimensions. One day, Pal demonstrated the extreme potency of Varma by application to a single Varma point of my friend Samer. In a flash, Samer was rendered immobile! A moment later, a soft yet swift touch by Pal allowed Samer to regain use of his body. This range of effect is not confined to the use of Varma as a martial art but rather is true of Varma as a healing art as well. Because Varma healing can be misused or misapplied, discretion and secrecy have always been essential. The responsibility demanded by it exceeds that of all other forms of energy and alternative healing. The requirements for an apprentice to be taught Varma healing are pure character, adventurous spirit, rebellious nature, and an inherent tendency toward humility. For these reasons, Siddha Varma healing will never be widespread.

Master-Student Relationship

The lineage of Siddha Healer Pal Pandian stretches back through the grand tradition of the immortal masters to the primal Siddha Agaysthiar and even to Lord Murugan Himself. His lineage is known as the *Bala Marga*, the Youth Lineage, because Lord Murugan is the eternally youthful son of Lord Siva and

His consort, Parvatti, also known as Shakti (see Figure 4 for the Siddha lineages). The longtime apprenticeship for Varma is not like ordinary instruction. The very foundation upon which the healing practice rests is formed by the divine initiations from the master. These profoundly esoteric yet powerful events infuse the student with the healing grace of the Siddhas. The master literally shares His own self, life force, and healing qualities with the students he chooses. Since the day of my initiation, I have felt Pal's presence guiding and protecting every aspect of my daily life and newly acquired health and infused within every particle of the healing quest.

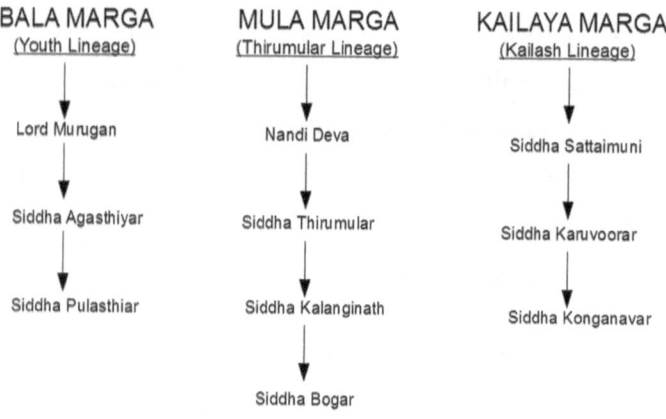

Figure 4. The Siddha Lineages.
There are hundreds of Siddhas, of which eighteen are considered primal. These above-mentioned lineages are available in the songs of the Siddha manuscripts. The placement of the other eight has not been confirmed textually as they largely hail from the Oral lineage.

Throughout time, the Siddhas have followed the strict guru-disciple tradition of passing on wisdom. This approach has ensured that the potency and authenticity of the wisdom remain today. Although a profound blessing, the relationship demands of the student the highest discipline, determination, and patience. As payment, the student must offer the utter destruction of his or her own ignorant, selfish, ego-centered consciousness. Without such sacrifice, the divine gifts cannot find suitable soil and environment to firmly take root and flourish in the garden of the student's being.

Above and beyond the characteristic traits required in the student, the most essential component of the guru-disciple relationship is that the teacher be an authentic master. Such a master has always been a rare treasure, and this is even truer in today's modern world. Discovering an authentic master is a profound blessing in itself, yet to be chosen by such a master for initiation and instruction is the rarest divine grace.

The legendary stories about how the Siddhas relate with aspirants have persisted throughout the ages. The common theme? The Siddhas are uncompromising with those who seek Them and Their teachings. Actually, the stories contain many details that show the Siddhas as confrontational, harsh, and abrasive. The Siddhas offer no warmth, intimacy, or comfort, and so the potential disciple would have no reasonable expectation of trusting

Them. They appear, to our minds and manner of approaching life, as utterly unreasonable. This is the mask that They wear.

By hiding behind masks of utter simplicity coupled with an abrasive manner, the Siddha ensure that they are difficult to find, much less to approach. Indeed, my first meeting with a Siddha was very unusual. Had I been in an ordinary state of mind, I would have seen only a filthy beggar suffering from extreme mental derangement, one who was totally ignored by all those around. Yet I was blessed to be in a different state of mind. What others ignored and avoided, seeing only as horribly dirty and ignorant, for me shone like a diamond among a host of human excrement. I saw a lustrous form with brilliant eyes whose madness conveyed Truth. Is it not itself crazy that in the appearance of absolute poverty, filth, extreme mental illness, and perhaps danger, I could see and experience only the purest love and most profound wisdom? The hidden reason for the Siddhas masking Themselves behind simplicity, madness, or abrasiveness is to ward off insincere seekers. Requiring people to look beneath the mask is a grand test to weed out unripe aspirants, for Their path requires that a student have uncommon courage and faith.

My Master and I

Pal Pandian's manner of relating with me has been quite opposite to the way in which Siddhas traditionally have interacted with Their disciples. The one traditional attribute he does embody is that of extreme simplicity, as he exudes the most ordinary manner. That alone is the mask that he naturally and effortlessly shows the world. Perhaps his warm, embracing, intimate way of relating with me flows from this core, this innate and almost-crushing humility.

What I am about to relate regarding our relationship is based solely on my own experience, and so it stands as a uniquely individual experience. Pal's profound compassion for me is such that he has blessed me with many Siddha paths rather than only Varma instruction. His showering of me with *Kaya Kalpa* (rejuvenation), *Siddha Tantra*, *Siddha Yoga* (Vasi yoga), and Siddha Varma concurrently has allowed an immense platform for the relationship to unfold. In the beginning of the journey into the healing realm, Pal slowly nurtured my capability of receiving other people with genuine compassion. This preparation began by cleansing and strengthening my body and mind and rejuvenating my spirit for my life's purpose. Over time, Pal took me into the esoteric dimensions of Siddha Tantra, Siddha Yoga, internal alchemy, and external alchemy.

If, for instance, our interaction had been confined to Varma instruction, perhaps his approach would have been much more impersonal. This strictness, he once told me, is how most Varma masters relate with their students. The reader is cautioned not to take the following description of Healer Pal's manner of relating with me as typical, as a representation of what they should expect if they seek out a relationship with a Varma master. Because we each are unique expressions, we experience unique journeys. The usual manner of a master is to make those who approach them apprentice for many years, working very hard in extremely menial, repetitive tasks. For whatever reason, Pal has always related with me in the most tender, patient, and intimate manner. With others, however, I have noticed that his countenance can be quite different. Why he should be so extraordinarily attentive to me I cannot explain, and certainly it is not due to any inherent virtue or attribute that I possess. My best guess is that we each receive what we truly need.

Once taken up, the Varma student's quest demands nothing less than total devotion to the path, an unparalleled willingness to disappear into the countless unknown realms of one's self, the relationship with the master, and the unending dimensions of Varma healing. Traditionally, a long apprenticeship is required, with twelve years passing before the student is taught the first application of a specific Varma point. Throughout the master-student relationship, the purification of the student's mind, body, and spirit stands as paramount to his or her learning. Without this purification, the comprehensive knowledge of Varma points, anatomy, physiology, psychology, and so forth remains impotent or simply "learned ignorance." The application of the knowledge would be devoid of genuine compassion and the capacity for enhanced wisdom and so would render diluted, if not dangerous, results.

The relationship between the teacher and student is an all-encompassing one to such a degree that no aspect of the student's life or being is left untouched. Caring for each and every particle of the student's composition and relationship with all of life and nature, the teacher guides the student to realms of immeasurable depth. The guru-shisya (student) relationship is undertaken in order to confront and eradicate all forms of inertia, prejudice, vanity, and insensitivity. The unending dimensions of divine love and reciprocity that ensue are beyond description. Early in my relationship with Pal, I asked him about the science of Chinese medicine and healing. I noted that Siddha Bogar had taken Varma healing to China, and I wondered if the Chinese systems contained such potency. After the usual natural, light laughter that is his nature to express, he explained that, indeed, in ancient times, these types of masters did exist. He allowed that perhaps such a master may remain hidden away in China. He then continued, "Even so, have you ever heard of any acupuncturist or other healer using their system for spiritual practice? But the Varma system has its own yogic practice and kalpa [science of longevity] practice for one's own salvation."

Through the devoted, long-term practice of Varma healing alone, the practitioner gains realization.

After the initial phases of serving a Varma master, as the instruction unfolds, the relationship between the teacher and the student is paramount. The student must be profoundly receptive to the teaching as well as to the healing essence that is transmitted by the master. This relationship anchors the student in the secret realm of the Siddhas and Their divine healing methods. Furthermore, this intimately felt and expressed relationship continues to develop throughout the healing journey and always serves as the foundation of the student's own healing capacity, ever-evolving instruction, and life course. It is never lessened, much less abandoned, in any manner, at any time, or to any degree. The spoken and unspoken communion contributes to the long and revered lineage of the Siddha healing tradition.

There is no substitute for this most essential tenet of transmission. Just as each person suffering from a disorder requires healing that is unique to him or her, each Varma student is drawn into his or her own relationship with a Varma master. Siddha Varma has never embraced classroom-like teachings or healing applications. This holds equally true for spiritual instruction. Yet it is not uncommon these days to see teachers of spiritual, yogic, and healing paths initiate groups of people into their various techniques. The problem is that each of us contains a singularly expressed constitution and life course, or purpose. Each of us requires a specific set of conditions, environment, and nurturing to fulfill our deepest potential. What follows such a rare possibility is a personally felt and personally lived nourishment of one's innermost, individual living. The result is a truly and completely fulfilled life.

The entire dimension of Siddha healing has undergone a reformation and unparalleled consolidation by Healer Pal. This is the direct consequence of Pal's years of dedicated learning under varied masters; his thirst for healing wisdom is unmatched. From this extensive learning, he has harmonized and integrated Siddha healing in a way that has never occurred before. The result is his own distinct expression of the extreme depth and breadth of the wisdom of the Tamil Siddhas.

Conversely, what is found today among most Varma teachers is a very dry approach to dispensing Varma instruction. They simply describe or casually list the Varma points. At times, they mention a few diseases. I call this approach dry or narrow, based on my observation of such teachers being capable of imparting any knowledge or understanding beyond the surface level. Devoid of deeply integrated wisdom, they are unable to describe even physiological logic with any clarity. In my experience, they are incapable of providing instruction beyond a mechanical demonstration of Varma points. They lack the experience and richness of the Siddha masters. It is the manual level of Varma application that these teachers are giving out to increasing numbers of students. The highest and most potent levels of spiritual healing, notably Amrita Kalai, are beyond them.

Preparation for the Road Ahead

I was recently asked a question about my first meeting with Pal: "Why did you not ask him right away about what had troubled you since childhood?" An excellent question. The whole reason that I returned to India annually was to search for resolution of my existential crisis. You would think that would be the first thing out of my mouth upon meeting Pal. But it wasn't. Meeting him for the first time, in his little house, I found myself unable to form any significant questions. In the short time we spent together that day, I had no problems with my existence. I was struck dumb, in a way. Just that morning, my back had been aching, but I felt no pain while I was with Pal. Another factor was that his presence cast over me a large aura of not only serenity but also a weird type of authority that came from the immediately felt sense of being in the company of spiritual perfection. This feeling isn't in any way like the authority of a boss over a servant. It is quite the opposite. The feeling of immense respect coupled with the most endearing quality kept me quite silent. Even throughout our years of instruction, I have found myself reluctant to ask some questions. They just seem impertinent. Pal shares so much with me, whether I am in India or the United States, that asking for more would be greedy. Still, I awaited spiritual instruction eagerly. The final, and most prominent, reason that I did not press Pal for an answer to that question when we first met is that, from that moment on, my body, mind, and life changed in the most wonderful ways. It was as if I were full from eating a feast. Asking for more food at that time was simply not necessary.

During those first years of my healing journey with Pal, I felt that he had yet to give me spiritual initiation. In fact, he had been preparing me, slowly and in his usual quiet, humble way, for the road ahead. I recall one day during the first year, after a class, he asked me to lie on a table. Without words and with only the slightest touch of his hand, I was swiftly pulled into a different realm. For how long I was gone or what he performed I am still unsure, but I do not think it was a very long time. When I came to my senses, I opened my eyes, slowly sat up, and realized that something dramatic had changed. It is a strange and beautiful experience to leave your body and mind in this way. Returning to them, one is aware that, for whatever amount of time has just passed, there were no thoughts, no object, and no subject. Just the most sublime peace. It was from this state that I emerged and noticed that my breath had altered. It was intoxicating! With each inhalation, the breath carried a palpable sense of energy into my body. Traveling downward, it did not stop at the lungs but continued all the way down to below the navel. Of course, the actual air only went as far as the lungs, but that which attaches to air (prana) was being absorbed in greater quantities and was traveling a new route. Tremendous gratitude flowed from me, and with tears of joy I did my best to thank Pal. Much later, I learned that is the first of the traditional yogic initiations. The master brings the student into his world and so prepares him or her for the personal spiritual journey.

Only in hindsight did I realize that the social (healing) and personal (spiritual) journeys had been skillfully braided together by Pal the entire time. It seems that, in order to have the high degree of sensitivity to practice esoteric healing, one's own consciousness must also become more refined. On a daily basis, Pal guided me, via demonstration, in the practice known as *Adangal massage*.

ADANGAL: A PARADOXICAL PRACTICE

The word *Adangal* is not easily translated into English and can perhaps be described best as sublimation. It is the chemical reaction that transforms a substance from the physical state to the gaseous state without the substance having to pass through the liquid state. Although this art is technically considered a form of the first level, it reflects a dimensionally higher and more subtle realm.

Since ancient times the Varma masters have applied, but only in secret, the method known as Adangal to people suffering from intractable diseases or mental derangements. This method is applied to bring an unconscious person to normalcy, even if the cause is unknown. Being of such potency, Adangal initiation is rarely given to a student but rather is reserved for one whose relationship with the master is extensively cohesive and deeply mature. Adangal is extremely rare in India: perhaps three or four authentic masters are capable of transmitting this wisdom.

An additional application of Adangal utilizes its effectiveness yet, paradoxically, seems a simple form of massage. From the perspective of a casual observer, this mysterious method may resemble a full body massage in which herbal oil is used. However, in truth, it has no resemblance to what we know as massage. The oils used are not simply herbs added to an oil base but rather are rarified herbs that are carefully selected, collected in remote mountainous regions, and then arduously prepared by being mixed in proportional quantities and heated with oils over a long period of time. Each of the herbal oils has certain properties. For instance, some formulations are used specifically on the head and neck, while other formulations are intended solely for the body below the neck.

Learning how to apply Adangal requires years of instruction and determined practice. The entire body is the platform, and many Varma points are included during the session. Specific movements and finely tuned geometric patterns of flow (*Yantras*) result in an astonishing predetermined format. The treatment always involves the healer's deeply introverted concentration. The complexity of the flowing methods demands that the healer rest naturally in a deeply meditative state while remaining intimately attuned to the person receiving the treatment.

Adangal is indeed a paradoxical practice and is challenging to describe in a clear manner. It is reserved for those whose bodies hold a disease, whether physical or mental, which has hardened into identification with the illness. Adangal softens and soothes not only physical structures but also the nervous system, energy centers, lymphatic flow, and various other aspects of the body. Traditionally, when the master reached the stage at which he became aware that his time on earth was approaching its end, he would instruct only his most trusted and closest disciple. This would be done in a room without windows and in utter secret. Such an application, which has such a high degree of potency and power to heal, also holds the potential for great harm if misused. Should a person not readily respond to manual stimulation (Systemic Vital Point Therapy), the application of Adangal is necessary.

A prime example can be found in the story of a five-year-old boy who suffered from moderate cerebral palsy.

His parents knew nothing of Varma healing, yet out of desperation they were willing to take him to our center in the United States. He was unable to pronate his hands, which meant that when he played peekaboo, his palms faced outward. In addition, he was incapable of using any of his fingers individually; as a collective, they remained close together and curved at the ends. His vocabulary was extremely limited, dominated by sounds rather than words.

Within just a few weeks of twice-weekly Varma healing sessions, he began to experience changes in his body. The first change was the ability to twist his wrists and hands in the normal manner of the game of peekaboo. Next, he was capable of pointing with his index fingers.

About a month after his first session, he spotted a single hair on the floor and, delicately and independently, used his forefinger and thumb to pick it up. He held it up to show his father, who stood there in amazement. The little boy's arms and hands responded to the healing first, followed by his speech. Approximately one year later, when I greeted him, he approached me and casually said, "How ya' doing, Steve?"

Cerebral palsy is a congenital disease that follows a certain course. Both modern medicine and Siddha healing agree on this, yet their views beyond that vary greatly. The Siddhas have long known that cerebral palsy is a result of a lack of nectar during the birthing process. While nectar belongs to the subtle realm, its physical manifestation is cerebrospinal fluid. Stagnation of this fluid results in stagnation of normal, healthy development.

When the subtle but vitally important Varma points, nervous system, and nadis are stimulated by use of Adangal "massage," the body is reminded of something. This forgotten something is the memory of healthy function. This memory resides in each of us, having originated in the embryonic stage of development. In the case of this five-year-old boy, the birthing process had blocked his body's intelligence from being fulfilled. The channels of life flow, the functioning of the dasa vayu, and the cerebrospinal fluid simply needed to be reminded of their originally designed movement.

The changes that took place in this boy are no miracles. The results follow ancient understanding, knowledge, and logic. Because this ancient viewpoint is different from our modern-day one, the temptation is to see the results as either miraculous or primitive. They are, in truth, neither. Rather, they are obtained from longstanding methods that have served humankind well for millennia. This simple wisdom of healing existed long before our current scientific methods were developed, overruled all previous approaches, and left us with a single, overly rational approach to health.

Chapter 6

Siddha Tantra

Living in Darkness

The year I spent at home involved an extremely full schedule. Although the demands of my corporate job had changed little, I spent the nights and weekends performing healing sessions. I overextended myself quite a bit. I was integrating Adangal, the full body work with Siddha oils that soothes and softens the nervous system, restores lymphatic flow, and provides suppleness to the bones and muscles, into the sessions. Integrating Adangal demanded not only more time but also a very high degree of clarity and sensitivity on my part. Away from the healing center, I had to be very careful with my diet, daily routine and, of course, attitude toward life. This attitude should reflect that of a healer in all aspects of life and point to a nurturing approach with all the various people and situations encountered. Applying this disposition while still engaged in the mundane aspects of life, such as work and social life, was my greatest challenge during that year.

By the time I returned to India the following year, I was severely exhausted. Little did I know what awaited me. Usually, my time there is spent with Pal, learning deeper aspects of Siddha healing. On that trip, introduction into the higher realms of Siddha healing would indeed occur, but the majority of my time would be spent in an entirely new way. My personal journey began in earnest. For five weeks, I lived in complete darkness and solitude in an underground chamber.

Living in darkness underground is a part of the Kaya Kalpa process, with its aim to cleanse the body and mind of impurities down to the cellular level. In the path of the Siddhas, the body is understood to contain the universe in microcosmic form, and thus its health, balance, and vigor are necessary before sweeping changes can take place. The universe, in its totality, contains all of the energy created, whether expressed or latent. The same holds true for the body in microcosmic form. Cleansing and purifying the physical frame allows these energies to align in their proper, potent manner. Without such grounding, the mind and body would be unable to assimilate the changes that take place. It is like having a profound insight. We hear, read, or suddenly realize something amazing, something with such clarity in the moment, and we just know it in our core. This something can change a huge aspect of our lives, at least in the moment. We feel it so perfectly, but then it slips away so that what we had known so clearly is replaced, clouded over. We cannot live it, because we were not capable of fully integrating it into our consciousness.

That which we had felt contained such immense power, transformational power, like an electrical device that cannot handle it, overloads with too much energy. We either burn up or simply cannot assimilate such power. While aching for radical transformation to live in an entirely new way, I came to understand the importance of physical purity. When anything is to be radically transformed, it must go through a protracted phase of transmutation, which is the change into another nature, substance, or form. In the ancient science of alchemy, the transmutation is from base metals, such as lead or copper, into gold. The lead would, by necessity, be required to lose all of its qualities in order to become the much more pure substance of gold. Those qualities that are not pure must be released before the transformation can occur. A parallel approach is undertaken for internal alchemical changes to occur in the mind and body. In order for the consciousness to be refined into the spiritual heights of enlightenment, the aspects of body and mind first must lose the impurities that they have accumulated throughout life. According to the Siddhas, alchemy applies not only to physical objects. To transform the body is known as *external alchemy*, while spiritual practices aimed at enlightenment are considered *internal alchemy*. In this way, long ago, the prince known as Siddhartha, who had lived his life in wealth and pleasure, found himself going through an intense process of transmutation that refined his common nature (like lead) into a refined state (like gold), and he became known as the Buddha.

The initial aim of the kalpa process is to bring out the conditioned patterns so that they can be eliminated. The first step is to break the identification patterns to which we have become attached. For example, my professional job required me to live by a fixed schedule, in a time-oriented fashion. To confront this, Pal first introduced me to the Kalpa house and had me live in a dark underground room in which there was nothing to do. He visited me twice per day to deliver lunch and dinner. In order to bring my body into greater balance, he provided gentle cleansing for the digestive system, sinus and head area, and eyes. Again, we see the cosmos in the body consisting of the five primordial elements, which are expressed in paired combinations as the three doshas of vata, pitta, and kapha, (air, fire, and earth). By having me live in the Kalpa house and providing cleansing, Pal brought the deranged constituents of my body into harmony.

Although the experience was challenging, I was delighted at the opportunity for extended rest and rejuvenation. Time alone and in darkness? I was all for it! My exhaustion had reached a critical point. I felt that sleep and escape from responsibilities were the best gifts I could have been given. When Pal told me how I would spend the days and nights, my happiness knew no bounds.

"You should spend your time like a newborn baby," he said. I stared at him with a puzzled look on my face. He went on. "How do babies live? They sleep, dream, eat, and play. That is all. Please be like a baby now."

The setting in which I had been placed made absolutely no demands on me. Living without the mechanical pattern I was accustomed to, I felt its lack. It is a feeling of suddenly having taken away from us something to which we are very accustomed, like a lover or a habit. The lack is noticed and acutely felt.

Initially, my reaction was very sluggish (*tamasic*), and I slept a lot. Occasionally, I became, in Pal's words, a little wild, meaning restless (*rajasic*). As my accustomed time-oriented pattern began to leave me, I started to feel a little lost, hence the varying, or restless, responses. By being deprived of the pattern, I felt nonexistent. I was learning firsthand that whatever I lean on, become accustomed to, or have expectations of, will, by its very nature, limit and constrict me. But I am the one who wanted and sought spiritual transformation. Transforming the base metal of ordinary consciousness to the refined gold of enlightenment is not without its challenges.

The Kalpa House

THE DOOR OPENS

A few days into the new routine, while Pal and I were sitting together, I told him that I had experienced a rather perplexing dream. It had been extremely vivid. All of the senses had been involved and, most notably, I could effortlessly recall every detail. Actually, the dream would not leave me alone. It continued to insert itself into my awareness. He encouraged me to tell him about the dream. I described it as follows.

The members of my corporate team, numbering about twelve, including myself, and our manager are on a hiking expedition in Egypt. We begin with a train ride to the starting point of the hike. The train ride is smooth. There is dust in the air, and the entire carriage is lit by blazing sunlight, which makes the fine particles of sand in the air take on a glittering quality as they swirl about and settle on every surface. Sitting on the right-hand side of the carriage is an enormous animal cage that has numerous compartments, each containing a different animal. Atop the cage sits a man, who is facing me and wearing typical Western-style safari garb. I see many varieties of animals in the cage and note that, although caged, they look healthy, well cared for, and at ease in their respective compartments. Although I am aware that almost every animal species is present, I can see only a jackal and a hyena in detail. The man is sitting cross-legged, and fascination swells within me. I find him and those in his charge irresistible. Approaching him, I begin to ask questions, but before he can reply, the train comes to a halt, and we disembark and begin our hike.

The manager leads us, and we each carry a small, olive-green backpack as we trudge, through scorching heat, across a hard surface that is covered with only a single layer of sand. To our left stretches the Sahara Desert, with its sand dunes whirled into brown-yellow motionless waves that crest in bunches akin to family members staying close to one another. In the distance stand the great pyramids, those monuments of the East that have for so long called out to adventurous Westerners to leave the comforts of their homes to taste the exotic. That which is on our right is of another matter. Walking only a few feet from the edge of a cliff, I glance down only to see ragged, sharp daggers of stone. Some of them begin just beyond the precipice, but the bottom is so distant that its end may well be the bowels of the earth. I feel a bit confused, because I had been convinced, prior to looking, that at the bottom were the Nile and her flowing sustenance. The scent of her waters remains in my nostrils. Returning my gaze ahead, to ensure that I am following the path blazed by my teammates, I notice that, uncharacteristically, I am at the back of the group.

After only a few more steps, I again look to my right. There the man from the train sits atop his huge cage filled with the animals. In that moment, I know that they are in a place of great danger. I stop in my tracks and notice that they are on an island that seems to float in the air some distance from the mainland where we are hiking, such that there is a considerable distance between us. No one else takes any note of the island or its inhabitants. I again look down and see the jagged, sharp, misshapen knives of dry rock and the infinity of the drop. Without hesitation but rather with absolute conviction from an unknown source, I loudly announce to the team, "I must go to that island." Immediately, in a chorus of concern, they demand that I refrain from such nonsense, as death is the only possible outcome. Ignoring the others, I leap from the safety of a continent across a chasm that I could not reasonably expect to successfully traverse. When I leap, I am acutely aware that, indeed, death is the likeliest result. But at the same time, I am fascinated by my desire and action. The act seems not impetuous but rather necessary. I recognize this feeling of absolute resolve as something that has lived deep inside me since childhood, like a secret life. Having long been confined by non-expression, this secret has managed to exit, with yearning and action, at this precise moment and in these particular circumstances. Staking its existence and my life, gambling everything, we two take our best leap.

There is no fear in taking the jump—only the flash of certainty and inevitability of its occurrence. However, the outcome of the jump provides ample opportunity for me to visit such emotions. I am hanging by my hands. The olive-green backpack slips off my back, and I look down past my dangling feet as it falls away. Its drop continues for so long that I become weary of watching, and I wonder just how vast the canyon is. The man jumps off the animal cage, approaches the edge of the island, peers over, and invites me to join him. I hesitate to pull myself up, scared by the island's twirling movement as it is buffeted by strong winds.

Although the dichotomy of my having taken the leap with a sense of certainty only to now be indecisive on the threshold of the leap's success should be obvious, I am in no mood to reflect on my inconsistency. The fear of alighting on such an unstable surface is shockingly real to me, and in that moment I cannot imagine anything more terrifying. The question I pose to the man, however, immediately intensifies my fear. I ask how we are to leave the small rock island. Calmly and matter-of-factly, he informs me that a helicopter will soon arrive but that its chances of crashing and killing us all when we take off from the constantly moving island are high. Presented with options of pulling myself up onto the island or continuing to hang over the edge, I am now even more fearful of climbing up. Eventually, the situation forces me to recognize the inevitable outcome, regardless of my choice. Now that death seems inevitable, a clear, determined response instinctively arises from the depths of my being and announces, in a thundering tone, "I don't want to die just now. . . . I don't know how to leave the body yet!"

I was surprised by Pal's response to my recounting of the dream. He was genuinely overjoyed with what I had related. I must admit that I was completely confused. Although smiling and laughing is Pal's normal manner of interacting, I had yet to witness such obvious happiness from him. Terribly confused, I thought, *It was just a dream, right?* What exactly is going on here? Frankly, I was humbled and almost embarrassed at the way he showered gratitude on me. Emboldened by his joy, I plied him with questions about the dream's meaning. He happily relayed to me not only the inner significance of that specific dream but also how the subconscious mind influences us in general.

Patiently, he explained how we live unconscious of our deeper selves, motives, and reactions. The realm of dreams is of vital importance in showing us how we really are living.

For example, he said, "In a dream, we can walk our dog down the street, take off our clothes, and put them on the dog. Of course, if we were to enact this in the waking state, we would end up in jail!"

Unconvinced of the significance of dreams, I pressed him further about them. When he told me that "the Siddhas say that we should laugh at our waking-state experiences and take our dreams seriously," a greater measure of both understanding and faith arose in me.

"Your dream is a beautiful one," he told me. "What does Egypt signify? It is the land of the dead. Being with your job and the people from it shows your willingness to die, to leave behind your ordinary life and mind, and embark on the journey."

To die is to transform from one state into another, much like lead must give up its lead nature in order to transmute into, or be reborn as, gold. Pal's speaking of my leaving behind my ordinary life and mind mirrored the releasing of impurities, long-held notions, and fixations. Because they cannot be carried over into the new state, they must go; their departure creates an opening in which rebirth, or the new, can take root. The majority of life today is spent in our jobs and with our coworkers. That part of life is also a major source of both achievement and tension, and so it was the area with which I had come to identify myself. Incorporating the attitude of a healer into my daily career, with its specific demands, had always been difficult for me. By some great turn of fate and grace, that was about to change.

The Dark Underground

Apparently that single dream opened the door for what was to follow. The next day I was initiated into Siddha Tantra. The journey is specific to each individual; therefore, it cannot be taught with any authenticity in groups, workshops, or classrooms. Nothing of one's entire life experience can be left out or discarded. Each particle of our makeup, nature, and constitution and every single experience we have had is fuel for the fire of transformation. In this way, we see the beauty of Nature, that everything that exists has purpose and is utilized perfectly and that nothing is ever wasted or deemed useless. This lesson that our greater surroundings ache to teach us is always present and is a foundational tenet of creation. Although the subconscious realms are full of collective and individual impressions, their very existence originates from the one Source. In Siddha Tantra, the tendency to exclude the inauspicious and cling desperately to what is considered uplifting and good is a limiting approach. The classic tale of good versus evil is woven into every aspect of society and our lives. Morality and pride on one side and guilt and regret on the other do little more than swirl in never-ending circles, drying up the fertile soil of our native potential.

Much confusion persists surrounding Tantra, because it has always been a path of extreme secrecy and what appear to be strange practices. The Siddha Tantra master grants initiation only to the qualified and does so strictly on an individual basis that reflects the aspirant's inherent character (*Swabhava*). This inherent character is born within each person as a combination of his or her past-life merits, fulfillments, and shortcomings. Only the Sat Guru, a perfected master, has sufficiently vast and penetrative vision of one's inherent character and qualities to give initiation that can take one to the goal.

Siddha Tantra enables us to transcend our stagnated programming—in fact, all of our limitations and every form of dilemma—and thus find our Swabhava and live in accordance with it. Tantra works on the dark, conflicting forces of the human psyche, which are united by the integrative approach of this sacred path. Wild knots of passion, agitation, emotional constipation or diarrhea, and the commonly insensitive approach to oneself all fall prey to the mysterious, shrouded path that Tantra unfolds. Tantra refines these gross passions by transforming them into the very sap of divinity.

From the very beginning of instruction in Tantra, a different sense of time and space is experienced. The reason for encountering changes in time and space is that Tantra works with the subconscious realms of both individual and collective scale. Here again, I take us back to the Siddhas' view that all of creation is contained within each of us. Many new-age movements and teachings like to trumpet how we are "all one." That is certainly true, but what is often overlooked is the unity of all things, both auspicious and inauspicious, that rests within our subconscious. This grand unity of a collective nature includes all of humankind stretching back to the beginning of creation and lives in the darkness of our being, the subconscious, in latent form. It is a vast dimension, so when we begin the journey into it, there is ample opportunity for incredibly shocking revelations. Within us lie huge amounts of energy in specific primordial patterns that are often referred to as archetypes, or models. When personified, these archetypes make up the pantheon of deities, with each god, goddess, or demon embodying a specific primal energy. These inclusive patterns contain within them all of the energy that exists, which is the reason that a solid foundation is required before one can encounter them. What is this foundation, and what is necessary in order for it to be solid? The foundation is none other than our own bodies, minds, and spirits, which must be purified so that they will not be overwhelmed by the confrontational nature of the archetypes. The foundations should be well balanced and strongly rooted so that we can assimilate the oncoming waves of energy. This is another reason that a perfected master, a Sat Guru, is necessary: only he or she is truly capable of preparing and then shepherding the Tantric student through the maze that ensues.

Of all spiritual paths, Tantra is the most misunderstood and maligned, due to its highly esoteric nature. Tantric masters rarely allow themselves to be revealed publicly. In earlier days, they carefully chose a few disciples, and their meetings took place in remote, hidden locations, such as deep in forests, in mountain caves, and in graveyards. In the hands of many, today Tantra is being used in the most perverse manner—as an excuse for sensual indulgences and transgressions. Indulging in sensual practices and taking a casual approach to opening the doors of the inner recesses and energy of the psyche are not only disingenuous but also dangerous. I have even come across those who call themselves as *Tantric sexual gurus*. These individuals are by no means gurus, and what they attempt to teach is certainly not Tantra.

> *The Guru who removes blindness, they seek not,*
> *The Guru who removes not-blindness they seek;*
> *The blind and the blind, in a blind dance, mingled;*
> *The blind and the blind, in a deep pit, together fell.*

(Siddha Thirumular, "Thirumanthiram," Verse 1680, In Pal Pandian, *Siddhas: Masters of the Basics* [Chennai, India: Pal Pandian, 2008])

Two Paths of Tantra

Tantra has two paths: the Left Hand path, or *Vama Marga*, and the Right Hand path, called *Dakshina Marga*. The Left Hand Tantric path is the adoration of one's passion without any suppression and is void of any cathartic approach. This path is rarely taken these days, since most of us already live an indulgent lifestyle. The Right Hand path involves *Upasana*, the worship of a prescribed personal deity. This is the approach into which Pal initiated me, specifically the *Sri Chakra Upasana*. The literal meaning of the word *Upasana* is "close to one's grounding," and the practitioner's specific deity is carefully prescribed by the guru. For those on a spiritual path, Sri Chakra Upasana is the most highly sought-after initiation, for it grants both worldly success and spiritual realization. It is an extremely rare blessing.

Although I had never heard of Sri Chakra Upasana before my initiation in it, when I questioned Pal afterward, he spoke softly to me of its extreme rarity. He informed me that, in the tradition of all of their practices, the Siddhas withhold a vital key. This essential component has never been written and can be given to an initiate only by the guru. This key allows the practice to be fruitful. Without it, one cannot achieve Siddhahood. When Pal told me this, I felt extreme gratitude and prayed that I should gain enough humility to be worthy of the initiation.

Surprised that I had never heard of Sri Chakra, Pal asked if I had any further questions about it before he left. After pondering for a bit, I asked, "What is the purpose of this practice?"

Pal's reply was immediate. "The purpose is to become acquainted with death. We must move through the fear of it. For this, we should become adept at consciously leaving identification with the body. Whenever we de-identify with our physical body, the mind identifies with the subtle body. So, normally, people are not aware at the time of their death are pulled from the physical body and, according to their karma, stay in the earthly realm. But when we are leaving the mortal frame, we have to de-identify with all of the bodies, the physical, subtle, and causal, because we should be in a de-identified state with regard to all the bodies. When alive, people are identified with their physical body. In meditation, they are identified with their subtle body, and when dreaming, they are identified with their dream body. The mind always likes to identify with a body, and so when death comes, they will immediately identify with their subtle body and then be stuck in the earthly realm. We should learn to live without identification with any of these bodies. That is why the Siddhas say, 'Have a dead man's eyes, and Walk like a corpse.' It is only in this way that, in the moment of death, we will not identify with any body. We already know our true Center."

Once again, in his always simple and humble manner and with the most ordinary of airs, he had granted divine gifts.

Sri Chakra Upasana

After his departure, I descended into the underground darkness to begin the Siddha Tantra practice. After repeating the secret mantra only a few times, I was surprised to see standing before me a playful girl of four or five years of age. Dark-skinned, with short, cropped black hair, barefoot, and wearing a summer dress, she beckoned me. Without hesitation, I followed her up the stairs to a small shrine. Inside the shrine was a statue of a deity with whom I was not yet familiar. By the grace of the guru, my journey into Siddha Tantra began with auspiciousness. She had revealed herself in my presence and blessed the practice.

> *The Divine Mother's Magic*
> *Is ancient all life itself.*
> *She existed before Gods and mortals,*
> *and She will exist after the great dissolution.*
> *Mother is pure energy in subtle form,*
> *but in time of need*
> *or just out of desire to play, She manifests.*

(Pal Pandian, *Siddhas: Masters of the Basics* [Chennai, India: Pal Pandian, 2008])

Spiritual experiences of all sorts were no stranger to me. Yet this was utterly unlike anything I had experienced before. This was no temporary vision or mind-induced state. Sitting in the darkness underground, I began the secret mantra. Only two or three times into it, my surroundings became altered. All of the senses were totally involved yet transcended in some fashion. The reality of the experience was no different than my typing of these words on the computer. It was as if She were simultaneously embracing my physical body and taking it into Her realm. In this fashion began the lessons that were to guide me through the darkness of the unconscious.

During the weeks that followed, Pal visited me twice daily to bring my meals and check on my health. At those times, we sat together and spoke. Most days he attended to me with his healing touch, unwinding and relaxing both my body and mind. Weekly he sent one of his attendants to give me a full body oil massage. I gradually became more invigorated, relaxed, and flexible both physically and spiritually. After the initiation, when I had become accustomed to the environment, he slowly introduced some activities. On occasion he brought me books to read or sat chatting with me for extended periods. The time I spent in the Kalpa house was the most enjoyable period I could have wished for.

Sleeping was no problem for me, and I indulged in it whenever the feeling arose. Because I was in a dark chamber, whether it was night or day made no difference. My choice of recreation was reading, so whenever I felt the urge to read, I lit a candle. I ate simple breakfasts of a few small apples and some herbal tea. Pal kindly provided me with wonderful reading materials about the great sages Bhagavan Maharshi and Shirdi Sai Baba and the Siddhas. Devouring these texts was an exhilarating experience, since most of them were rare or out of print. I was to avoid sunlight, so after each meal, I descended into the underground chamber to read, rest, or sleep. Spending time in this way, my mind gradually unwound its tensions and tendencies to be obsessed with time. Because I had no schedule to keep, a softness entered me. The softness bestowed a sense of flexibility and receptivity that I never dreamed possible.

Rivulets of the Absolute

Shirdi Sai Baba

Mere days after my encounter with the Goddess in child form, *Valai* in Tamil and *Bala* in Sanskrit, I had just finished breakfast in the upper room of the Kalpa house. The day seemed similar to the ones before it, but then something different happened.

Goddess Valai

I peered out the window and noticed a half-ruined ancient building across the courtyard. Despite the instruction to avoid sunlight, I decided to investigate. When I entered the crumbling structure, I was surprised to see that it consisted of several rooms in addition to the front one, which was a kitchen. Continuing to inspect the building, I walked to an adjoining room and stood shocked at the sight before me. Lying on the floor were a gigantic Komodo dragon and, next to it, a small kitten. Both were inert and had their eyes closed. Out of concern for the kitten, I decided to test whether the dragon was dead or simply asleep. I grabbed a nearby chair and tossed it into the room in order to create enough noise to elicit a response from the dragon. To my surprise and utter horror, the dragon immediately awoke, locked its eyes on me, and proceeded to attack.

I fled the scene in absolute terror, racing across the courtyard to the Kalpa house. I was able to get inside and close the door just ahead of the determined beast, but I knew that the door would not hold against the size and ferocity of the dragon. I grabbed the mobile phone I had been provided with and attempted to call Pal. I knew that my only hope would be his immediate arrival. But as I looked through the window and watched the dragon's methodical approach, a feeling of terror began to overwhelm me. Try as I might, I could not properly dial the numbers on the phone. My mind was racing, my body had broken out in a cold sweat, and I was shaking uncontrollably. Frozen by fear, my body was utterly locked into inaction, and my mind was capable of only a single thought pattern: "Shit, shit, shit! I'm going to die a horribly long and painful death!"

Suddenly and simultaneously, two things happened, neither of which did I find odd at the time: a motorcycle, ridden by a young girl wearing a half sari, pulled up to the side of the dilapidated house, and the dragon disappeared, taking with it all of my terror and even any notion of its existence. All of my fear vanished and was replaced by an overwhelming curiosity about the young maiden, who could not have been much more than sixteen years old. Observing her actions through the window, I saw her enter the house and begin preparing a meal for herself in the partially destroyed kitchen. Soon enough, carrying a bowl of vegetables and noodles in her hands, she walked across the courtyard and approached the Kalpa house. I promptly opened the door and invited her in.

Delighted at the prospect of such lovely company, I patiently waited and watched as she began to eat with chopsticks the meal she had made. As she sat atop a brick pillar on one side of the room, I sat opposite her on another. She wore a half sari and jeans and had long, straight black hair. She remained silent and swung her legs over the pillar in a relaxed, playful manner. After a time, she looked at me and asked, "Do you like it here [in the Kalpa house]?"

I replied, "Yes. Very much." I became aware that I was not only grinning broadly but was also extremely happy for her company and totally transfixed by her appearance. I could not take my eyes off her for even a moment.

She continued, "That is good. I used to live here."

We continued to exchange words for a while yet, of these words, no memory was allowed to remain with me until I asked a pointed question. Our chat had led me to something that I was sincerely interested to know about her, and that she, in turn, was waiting to inform me. "What is it that you do?" I inquired.

"I instruct children," she replied.

Again, I felt a thrill move through me and could not escape the profound joy that I felt in her presence. Soon I had the overwhelming desire to move closer to her and, for some reason, felt compelled to take a close look at her face. Strange as my desire to approach and examine her in detail seemed, I was aware that she was allowing me this indulgence and that her doing so was nothing short of the bestowal of an extremely patient blessing. Standing before her, I noticed the radiant, thin shape of her body and the beautiful black hair framing her face, and I then got quite close and stared into her face, straining to see her exact features. There were none. Her face was a simple orb of radiant white light. She took Her leave by dispersing into ever-smaller orbs of golden-hued light, leaving behind the smell of fresh flowers and a throbbing radiance that was both felt and seen.

In the few short days I had spent at the Kalpa house, She had matured from a little girl to a young virgin. The form of the maiden transfixed me, because Her presence radiated such heavenly beauty. When one has authority over us, we wish to avoid their disapproval and seek their approval. Except when we are very small and with our mothers, we do not associate love with authority. In this case, however, these typically perplexing attributes of extraordinary authority and profound love did not confuse me. The naturalness of our bond did not seem odd to me. Her appearance, scent, clothing, and radiance both drew and bound me to Her. Living in simplicity, predominant darkness, and solitude had left me increasingly vulnerable to Her influence.

When I opened the heavy plank door for Pal that evening, I was eager to relate the encounter and learn of its significance. The tropical nights were only a little less sweltering than the days, but when I was aboveground, I wore the usual long-sleeved shirt and pants. Indian mosquitoes, it seems, find my flesh a delicacy. The particular routine of sitting opposite each other on the floor and smiling while gazing downward in beautiful silence ensued.

Breaking the silence, I told him of the maiden's visit.

He asked, "What do Komodo dragons mean to you?"

This was easy for me to remember. "I saw a BBC documentary on them just a while back, Sir. Two things both fascinated and horrified me. One was how they would wait for their prey to die and rot. When the insides had liquefied into a black paste, they would then feast. My other memory is of a man walking through the high grass of an Indonesian island with great care. Despite his caution, a dragon appeared quickly and bit his leg. While suffering intense pain, he continued to walk, attempting to escape the beasts that were methodically trailing after him. It took several days of extraordinary agony before he was rescued. All the while, ever-increasing numbers of dragons followed him, waiting for him to become totally paralyzed. If that had happened, they would have begun feasting on him."

He laughed and said, "Good."

Apparently, my terror about the Komodo dragon, followed by Her visit, had created a type of opening inside me. Although Pal had already spoken to me of being acquainted with death as necessary for spiritual ascension, I was not prepared to meet such fear directly. My fixation with living in a routine had to be broken so that a new approach could find room in me. The Kalpa house, Pal's healing touch, the pure diet, the predominant darkness, and the solitude all aided the process. In response to my query as to how this combination is so effective, he replied, "Only when this pattern is emptied can something new be poured into the vessel. To bring something new, we must first die to the old. This is true for the body as well; if you want to be twice born, first you must die."

Turning my attention back to the maiden, I asked about Her in detail.

"What did She mean when She said that She used to live here and that She instructs children? Does this mean that She is a teacher, Sir?"

"Yes," he replied. "She is telling you that you are now in Her house, where She lived. And, certainly, it is a good sign. When She stated that She instructs children, that is exactly what She does. We are children to Her, children whom She teaches."

We spoke more about Her, and from that discussion I learned that Her having matured so quickly, as she had during my short time in the Kalpa house up to that point, was very rare. Further,

Pal stated that usually the path is one of "thorns" and includes ample tears.

After laughing louder than usual, Pal continued. "Your path is more like one of roses. By the grace of my guru, so was mine." Knowing to my very core why the Upasana was flowing quickly and gracefully, I could only gaze at him, my eyes mist-filled and my throat tight.

In between Her visits, I read everything that Pal brought to me. Yet the one book I had carried from America (*Siddhas: Masters of the Basics,* by Siddha Healer Pal himself) I read repeatedly. Although it is a voluminous 600-page book, I pored over it again and again. Having read the same passages before, I gained a deeper understanding each time I revisited them. Never before had an actual authority put pen to paper to reveal the core aspects of the Siddhas. Cherishing this book for its depth and astounding transformative effect, I was reading a certain chapter for the third or fourth time when I fell into deep reverie, like a waking dream.

Dressed for work and driving the company car, I take a detour before making my first sales call. In the small town where I reside, I have decided to move the Siddha Varma healing center to a new location. Arriving at the new location, I see that it is an older house on a scenic street with beautiful trees near downtown. Searching for the key to unlock the door, I am excited to inspect the new building. When I enter the main room, which contains no furniture, I am taken aback. Sitting cross-legged on the floor is a woman, perhaps in her late twenties, with her young daughter. They are of Indian origin, are wearing saris, and eating a breakfast of idlis, sambar, and coconut chutney. Neither look at me, so I quietly sit on the floor at the opposite end of the room.

Using only the right hand to eat, as is the custom, they swirl the last portions of their meal. Rising and then exiting the house, they neither look at me nor acknowledge my presence. Immediately after they have left, I sense that a visitor has arrived. I open the door and am delighted to see that Pal has come to see the new healing center. I invite him in. Before I even close the door, I spy an unusual figure.

Sitting on the ground and leaning against the house opposite the healing center is an old, wrinkled woman also of Indian origin. She is dressed in a filthy sari. Although it was once some bland color, it is now a faded, worn, gray rag. Next to her is a large round pot with the usual broad opening at the top. She is staring at me with narrow black eyes in a severe countenance. I cannot possibly imagine who she is or what she wants from me, but I am certain that she wishes to communicate something. Quickly, I think that she may be a beggar and want some rupees. I feel slightly uncomfortable with this thought, and I shut the door.

I turn my attention to Pal, and we wander through the new healing center. In each room, I ask for his input on its purpose. After our tour, Pal concludes that it is indeed a fine location with a suitable layout. Delighted at his assessment, I set off to pack up the contents of the old location. I tell Pal that I will be back with everything in a bit.

Upon exiting the building, I am face-to-face with the old woman. Nothing has changed in her appearance. She is still sitting in the dust, and her eyes again lock with mine. I continue to stand there and look at her. I cannot imagine why she continues to sit there and stare at me. Somehow, I know that she is waiting for me. As to why, I have no idea. Eventually, I walk to my car and drive away.

When I related the reverie to Pal, he replied, "You do not have to stay here in the Kalpa house any longer. She has matured and now has come to bless you in your home. This blessing She has given for your work, Varma healing sessions, and life."

Humbled and grateful for the wonderful news, I was also reluctant to leave the house and the darkness of the underground chamber. The easy routine and rest had been so restorative that I was not yet willing to resume my normal activities. Thankfully, Pal said that it was fine for me to stay for several more weeks if I so desired.

My diet and routine were kept pure throughout this time. The purity had cumulative effects on both my mind and body. Lightness, clarity, and mental sharpness grew daily. I was comfortable in my surroundings and with how I spent the days and nights. The flow of the Upasana nurtured within me a greater sense of awe. Reading was the only external activity I bothered with on most days. I had brought a book with me that related stories of Bhagavan and animals. For some reason, reading that book seemed to open up an entirely new relationship with Him. I was entranced by the stories. Sitting in the underground chamber with a single candle for light, I was absorbed in reading a particular passage about Bhagavan and squirrels, and then I experienced another waking dream.

I close the book and use my finger as a bookmark. My eyes are closed, but a light comes, accompanied by a warming sensation and a sense of the slightest movement.

I look down at the book with my finger between its pages and sense that I am outside. Looking up, I see Bhagavan Maharshi seated on His divan in the Old Hall of the ashram. Just outside a small wooden fence, a host of people—including myself—are peering at him. At Bhagavan's feet sit two identical girls with long, wavy black hair. Both elated and surprised by the sudden change of environment, I touch the book again and look about me. The ashram is as real to me as the Kalpa house. Before I am able to go any further into mental analysis and comparisons, the maidens approach the fence, open a gate, and invite me in.

For a moment, I wonder, Why only me and none of the others? but that thought is quickly washed away when I realize that I am about to be granted a most cherished wish: to sit at the feet of Bhagavan. Silently, the maidens instruct me to sit facing Him. There is one other there, a thin man of Western origin whom I do not recognize. He prostrates himself to the Maharshi and takes his leave. As he does so, I take the opportunity to closely examine the two attendants. Like the Goddess who saved me from the Komodo dragon, they have no human facial features. Their faces are the radiant orbs of white light.

I am sitting. My eyes transfixed on the form in front of me. The room filled with the most palpable Presence. Silence felt in every cell of my body. My mind does not merely stop—it ceases completely. Has it ever existed? His face slowly turns in my direction. Tears of bliss spill forth from my eyes. His eyes are fixed not on me; they are gazing through me into infinite space. Now He is felt everywhere. As everything. My body, the space around, there is no difference. No other. My face and chest are soaked with joy.

There is the slightest of vibrations, and I am back in my chamber in the Kalpa house. The tears of bliss are still flowing from my eyes. My shirt is soaked, and the book in my hands feels exactly as it had a moment earlier.

When I had regained a sense of my surroundings in the chamber, I had the feeling of being an infant, soft, warm, and just having been caressed by its mother. The tears that soak my entire face and torso spring from the grandest feelings of awe and the most sublime happiness imaginable.

In the evening when Pal visited me, we spoke about the encounter with Bhagavan.

He asked, "Was this the first time you have been with Bhagavan?"

"Yes, Sir."

"Good. He has come to bless you. It is a good experience."

We both sat silently and looked at the floor. He spoke softly and, although his words were directed at me, he seemed to be speaking to no one in particular. "This practice is to give you gnana, enlightenment."

He had delivered my dinner, and before he left, we also spoke of worldly matters. In his always courteous and caring way, he inquired about my comfort, health, happiness with the food, and so forth. Continuing, he detailed the plans for the following year's visit to the Sri Meenakshi temple in Madurai and then on to the Satti Swami shrine.[3] He continued, "Then the trip to Rameshwaram. There we can propitiate the ancestors." Ancestors are given little importance in Western society and religions, but they play a central role in the ancient ones. I had come to learn the importance of ensuring that one's ancestors are freed from the earthly realm so that both they and we may continue our journeys unhindered.

After our conversation for the evening, I accompanied him outside to his motorbike. The tropical sky was filled with glowing planets and twinkling stars. From the surrounding houses came the sounds of clanging pots being cleaned after supper and the rhythmic Tamil chatter of the women finishing their nightly chores. The smells of incense and cow dung floated through the air. As we both stood silently, heads tilted up at the heavens, again I heard Pal say to the space in front of him, "The practice will give you gnana."

---

[3] The Mahasamadhi of Satti Swami holds particular relevance. Pal Pandian writes of this eloquently in his book, *Siddhas: Masters of the Basics*.

Rivulets of the Absolute

Golden Pillar-Sri Meenakshi Temple

This golden pillar acts as the link between Cosmic energy and earth energy. It has 33 rings symbolizing the human spinal cord. This kind of pillar is found in all ancient temples in Tamil Nadu, situated right before the main sanctum.

Most of the days of the final two weeks of my stay were spent at Pal's healing center, Dwarka Mayi. Receiving deeper instruction as well as training in more esoteric practices, I was gradually brought into a more external mode. Because I had spent the previous month mainly in solitude, both my mind and body had to be brought into the more usual manner of life before I returned to the United States. In this way, Pal's attentive care allowed for a slow return to ordinary routines and less introversion.

While the Kaya Kalpa process during the stay in India had an effect on my mind and body, the return to the corporate job and typical Western lifestyle would need to be balanced by the continuation of Kaya Kalpa in order to simply maintain what had been achieved. Again, the requirements of having to use an analytical approach during a large part of the day meant that the rejuvenation of my body would require a unique path.

Chapter 7

Shadows of the Psyche

Rotten Things

The key to immortality is hidden in rotten things.
—Pal Pandian

The Siddhas' ancient art of rejuvenation is legendary in India and, as such, many misconceptions about it prevail.

"What is Kaya Kalpa really, Sir? And what is meant by rotten things?" I asked Pal.

"In ancient times, Kaya Kalpa was used to restore youthfulness and even to attain physical immortality," he replied. "Many people think it is only for this, and so they focus on the body. This is a mistake. Gray hair or wrinkles, these I am not concerned with. It is the spirit that should remain youthful. We should remain youthful, flexible in the mind and spirit, not fixed in any way. This is the true spirit of the Siddhas and how they met life."

Indeed, when Pal first informed me that he would be providing me with the alchemical medicines, I asked him about their purpose.

"To ward off all disease and increase longevity," was his short reply.

From our interactions, I knew that the purpose of maintaining a healthy mind and body was to extend the life span so that ultimate realization can be attained, thus breaking the cycle of birth and death.

> *Where you have fallen, there you must stand up.*
> —Pal Pandian

This foundational theme of the Siddhas is particularly relevant in tantra. When I went to Pal exhausted and with a rigid approach to my life's routine, those very patterns were the ones he patiently had me encounter first. His gifting me with an entire milieu, or environment, in which I would be able to face my existential conditioning and begin to transcend it revealed his unknowable wisdom and compassion. By having me reside in darkness, solitude, and with an empty schedule, he tastefully pushed me to encounter those aspects of myself. Simultaneously, he used his healing touch to give balance to my mind and body so that I could digest the changes. I had "fallen" into an ordinary, time-bound, goal-oriented approach to life. Being made to face it directly, while lovingly supported, brought me out of it.

The "rotten things" in which my key was hidden were that same mechanical mode of living. The approach that I had adopted held within it the very momentum, the actual energy, to transcend it. By utilizing where and what we are, tantra transforms us. Only the wisdom of the guru can see such things in a student. Only the guru's compassion can release the transformative nature of our limitations, locks, habits, and addictions.

Each one of us has many such "locks" in our subconscious, but Siddha Tantra says that there is one primal knot, one essential lock, that must be addressed. Different for each individual, this intense lock is the door through which we must walk. Worshipping a personal deity, dreams, visions, and visitations from the Beyond may appear odd to modern society, yet there is beauty and logic in this journey.

Deities and Knots

The gods, goddesses, and demons are the personifications, the grand archetypes, of all of the primordial energy patterns of the human psyche—*all* of them. The guru's choice of personal deity for a tantric practitioner is no random choice, for the deity itself represents the lock. Furthermore, each deity has two faces, one benevolent and the other fierce. All aspects of ourselves and where we have fallen, which comprise our own primal knot, are to be experienced. Here, in this very ground of our most basic attachment, we are to stand. This rotten thing has stagnated within us in the dark. Our courage to stand and tread the path by facing ourselves as we actually are provides great benefit. Pal explained to me that there is a tremendous amount of energy tied up, held, and lying latent in the primal lock, or the primal knot. He described it as follows:

> *This primal lock has a hidden enlightenment experience within it. When you become fully conscious of it, finally there is no residual, no more fragment of mind. This we call enlightenment in Siddha Tantra.*

Taking My Leave

With my body more flexible and stronger and my mind relaxed and detached from its time-oriented approach, the departure date arrived. Taking my leave from Pal is always an emotional experience. Deep feelings of gratitude inevitably surface as an inability to express in words what I feel. As is usual before my departure, we spent some time sitting on the floor alone, facing each other. In his typically graceful and gentle manner, he handed me a small gift that was lovingly and delicately wrapped. Upon opening it, I see a small brass Ganapati statue. Although normally depicted holding other objects, in this case the elephant-headed god was playing a flute.

"To bless your practice of Vasi induction," Pal said in explanation.

Among all of the tender care and divinely graceful initiations he had showered on me during that visit, he had also bestowed prana, *swara*, and Vasi yoga induction.

"Oh, Sir," I choked out between tears, "thank you. I am so grateful for everything. All I have, I see now you have given me, Sir. Thank you, I am so very grateful…" was that all I was capable of before emotion made speech impossible.

As I regained composure, we continued the cherished moment together. Time slowed to a halt. The air around us ceased swirling. Powerfully felt silence was interspersed with softly spoken words of thanks. From Pal came simple yet beautiful encouragement. More silence and its pulsating throb. Wide eyes. An absence of blinking. Slowly moving breath. The two meeting in space. Only one face with tears of unspeakable gratitude.

It would be almost two years before I could return to him, as the career demanded my extended work before another long holiday. Normally, this would have seemed an unbearably long time. Although the wait was not easy to accept at first, the tantric practice of Upasana with the Divine Mother continued its astounding flow. It nourished me by keeping my focus on its unfolding. The constant communication—both within myself and by worldly electronic means with Pal—held, comforted, and, of course, guided me. Continuing with the practices he had given and speaking with him were crucial as the path unfolded. The dark realm of the subconscious was opening, and its revelations offered ample instances of shock.

Every time I returned to the United States from India, I would resume the corporate job during the week and fill my free time during evenings and weekends with healing sessions. Because I had been gone for two months, clients, friends, and family often asked similar questions. Invariably, the same two questions would be posed to me.

"India, huh? Why? What do you do there?" Or, "Oh, you just got back from India! Do you do yoga? Is that why you go there?"

Never quite sure how to answer their casual queries, I most often offer something brief and simple: "Yoga? Yeah, something like that."

I have never been shy about speaking of my experiences, but the problem of how to reply is twofold. First, I have tremendous passion for the healing and spiritual paths. Second, it is not easy for me to explain those paths in a brief, simple manner. Therefore, I must gauge the level of actual interest of those who ask in order to determine how much I should say in reply. Once I get started, if the person is truly interested, the conversation can quickly become passionate and lengthy.

The Healing Center

The best time and place to answer any and all questions in depth has always been at the healing center. People go there specifically looking for solutions to health issues that have continued to plague them, often for a very long period. When I returned from this visit to India, balancing the career, healing sessions, personal life, and spiritual practices was becoming easier and more natural. Pal had long emphasized the importance of relaxing into each aspect of life with the same light, consistent attitude of a healer, an attitude of perpetual learning. Embodying this open-ended curiosity for each particle and moment of life leads directly to the release of all expectations. It means giving no thought to the results of an action but rather simply waking each day and consciously flowing with the tasks that are given. This very attitude is reflected in the *Bhagavad Gita*, when Krishna exhorts his disciple Arjuna that he should "seek to perform thy duty, yet lay no claim to the fruit thereof."

I must confess that it took quite some time for this attitude to take firm root in the more mundane aspects of daily life. My work at the Siddha Varma healing center nourished this healing spirit. My spirit was nourished by working with others who were suffering and then observing the health to which they were restored. This feeding of the spirit within slowly colored the rest of my life's responsibilities in the same shades and hues. At times people would go to the center with long-held, deeply rooted disorders. Others showed up with issues that had begun only recently.

While at the Siddha Varma Healing Center in my home city, one day I had just finished my sessions. As I was preparing to leave, a middle-aged man walked in. He said that he had seen the sign out front and wondered if we could help him. He had been experiencing severe pain on his right side for several months.

The pain originated above his hip bone but below his rib cage, and his doctors could find no solution for it. They were baffled, he said, because there were no bones or specific muscles to which they could attribute the pain. Massage, chiropractic work, and physical therapy had not provided him relief.

"I work for the city, Steve," he told me, "and you can see my truck outside. Getting in and out of it all day is killing me. The pain starts here and shoots down my hip all the way to my foot. I'm moving like an old man, and the pain has gotten even worse in the last month.

From his explanation and description of where the problem originated, it was obvious to me that the prana (upward moving air) and apana (downward moving air) had mixed and were stagnated at a specific Varma point. I began my session with him by performing a stomach massage to separate the five major vital airs—prana, apana, samana, udana, and vyana. After the stomach massage, I worked on four more Varma points—vala kumuli, vayu kalaam, nangana pottu, and per el.

After no more than ten minutes, the man sat up on the table, opened his eyes, and looked around. With eyes large, as if he had just woken from a most pleasant dream, he smiled at me.

"How's the pain?" I asked.

"Actually. . . there isn't any right now."

I told him to let me know if the pain stayed away and stop by if the pain came back. I gave him my card and informed him that he could call me if he needed any further help.

Three weeks later, the same man walked in again. He expressed his gratitude and told me that the pain was gone. He was so happy. He was able to work without any problem, and he was spending his free time bowling with his friends again, something he loved and had missed.

Although witnessing someone gaining quick resolution to a health issue is always wonderful, the most satisfying part is how the improved health affects the person's life. The man was able to involve himself in both the work and recreational aspects of his routine, and his life continued without the blockage that had arisen. Left unaddressed, it may have slowly built or spread into something worse. When the life forces encounter a blockage in their flow, they adjust around it in order to compensate. We, in turn, modify our lives accordingly. When this occurs, our subconscious registers the imbalance as "normal." Living in this way, our minds and bodies then take on a new identity. Accepting mental and physical disorders into our being and assimilating them as normal is both unfortunate and unnatural.

Not all diseases appear as physical pain or seem severe at first glance. However, they can build up and become significant both physically and mentally. This insidious encroachment on our well-being holds the potential to alter and negatively affect an entire life course. The following is one case in which I saw this quite clearly.

Hypertension (high blood pressure) is a common affliction. Modern approaches cannot heal it, and so they aim to "control" it by use of various medications, all of which the patient must continue to take for the rest of his or her life. Not only are the medications expensive, they also carry unwanted side effects. Of course, if not addressed, hypertension can cause great harm to the body. On occasion, the condition can become very severe. In these emergency cases, the person is hospitalized. After such an event, a physician who is familiar with me and our healing center referred a man who was suffering from hypertension.

The man was just thirty-seven years old, but his doctor, upon registering a blood pressure of 238/138 sent him to the hospital via ambulance. By the time he was released, he had been placed on five medications and was taking them four times per day. Even with the medications, his blood pressure was averaging 195/104, well above the normal range of less than 135/85. His blood pressure had been elevated since he was nineteen years old, but he had only recently sought medical attention.

During our first meeting, I learned he also suffered from extreme hemorrhoids and sleep apnea. Excess weight was an issue, but he also confirmed that hypertension and early death from cardiac conditions ran in his family. When we spoke a bit more, he confessed that he was determined to regain his health and that, to that end, he had been asking his doctor if he knew of any alternative methods. Then, his eyes brimming with tears, he told me that he wanted to live a healthy life because he was very much in love with a beautiful woman he was to marry.

"We want to have children, Steve, and I want to be there as they grow up. But even with all these medicines, nothing is working, and they make me feel terrible. I'm afraid. A heart attack could come at any time." His openness and sincerity tugged at my heart.

Lowering blood pressure by treating Varma points is quite straightforward. In this case, however, the condition had hardened into his body's identity and came from a deeply rooted genetic, or karmic, source. It would take some time for his body and mind to release the identity. In order to release that identity, first a new identity had to be introduced. Just as important, he himself had to not only accept the new identity but also consciously maintain it until it became natural.

After our first two healing sessions, he said that his hemorrhoids had become even worse and that his sleep had not improved. After a session of Systemic Vital Point Therapy, his blood pressure decreased but then elevated again the next day. We needed to alter our approach to his treatment. In addition to Systemic Vital Point Therapy, we began energy healing sessions, or Amritha Kalai.

Within two weeks, his hemorrhoids were gone, his sleep had improved, and his blood pressure was consistently in the 175/95 range, still above the normal range but improved. Continuing on the treatments for another three months, we incorporated some simple lifestyle adjustments. We asked him to refrain from eating meat and drinking alcohol and to begin a light exercise routine of daily brisk walking. Moving his body for a short *time daily was an essential component, because his constitution was kapha. Being strong of body and grounded in nature, those of kapha, the earth element, slip into inertness when overwhelmed. This situation, in turn, leads to them gaining weight, which exacerbates illnesses such as hypertension.*

After those additional three months of treatment and before I departed for India, his blood pressure readings averaged 140/80 (approximately normal), the five medications had been cut back to three, and he was taking the medications one or two times per day rather than the previous four times per day. In due course, he would be able to discontinue these remaining medications. Because the condition had been with him for his entire adult life, it would take some time for his body to remember its natural state of existing with normal blood pressure.

The man's mind, body, and life routine had accepted the disorder of hypertension. When life's circumstances resulted in him encountering his destiny of having a loving family, he was forced to acknowledge the illness. In this way, She, life, nudges each of us to recognize where we have fallen. These falls are our inherent limitations. To the degree that we give in to victimhood and remain stuck in repetitive patterns of self-limiting conditions, we continue to suffer. We suffer until the day comes that we realize that we are failing to live and to embody our life's purpose. Yet the suffering experienced is often necessary learning. Through the suffering, we can become softer, less arrogant, which creates an opening within us to learn more about ourselves. Once the opening has been created, we are filled with fresh inspiration, and we discover our latent powers. The power of the body to heal itself is one such hidden jewel. With correct and sensitive reminders of the body's inherent blueprint of health, even genetically predisposed, or karmic, imprints of disorder can be left behind. Witnessing this man's unfolding and embracing of his body's return to health and its reflected nature in his mind brought me great joy. Healer Pal's gift of Siddha Varma healing offers a platform for interacting with other people in this lovely manner. I can think of no other way that I would ever wish to spend my time and energy.

These two years between visits to India were spent, as usual, between balancing the corporate job and healing sessions. All along, the personal journey of tantra continued. That it unfolded whether I was sleeping or awake did not really surprise me. What many would consider mystical experiences occurred almost daily, often during the most mundane activities. My maintenance of a busy schedule and fulfillment of my responsibilities was no barrier. In time I would learn that the busy nature of my life was actually very helpful in the personal spiritual journey that was unfolding. In this way, the practice of tantra is inclusive, while the practice of yoga is exclusive.

The many spiritual practices generally fall under the two main categories of tantra and yoga. Which of those a person is to follow can be determined only by the guru, because if we look at ourselves, we will see a mixture of the predispositions for both. In truth, each of us has all of the paths (yoga; tantra; gnana, or intellect; and *bhakti*, or devotion) within us. However, one of those paths is the predominant path, the one for us. In this way the guru does not give a person a path to follow but rather reveals the path from within the person.

Unraveling the Knotted Mind

Both paths—yoga and tantra—have as their aim to dig deep into the mind in order to see its primal face. The person who is to follow either path inherently possesses a particular core inclination. The inward-minded are reclusive and contemplative and tend to run away from worldly ties: they are of the typical yogic mind. Those who love the world and its pleasures and enjoy its vibrant colors belong to the path of tantra. One who follows yoga confronts his or her existential conditioning, or existence. Closely tied to the body, the conditioning the yogi encounters includes his or her need to breathe, eat, excrete, and so forth. Conversely, the tantric practitioner has his or her existential conditioning wrapped up in conditioning of an acquired nature. This conditioning may well include family, job, lover, trauma, addiction, or whatever else the person is intimately attached to. To follow this path, the person should have a deep, long-held attachment, but it must be one that they have truly lived for an extended period.

"I can work with this lock and give them tantra," Pal said to me.

The tantric thrives on passion, and this is the tantric's madness. This madness implies going beyond the mind's patterns. This mad urge drives the tantric in search of a beloved, his or her beloved, in all. Thus, the tantric is subjected to numerous upheavals. Of course, the aspirant is still ignorant of what he or she truly seeks and so has not a clue as to where the beloved is hiding. The path of tantra is all about guiding the aspirant to his or her true beloved, or inner shadow. Tantra calls this shadow the darker one.

I was guided in search of my beloved, this darker one, because the guru had set forth an environment for me to follow when I returned home from India. The "classroom" was none other than my day-to-day life. Evolving through my experiences and relationships in the world, I found my heart deeply entangled in all of the circumstances of life. The journey had begun, and every day I found that there was no place to hide, no direction in which I could retreat. Upon awakening each morning, I found myself embarking on a fresh day filled with the routine of standing up where I had fallen. My habits, my choices, my attractions, my aversions, my weaknesses, and my strengths all continued to build the web in which I lived. In this web that I wove each day, my learning and inner evolution happened. Long before meeting Pal, I had heard that tantra can be thought of as a fabricated web. I used to wonder what that could possibly mean.

Although Pal had initiated me into Siddha Tantra, I did not know much about it at the time. I knew only what I had read or heard about it secondhand and, frankly, those sources had been utterly inaccurate. Thus, I really knew nothing about tantra, especially the authentic tantra of the Siddhas. Completely naive to its concepts, theories, and any notions of what I was experiencing, I nevertheless felt its effects. This naiveté was itself a tremendous asset and blessing. Had I been born in India, I would have been familiar with the stories and legends. I also would have been aware of the vision quest that ensues. My ignorance of the journey I had begun aided me in moving through it at a quicker pace. Pal withheld all theory until much later in the journey and, out of respect, I asked him few questions about it. Besides, the experiences were so overwhelmingly uplifting that I did not feel the need to know the specifics. On one occasion, I did pester Pal about the tantric path and why some people are seen by the guru as fit to follow it but others are not. His reply came in the form of two stories. The first was about a Frenchman who went to Pal in despair a few years earlier:

"He experienced his life as empty and boring. Having lost his spirit and love for life, his heart wept in anguish. His longing kept taking him back to his teens, to his spirit back then. I asked if he had taken any drugs

or alcohol in the past. He admitted he had. I asked if he had taken it for a period of time and if he had taken it to forget himself. He had. I said, 'Good, you must immerse yourself in the beauty of life.'

This is tantra.

As he was already playing the saxophone, I suggested that he could immerse himself in life through music. His passion for music and musical instruments gradually brought his spirit back to life. He began to feel his madness once again—this time through his musical instruments."

Pal's second story was about one of Pal's friends:

About ten years ago, a friend of mine wanted to renounce the world and take the orange robe. He wanted to become a sadhu. While he was trying to embark on this path, he met a girl. He fell in love with her, but the girl did not fall in love with him. She quite plainly turned him down. His mad love for her took over. He could think of nothing else. Not concerned about his recent decision, forgetting society and his reputation, he followed her everywhere. It was as if nothing else existed.

One day as he tried to speak to her, she spun around, angry, shouting, and raising her hand at him. A group of people stood and watched. That moment changed everything. Not only did he stop pursuing her, but he also gave up his job. He sat himself before Bhagavan Ramana Maharshi and the Goddess. He sat there day after day, immersed in a failed state of mind but with a longing for love. Without a care about earning a living, he just sat before Them. Grace answered him. Grace came in the form of Goddess Valai, and his journey began.

Both of these stories demonstrate a tantric mind set of hearts that had not found expression, or fruition, because of a failed first love. This mind set of the tantric is a like a carriage drawn by passion. Bypassing boundaries and norms, it strives to reach newer heights to experience creative excellence. Addiction (not necessarily negative) is one such form of over-enthusiastic passion. Such excess is the "dark side," dark as in unconscious, because the person is unaware of its presence within him or her. Residing in darkness, one requires a wake-up call from life in order to shake loose the inertia and begin the first teetering steps. More often than not, this wakeup call comes from a strongly felt life experience. Its lesson is humility. Authentic humility is born of the shock of experiencing one's own limitation. Such a shock must be sufficiently strong that we loosen our grip on what we think we know, who we think we are, and what we think anything means. This allows for a few habitual patterns to slip away and take a bit of arrogance with them. Eventually, the emptied space can hold hope and promise of a new platform to rise from the failings of the old.

And no one pours new wine into old wineskins. . .

—Jesus Christ (Mark 2:22 [New International Version])

Throughout the two years before I returned to India, countless visitations, visions, and dreams continued to expose and transform the subconscious. My life was a busy one, yet the grace and blessings of the guru never ceased. Upon meeting deeper aspects of his or her shadow, the tantric can expect to be forced to resolve them either in life circumstances or as part of a vision quest. My good fortune has been that such encounters, almost without exception, took place within my consciousness, causing little disturbance to my life routine. The Mother showed Herself to me repeatedly to instruct, guide, and oftentimes just to spend time with me in a playful way whenever the journey became intense. Looking back now, my journey seems to have been so effortless, but that is rarely the case. Pal has told me more than once that following the path of tantra, like all spiritual paths, almost always takes a long time and that many who begin the quest find its pace so tedious that they abandon it. My uniquely deep and affectionate bond with Pal is the sole reason for any success I have achieved. A particular instance that I can relate occurred one evening when I returned home after a full day's work, ate dinner, and then began my nightly routine. That routine consisted of a precise Siddha mantra and meditation, which was relaxing in a most natural way. In the fullness of the silence that ensued, I experienced the following encounter as a waking dream:

I am walking alone on a dusty road, my eyes transfixed by the beauty in front of me. Thoughtlessly, I pace so lightly that it seems as if my feet merely approach the ground. Rather than making contact with the earth, they get ever so close to it and then swim up again only to repeat the movement. Briefly noticing this swimming motion, I recognize the lightness of my entire body. I feel no shred of tension, tightness, or even the slightest notion of a difference between my body and the mountain at which I gaze. Pacing along, still married to Arunachala, the holy hill, in this way, I am returning from Dwarka Mayi, Pal's healing center.

Rounding a bend in the road, I notice that I am no longer alone. Standing by a fence in front of a house is Papaji, a devotee of Bhagavan Ramana Maharshi. As I approach him, we smile at each other. Immediately, I begin to tell him about some strange mathematical invention that one of my relatives is attempting to create. His interest is keen, and we speak for some time while standing there together. Eventually, he asks me to sit on the grass with him. We sit facing each other; his back is to Arunachala, but I am facing it. Our conversation about the invention continues, and he plays with the model that I show him.

While he talks, I look at him, and my mind is suddenly gripped with an overwhelming inward pull. My eyes close, and every one of my previous thoughts flashes before me in a visual manner. Simultaneously, the incredibly solid realness of "I" stands and exists in silent observance. The running river of thought patterns gradually slows and loses its density. And then..., all attention is withdrawn from any thought or pattern and anything external. Spontaneously from within, "Who am I?" At the same time, the sense of "I" grows, sucking all awareness into It. "I, I, I" throbs repeatedly, alone, and then simply "I."

A grand flash. Light yet not light. Conscious and unconscious. Being and non-being. Silence yet beyond silence. No movement, no stillness. No thoughts, no thoughtlessness. No "I."

After I had slowly regained awareness of my surroundings, a single pattern was available to me—there is no "I"—there never has been. I sat there in a state of glowing silence for some time, because there was nothing else with which to contrast it. The following day I related my experience to Pal.

"What could this mean?" I asked. "I have never felt any strong connection or feelings toward Papaji, Sir."

"Papaji is one who brought Bhagavan's teaching to many Westerners. So it is in this form that Bhagavan has come to you."

Surprised by his response, I asked further about the ordinary conversation that had preceded the powerful event portion of the waking dream.

He explained, "When people would come to Him and ask questions, Bhagavan would, on occasion, ask them, in return, who was asking this question, having this thought, and so forth. But it was not just a question that He was asking or a teaching. Rather, it was initiation. This is how Bhagavan initiated many of those who came to him. Bhagavan has come and given you initiation."

"How strange," I said. "All those years in the past of practicing self-inquiry, and yet this was so powerfully real. And it just happened, out of nowhere!"

This seemed to amuse him.

He laughed and then said, "Yes, it happened not as a practice, because it does not follow from the conscious mind's way of practicing anything. But now it is seeded in your subconscious, and we can look to the day when your subconscious brings out the question spontaneously."

Daring the Turbulent Waters

This incredibly divine encounter strengthened me to continue the journey. That strength was needed, because the sacred path of tantra has two modes. I had been immersed in the first mode for some time, yet the second mode still awaited. Actually, at some point both modes will surface. The path of tantra is not a linear journey in which the first mode ends and only then does the second begin. Rather, the two modes intertwine and so further confuse any manner of mental or intellectual understanding. My mind could not make sense of where I was or where I was going. Yet the changes that were happening in me and in my relationship with the world were undeniable. Every particle of the unconscious that I encountered lightened the burden such that I was beginning to see the world and myself differently. The associative memories were being erased.

The entire mist-filled beauty of this journey is the preparation to meet one's beloved, to uncover one's unconscious and see its face. Then we can recognize our beloved. Entirely falling in love in this way is none other than coming to know who we are. This initial phase of tantra is called the *shadow work*. The second phase of tantra is the journey behind the shadow unconscious, or the realm of the contra-sexual aspects of the mind, of the psyche.

> *At the level of the Self, we are neither male nor female;*
> *we are beyond.*
> —Pal Pandian

Before practicing shadow work, we live oblivious of our own truth. Ignorant, we go through our lives veiled by false beliefs. Our self-images are clouded, nothing more than phantoms of our own choosing. Although the phantom is everything convenient and comfortable, we are incapable of recognizing that this manner of living is itself the cause of our suffering. *All* of our suffering.

This relying on the known, blindly following the herd, and the reflexive choosing of only convenience and comfort is not the truth of who we truly are. These are but the combined dark realms of the human psyche played out over millennia. Confronting this reality and realizing what we do is shadow work! Shadow work begins as soon as we start to look into the deepest, darkest realms of our unconscious. This arduous phase enables us to feel our true inner essence and experience the joy of who we really are. As much as this work sounds rather unpleasant, it is also extremely grounding. Pal's platform that he gracefully constructed helped me to begin to break out of the confines of mundane living. He did so in order to teach me about the infinite dimension of my own being, where my beloved awaited. As my beloved continued to beckon me, my longing grew. Without shadow work, the journey cannot even begin. The shadow is the door to the unconscious. In shadow work, we encounter personal traits such as self-esteem, arrogance, fear, timidity, doubt, suspicion, and viciousness as well as generosity, love, adoration, trust, integrity.

Just as most people remain caught in their shadow dynamic, they are equally trapped in seeking their inner partner in the outer world. We fall in love with our projections, the ideal woman or man. We soon discover that the partner of our dreams are human beings who have faults. Although some couples manage, through patience and hard work, to contain the contradiction and stick together, for many the disappointment leads them in and out of relationships. They replay the same drama. Yet the lover we truly seek is hidden within ourself. The beloved is the god or goddess that calls and entices each of us into the arena of love. The beloved exudes an enigma that stupefies the mind. To meet us, the gods and goddesses take on human form, but their true nature belongs to the Beyond. The birth of a relationship with our inner masculine aspect or inner feminine aspect is a crucial part of Siddha Tantra.

Up to this point, the encounters that, during my journey, uncovered suppressed traits have not seemed so frightening. Yet our inner kingdom is guarded by mighty forces. These powerful energies stand guard to scare away the unfit, the common-minded and casual aspirant. The shadow unconscious leads to a mysterious inner world, a place out of bounds for the common-minded aspirant. Those unworthy of walking the dimly lit lanes of the inner land remain engulfed in the shadow dynamics. Meeting our shadows is a head-on confrontation with the evil side of our self-created ego identities. The only way ahead is to reclaim ourselves. Pal's own tantric teacher once told him, "If you have to follow tantra, you must have neither fear, disgust, nor guilt."

CHAPTER 8

The Abyss

It is painful to realize how we actually feel and think. Hate, bitterness, venom, wrath, rage, or envy. Walking through both the personal and collective unconscious of humanity requires great commitment and courage but, most of all, the guidance and protection of the guru. Without the loving embrace of the guru, I would never have been capable of encountering the darker aspects of the unconscious, for it is a devastating encounter. Indeed, it is our false image, the one in which we have walked around the waking world for so long, that makes the encounter devastating. In this exact regard, were Pal's words to me: "The courage and humility it takes to survive this . . . well, is to be seen."

Deeper shadow work deals with human trauma, and here the guru works with great care and finesse. The platform created by the guru's grace unlocks the deeper unconscious, or trauma energy. That little, dark demon awakes. During my shadow work, I was surprised by the presence of trauma energy and the depth of its darkness. Yet once that energy is awake and active, we must live with it in order to visit the darkest corners of our psyche. There is no turning back. All obstacles must be crossed. The circumstances either are created by the guru as part of the aspirant's daily life or experienced by the aspirant as a visionary journey that comes from the grace of his or her deity worship. Either way, the resolution is always entirely experiential and in no way intellectual. The aspirant must experience all of the stages of the fear in order to know that fear and his or her own true face.

One night, after having had a rather difficult day, I prepared for bed, lay down, and was about to step into this arena of facing both my fear and myself. Yet before I could even close my eyes fully, I was forced—or rather, pushed—into a familiar working environment. This was no dream. All of it occurred in the most real way: I saw, heard, and felt it all with my own senses. The suit and jacket I wore were from my wardrobe. Immediately, though, I sensed that something was off, something was dreadful. At first, I thought I was just feeling tired or in a crappy mood. But once I looked around me at other people, I began to sense and then feel for myself a very real sense of dread.

Everyone is rushing about a city street, and I am one of many people entering a building. I approach the elevator that will take me to my final business meeting of the day.

The Abyss

I realize that humankind is caught in a terrible state of duality, of living double lives, and what is troubling me is that none of us pays it any heed until there is darkness. Even more unsettling is that there appears to be no one capable of escaping this dilemma. Much like in the movie Groundhog Day, *the repetitiveness of our lives is being lived over and over again, and try as we may there seems no escape. We are living an inevitable sequence of collective destiny. When there is daylight, it is unquestioned, and we go about the trivialities of life with zeal. But when darkness comes, a terrible, inescapable reality exists for us all. I realize that ignoring this duality any longer is just stupid. I become agitated yet confused, so I feel frozen, unsure of how to react and what to do next.*

This brutal truth of human existence haunts me even as I hurry to squeeze into the elevator before its doors close. Once inside, I examine the others around me. The men are dressed in similar suits and ties, and their trench coats are spotted from the cold drizzle outside. The women are wearing their hair up, and their delicately painted faces and their suits inevitably display slightly more color than do those of us men. Well, except for the occasional loud tie that, invariably, is worn out of a compulsion to satisfy the relative who somehow thought it to be in good taste when gifting it.

The strangely uncomfortable silence that seems mandatory in an elevator only underscores my agitation. I can feel it not only in myself but in those surrounding me, and it is so pervasive that it seems to have a strong, almost invasive, odor. The distance from the nose to the brain is very small, so what I, like us all, am attempting to ignore rushes to the forefront of my awareness: We are not people. The elevator doors slide open, and I wait for my turn to exit. As I stand there, the anxiety that should be present only during darkness is creeping in. My knees begin to feel weak and my head light. Doing my best to push aside the inevitable, I step into the office's atrium, feign normalcy, and search out the meeting room.

The business meeting takes longer than I had expected, and afterward everyone is in the usual hurry to go home. We all feel that it is somehow better to be in familiar surroundings once the sunlight has departed for the day. As I again stand in the elevator, with different people wearing similar clothes, the air is thick with growing dread. I admit to myself that we all know or, at least, should know that where we are makes no difference to the darkness. The mood is markedly different during the elevator's descent than it had been just a few hours earlier. Facial muscles are strained, and eyes are wide, staring into the space in front of them as if afraid to look anywhere else. Another flash reveals itself to me: being in a crowd of other people is of no help at all. Doubting the truth of such a thought seems the most likely course to follow, since it seems that no one has ever voiced such insanity. Everyone gathers during the dark. We all know that not only is there safety in numbers but only together will we ever learn to escape the inexorable daily routine. Then it happens. The elevator stops between floors, the doors incapable of opening, and the customary ritual begins. Darkness has arrived, and the Beast has sole reign until the sun rises in the morning.

The custom and virtual social demand that strangers not speak while in elevators immediately vanishes. Everyone begins to rapidly indulge in methodical attempts to survive for one more day. "If we all just keep speaking, he will pass us by, since making noise shows we aren't hiding from him" is the first theory put forth by one of my fellow passengers. "I think singing would be best, as he can't stand good spirits," offers another. "Don't be ridiculous. Prayer is the only way we'll make it until the light reappears." The conflicting suggestions set off serious debate. The fear that had been subdued and repressed comes out of each trapped passenger, and the odor that I had sensed earlier seems to have taken shape and substance in front of me. It strikes me now that earlier each person had looked like a half-dead yet well-dressed corpse, because it seemed to take virtually all of their energy to distract themselves from the intense fears that live inside them. What had been just a thought has now shown itself as literal form in front of me. We are not people.

By the time darkness leaves, several of my elevator companions have been grasped by the teeth of the Beast and hauled away screaming in tones unrecognizable as originating from a human. The remnants of the group resume our emotionless, reserved masks and begin another period of light in which we will use all of our life forces to temporarily forget what just occurred.

The next night of darkness follows exactly the same script except that this time I am in a hospital rather than an elevator and am surrounded by a different group of people. The ritual resumes, with countless theories being proposed for how to avoid the Beast. I become convinced that no one actually believes that doing so is possible. This recurring custom is simply the only socially acceptable manner of dealing with life. "Never again," I tell myself. "Never again will I seek out or be left with others during the darkness. I have got to be alone." Night after night, I seek solitude. But my search is to no avail, because others always find my hiding place, speak incessantly of their fears and their theories of how to escape those fears, and eventually are mauled and carried away.

Finally, thinking that I have found the perfect hiding place in a barn in the countryside with not a soul around for miles, I cover myself with hay and wait. To my chagrin, others come, seeking the possibility of solace. As I watch them and listen to them, something happens to me: I realize the utter foolishness of all attempts to hide. Among those who come to the barn for shelter this night is a family with small children. Offering flimsy reasons that they are safe, the parents try to get their children to close their eyes and sleep. The parents' lies are perfumed with noble intentions. Motivated by extreme nervousness born of the impending doom, everyone begins talking incessantly. Even in the isolated barn, the Beast comes. The entire family, including the children, whether asleep or not, is taken. After the family, which had been huddling just in front me, is torn away, I snap. The fear of the unknown that stalks humanity has become so incredibly hopeless to me that I cannot bear another moment of repeating these fruitless habits of humankind.

Like a broken vessel that no longer is able to serve its intended purpose, I feel incapable of hauling society's water pulled from the putrid banks of the stagnant, polluted streams of collective decorum. I can no longer tolerate the useless exercise of theories and psychotic bargaining that is considered normal behavior. I decide that never again will I repeat this exercise of stupid futility. Instead, I rise to seek out this Beast and have it done with one way or another. The remaining souls screech and scream in attempts to dissuade me from acting "crazy." As I continue to walk away, they turn to insults, accusing me of abandoning them and calling them insane. Finally, they wail that I must be evil itself, like the Beast. All of their pleas fall on deaf ears, for I have seen and heard enough to know that even during the light no one is truly alive. We are incessantly and cruelly ruled by humankind's suppressed fears, which have clouded over our entire lives and only present themselves during the times of darkness, in the form of the Beast. Humankind is enslaved. I have decided that it would be best to allow the Beast to devour me now, and get it over with. At least I will obtain some small sense of satisfaction from getting to look at this monster before it tears me to shreds and feasts upon me. It will be better to face the Beast than to hide from it for the remainder of "life."

Finding my way to the Beast is no easy task, but I eventually locate the mountain containing the lair of that which haunts all. Upon entering the lair, I am fearful no longer. Even more pleasantly, I do not have to hear the useless philosophies of others. On either side, mountains of human bones stretch higher than the tallest skyscrapers. Snow swirls about the floor of the cavern, which appears to encompass the interior of the entire mountain. Intense curiosity rushes into my mind, fills my body, and propels me forward. Best of all, I am no longer hiding! When I round a corner of one of the enormous piles of bones, I see the Beast. There is a brief pause, during which I am unsure of the wisdom of being unafraid, for I have never imagined the size and ferocity of what I am now facing.

The Beast fixes his green eyes on me while slowly arching his head down from a tremendous height, until we are face to face. Although I am acutely aware that I am minuscule in comparison to the Beast, I feel only the deepest resolve to confront him and see what happens. From its reaction, I realize that courtesy and social skills are not his strongest suit. Perhaps its attitude is due to my intrusion into his place of refuge. Clearly unhappy that I have invaded its lair, he nonetheless refrains from attacking me. After we have stared at and inspected each other for a time, he asks why I have come. Oddly, I now feel comfortable, and I proceed to sit on the floor and inform him that he knows why I am here.

His unhappiness is intensified when he informs me that he cannot ever devour me and that we have reached a truce. The euphoric feeling of this truth lifts the burden of lifetimes from me, and the feeling of having been washed clean, reborn, and invigorated courses through my veins and lifts my spirit. What he speaks to me next is even more revealing, however: "But I will continue to haunt, destroy, and devour humanity." Looking at him, I become aware that he expects me to condemn him and fight with his decision to act out such atrocities, whether from a moralistic stance or a humanitarian one. Instead, in that very moment, something wonderful that I never could have expected happens: I understand him completely.

We often encounter our dark unconscious in our dreams. The dark, menacing figure that stalks us is our own rejected self. Like abandoned children, these dark aspects sometimes relate to us through anger and aggression. They stand in the dark, starved of affection and craving the sunlight of the conscious. The more we fear them, the more we cling to a false ego identity. This is nothing more than a creation of our choicest traits. Facing them and stepping toward them dissipates their intensity.

Shadow Work Continues

The inner foundation built by shadow work is of immeasurable value. Shadow work opens the gate to a spiritual life. A strong, stable foundation ensures a deeper journey. Intensely valuable psychological experiences and high states of consciousness become available only from a strong foundation. Without stability and strength, the same journey can turn into a nightmare for the psyche, and our lives can suffer dangerous calamities. Shadow work is essential for creating an emptied, uncontaminated vessel, one whose inner space can be used to awaken our divine nature. The work is laborious and long. There is no easy way out.

The outward search for one's truest self takes other forms, and its costs are both energy and inner potential. We play out this search by seeking approval and comfort in all aspects of our lives—relationships, friendships, and careers. In short, we demand everything from other people yet ask nothing of ourselves. In this way, we live in our shadow and so give away our power of perception. Consider the following example:

"The office in which I work is run a by strong, authoritative boss. He scares the crap out of me. His voice is deep, and when he's upset he yells in a loud, commanding voice. I feel like no matter what I do, it's never enough for him. It seems like he can see through walls and is watching my every move. I can't stand going to work every day and can't wait for 5 p.m. to get the hell out of there."

There is nothing wrong with this person's boss. He is just acting as what he is—a boss. For this person, however, his boss's presence is discomforting and intimidating. It prevents him from being relaxed and functional. This person's response to authority is unnatural. Is it not unnatural to give away one's own power, freedom, and happiness to a falsely created external source? This belongs to the person's shadow unconscious, but he has projected it onto his boss.

We also tend to project the shadow unconscious onto objects, as in the following example:

A man loves motorcycles. He is consumed with curiosity about every aspect of them, and the thrill of motorcycles pervades every part of his life. He thinks and dreams about buying the next biggest and most powerful one. His craze obviously influences the way he thinks and the way in which he lives.

What is the true face of the shadow unconscious hiding behind the man's obsession with and addiction to motorcycles? He is screaming for unrestricted freedom!

The projection symbolizes what we are saying within. However long and deep the roots of our unconscious run, the shadow survives only as long as we are unconscious. But there is more to the tale of our tendency to project. By projecting, we shirk responsibility, the responsibility that comes with inner power and potential. As we withdraw our projections, we are flooded with inner power and freed potential. With this enhancement comes responsibility. In addition, now that we are conscious, we can no longer blame the boss for our timidity or seek freedom by riding motorcycles. Now all of our failures are our own. It is time to be truthful to ourselves. Shadows are not always unpleasant or negative. Hidden within a shadow may lie some dormant creative potential or deep spiritual quality. These positive aspects cannot surface without the proper foundation.

Today's materialistic environment is rather constrained in this sense. It offers little to support such a foundation; surviving in today's society requires only a narrow set of qualities. Even if we have those qualities, much of ourselves is unconscious. Traits such as competitiveness breed a singularly achieving type of mind set. Even children are encouraged to develop and display disdain, cruelty, superiority, and anger in certain environments, such as sports and academics. In other environments, they are admonished for expressing such qualities. This imbalance is directly addressed by Pal when he wrote the following in his book, *Siddhas: Masters of the Basics*:

> *Our materialistic and mechanical culture is in collective denial of the mystical realm. An inner mystical experience has little value in the overly rational (left hemisphere) approach and automated lifestyle. All souls born with such traits that are inclined to a spiritual path suffer. Their inclinations remain bereft of nourishment. What is most precious and fulfilling they don't live to experience and if by chance they do, they face the collective denial of the world.*

These words by Pal struck me deeply. I had been searching long and practicing various methods. Prior to meeting him, I had often felt outcast, odd, and a stranger in a world that appeared to be opposed to my deepest cravings. Through tantra, I came to learn that positive traits lie buried within oneself. One such dormant creative potential lying in wait for me was the ability to write this book. When Pal asked that I begin writing a book,

I had no idea how to proceed. It was only my trust in him that allowed me to begin and continue doing so.

A few years earlier, if I had been asked to add another task to my daily routine, I would have balked. Where would I find the time? Where would the energy possibly come from? Indeed, some years earlier, Pal had suggested that in the future I should write about both my experiences and the Siddhas in general. His loving, attentive care cleansed, strengthened, and molded my mind, body, and spirit to such a degree that when he eventually said that the time was ripe for me to begin writing the book, I took up the task rather naturally. He had taught me how our energy, when spread out to include the various appropriate actions of life, always serves us well.

"Each of us will have a certain amount of energy available to use each day," he began. "What often happens is we misuse it and so accumulate what people like to call stress and then, of course, feel drained of both energy and aspiration for our lives. But it is very simple. If you have or focus on only one area or task each day, it will require all of your energy to fulfill it. It will drain you, and even if you had been previously fond of it, it will change into an unpleasant and stressful activity. Life knows us and responds to us intelligently. How does She do this? Each day, when we live appropriately, all the activities will ask from us only the energy that we have to spend that day.

"If a person gives all their attention and energy to one task (for instance, a job), they have chosen to invest all of the life energy into that area at the expense of all other areas. But you also know by now that we each possess natural limitations. Where will She show us our limitations? In this same area (in this instance, the person's job), the job will require all of the person's energy to complete it, since it has been given their entire focus. On any day, all of the person's available energy will be demanded in order to fulfill the responsibilities of their job. Usually, the demanding nature of the chosen area is seen as many obstacles presenting themselves. Such obstacles are often seen in troubled relationships. Whatever is needed for us to spend the energy that we have dedicated to the chosen area will be demanded by it each day.

"However, if we have several varied areas or tasks that we wish to participate in, each will demand only a portion of our energy. A much smaller amount will be required to fulfill what we set out to do in each area than if we focused solely on that one area, and the problems seem much less solid and much easier to solve. Again, this is because when we live in a conscious way, we are not fixated on a singular, obsessive mode. Life asks us to participate in all her colors and to use all the gifts we possess. So please live in this way. Give yourself to the many activities each day in the amount of time and energy available to you. All will happen naturally and turn out fine."

"That is obvious now, Sir!" I exclaimed. "I can see this, and it makes so much sense. If I give attention and time to only one thing—say, my career—then naturally I will feel like it demands so much from me. It's like I would be making it into this huge challenge, and I would feel that it gives me so many problems and leaves little inspired action for anything else."

"That is correct. Life will take from us each day only the level of energy we possess. If we spread this attentive focus across several varied aspects of life, She will still take only the amount that we have. When we involve ourselves in all areas that present themselves, each will then take only a part of it. And in a most natural way."

Once Pal spoke these words, so much of what he had been attempting to teach me about approaching my life became clear. Although I had no experience or schooling in writing, I nevertheless began to write the book. Before long, I started to really enjoy the writing and found it a relaxing way to spend my free time. Frankly, I was not very good at it, but that did not matter. By the time I was able to visit India again, I had written hundreds of pages. That most of it would never make it into the final version made no difference to me. I had found the taste for writing. By the time I arrived in Tiruvannamalai that year, I had developed a new passion. What awaited me and would be revealed during this visit, I had no way of knowing.

CHAPTER 9

Blossoming of the Tradition

The pace of life in South India is unlike any in the United States. It takes a few days for me to relax and fall into the slow approach. However, the pace is by no means lazy. The people are forced to work hard, by circumstances that lack resources, funds, and development. It is common to see the rice farmers hauling their crops into town on bullock carts in the same way that their ancestors did a thousand years earlier. Roadside vendors of fruits and vegetables, chai stands heated by charcoal and lit by ghee lamps or kerosene lamps, girls and women carrying water on their heads every morning—these persist as daily reminders of a wholly different yet fulfilling lifestyle. They all have much work to do and use the strength of their bodies to complete it. Why should there be any rush when each day is the same? Their lives are simpler than the lives of Westerners. Devoid of so much technology, they are more in tune with nature. Greeted annually by their easy ways, ebony skin, and gleaming white teeth, which are so often visible due to their natural tendency to smile more than we Westerners could ever dream of, I am beyond happy to return there.

"You have done well with the writing. I am happy to see our tradition come into book form for the people of the West," Pal said to me shortly after I had arrived.

Eager to present the first draft to him, I had brought it with me. Although we had spoken often about the project during the past year, he had not offered much advice. During the flight back to India, I had looked over the draft and had serious doubts about its form and substance. Secretly, I harbored the wish that I could spend most of my visit working on it and getting recommendations from Pal about how it should unfold.

My wish was granted: each morning for two months, I went to Pal's healing center, Dwarka Mayi, and was encouraged to sit and type away on the computer. It was a glorious time. Pal sat on the floor across from me, attending to his patients, preparing and dispensing medicines, directing his assistants, and greeting the various seekers and well-wishers who streamed into the small town to meet him. Interspersed through it all were our frequent and, at times, lengthy breaks. During these breaks, often while we sipped chai or ate small snacks procured by Shahul, he would take me deeper into the secret dimensions of the Siddhas. At other times, Pal patiently guided me on how to address particular subjects in the book. In turn, I asked him many questions about a variety of subjects. After my understandings had been cleared up, the words flowed much easier.

One day while I was typing, Pal sat down next to me. We were the only two in the clinic at the time; the others were busy outside cleaning and preparing herbal remedies. The rhythmic pounding of the large mortar and pestle and the occasional passing rickshaw were the only sounds. As I looked up, he greeted me with his ever-present, warm smile. Over the weeks, he and his life partner Amrita reviewed the draft, offered clear advice and encouragement, and then kindly read each draft as I made changes. The book had completely transformed. Although they sometimes made rather general comments, their aim seemed to be to assist me in finding a way of putting my personal experiences onto the book's pages. This took a good amount of time. Each morning I would arise at 3:00 a.m. and write away in my little room, drawing inspiration from their kind suggestions. Five or six hours later, I would eat breakfast and then go to Dwarka Mayi, hand the newly printed drafts to them, and await their critique. It was not unusual for me to rewrite an entire section throughout the day, based on their critique, and then attempt to start the next section. I would then rise early the next morning to repeat the process.

Sprinkled throughout the days were our discussions of various matters ranging from my questions about tantra and healing to the writing. As we sat together one day, Pal began to speak about a subject that I had been trying to put into words but was having difficulty making readable. The time had apparently arrived for him to clarify a subject that can best be described in a single word: yoga.

Siddha Yoga—The Pinnacle of Yoga

"You have written of the many yogas and have asked questions," he began, "but there is an even more important question that you have not asked."

"Oh, yes, Sir?" I had no idea what that question could be, but I was excited that he was about to reveal it.

"Of course, you know the word *yoga* is a very general one, much like energy or prana. But today it is associated with only the practice of body postures, or *hatha yoga*. Please write about this, and clear up this simple matter."

Due to the rapid growth in the popularity of the practice of hatha yoga, I had long been aware that most Westerners think only of those body postures when they hear the word yoga. The literal translation of yoga is "to yoke" or "union." Yoga actually means to join or unite the individual soul with God. The broadness of its definition necessarily means that it encompasses vast disciplines. The hatha yoga to which we in the West are accustomed is meant to work with the body as a means of strengthening the practitioner and encouraging him or her to move beyond the physical. It is useful in the early stages of spiritual practice for those who have difficulty confronting the mind through meditation. That it can enhance physical strength and balance is a wonderful side effect.

Many of its teachers assert that its origins lie in the treatise *Yoga Sutras*, which was written by Pantanjali. What is rarely known is that Pantanjali himself was a great Siddha from South India. His work, which describes the essence of *ashtanga yoga* (the eight limbs of yoga) places very little emphasis on hatha yoga. It is recommended only for the very beginning of one's quest. Having visited his Mahasamadhi, or shrine, within the great temple in the city of Rameshwaram, I can attest to his profoundly felt presence. As one of the eighteen Tamil Siddhas, Pantajali's *Yoga Sutras* was put into written form for the benefit of the masses. It focuses on the proper conduct and purity of character far more than on yoga postures (*asanas*). Although hatha yoga is excellent for improving the strength and health of the physical body, its main purpose is to relieve one from bodily discomfort or weakness. The practitioner can then proceed onward to where one's limitations truly lie—within the mind and spirit.

The actual goal of yoga is to enable one to transcend every form of limitation and return one to the Source, to merge the individual soul with the Universal Soul or God. To this end there are many forms of yoga, each focused on a different practice: physical postures (hatha yoga), sense withdrawal (*pratyahara*), breath regulation (pranayama), the formation of geometric hand patterns (*mudra*), meditation (*dhyana*), devotion (*bhakti yoga*), wisdom (*jnana yoga*), the performance of auspicious deeds (*karma yoga*), the chanting of sacred syllables (*mantra yoga*), kriya yoga, *kundalini yoga*, *agni yoga*, *amritha yoga*, *tantra yoga*, *nada yoga*, *atchhi yoga*, *kapala yoga*, *raja yoga*, ashtanga yoga, and *swara yoga*. The pinnacle of them all is *Siddha Vasi* yoga. This is the yoga practiced by the Siddha masters.

The Quest of the Ancients

"How and why did our ancestors discover the need for all of these paths?" Pal asked me rhetorically.

OK, here we go, I thought. I saved the document that I had been working on, closed the computer, and settled in, knowing that he was about to regale me with wonderful details.

"When the first humans wandered out of Africa long ago, they would have followed sources of food and water. The ocean, rivers, and lakes offered easy ways to gather food and certainly water. Hunting and gathering food would fill their lives and leave them little time to do anything else. Over time, the desire and ability to settle and cultivate crops occurred. From there, it was possible to build more permanent structures to live in. Residing in huts and tending to their food supply, our ancestors began, very slowly, to notice their environment from a different perspective. Nature, as She often does, would on occasion force them to pay attention. Speaking to them through natural calamities of rains, floods, shifting waterways, drought, and so forth, She required them to notice something more about their lives.

Observing their greater surroundings, particularly Nature's upsetting ways, humankind came to the understanding that something greater than themselves was at play. They were forced to understand that their own lives were dependent on the forces of nature. It was then that the first important shift happened for our ancestors: They began to worship these higher forces. This worship was natural to them, because they recognized that all these forces had their own independent and inherent intelligence. As people, they could not influence or change them. From this understanding, they gave them the names gods, goddesses, and demons, and deification persisted, because India is a naturally religious society. In the West, they came to move towards science, so the names were shifted to that understanding."

Pal went on to explain that the effect of living at the mercy of outside forces influenced ancient people to eventually look deeply into their lives and themselves for answers. Of course, someone who is busy just trying to survive does not have time for or care much about philosophical musings. That only changes when times are good enough that people have the free time to look and think more deeply.

"Even today, when our lives are abundant and easy, we usually feel satisfied and think that life is good and will continue on like this. Until it does not. Through crisis, we find ourselves, and our attention is drawn beyond its normal scope. From there, we examine the larger environment of our lives, our greater existence. In the same manner, our distant relatives enjoyed, for the first time, some relaxation when their crops were fertile. They had enough food and the ability to stay in one place. They were able to feed and shelter themselves. Life was fertile. Until, of course, it was not.

"Droughts, floods, and other natural disasters easily shook their sense of fertility and replaced it with a feeling of fragility. This would make them realize that they were dependent on higher forces. Mountains were worshipped; their size and abundant resources held both obvious enormity and mystery. The sun, moon, rain, and all of Nature's ebb and flow upon which they were dependent became objects of worship. In this way, their lives flowed with a greater sense of their role as a part of Nature. They slowly came to know how She moves all things. This movement has dual expression in that it both gives life and takes life. In time, this felt connection was strengthened by their worship.

"Better able to feed themselves and feeling integrated with nature and her forces, they again enjoyed the feeling of satisfaction. This, in turn, led to more time to observe and notice the deeper aspects of life. And to ask questions. Life seemed fine to them, but when they looked more closely they noticed sickness and disease. Discovering plants and herbs, they began to develop medicines and healing.

"This, of course, forced them to confront Nature's major limitation. Upon noticing the inevitability of death, our ancestors would have plunged into the deepest of questions: What comes after this? Where do we go when we die? With the inquiry into death and what may lie beyond, the journey into yoga began.

"By this method of discovery, all of the forms of yoga would be created over a long period. Our ancestors took this journey. They would have had no idea of the goal or the outcome of such an undertaking. But the beginning? That which was the most basic and knowable to them: the body. Not surprisingly, hatha yoga, the practice of bodily postures, was the first yoga developed. Traveling the path and eventually mastering the body, our ancestors once again found a limitation. The darkness within the mind remained.

"Next, they would have to travel into the mind. The natural evolution of the yogas and spiritual practices continued. Humankind's first yogis, the Tamil Siddhas, continued to live in their journey and so raja yoga, for the mind, and ashtanga yoga, for the guidance of conduct, were among the next to be developed. They are prime examples of yoga for the mind. They scrub away the darkness. Traveling this evolutionary path to its next barrier, our brave ancestors found the limitation of energy."

"This reminds me of a story you told during my first year with you, Sir." Taking advantage of Pal's pause, I wished to clarify if the story was a good example of where we were in his recounting of the Siddhas' history of yoga.

A master is followed by two of his closest disciples. He is leading them on an earnest journey whose destination he has yet to reveal. With great love and admiration for their guru, the two devotees had set out with him two days earlier. Trailing him wearily along the slopes of a steep, forested mountain, they find it almost impossible to keep up with the swift, sure-footed master. Glancing at each other and stopping to sit, they finally find the courage to speak up. "Master, we cannot walk another step. For two days and nights, we have walked with barely a pause. It is impossible for us to move any farther. We must stop here and sleep for the night."

Eyeing his two disciples with compassion, the Master replied, "Yes, of course you need your rest. Please lie down comfortably here, and stay for the night. But be careful," he continued as he strode away, "for there are many man-eating tigers that live here and travel this very path!"

Immediately, both of the disciples jumped up and hurriedly ran after their guru.

When they had caught up with him, he looked at them and asked, "What is this? Only a moment ago you could not move a step more, and now you are running so easily. What has happened?"

Embarrassed, they remained speechless, staring at the ground in front of their master.

Pal laughed gently at my retelling of his story and, with twinkling eyes, let me know that he appreciated my desire to reminisce.

"Yes, that story surely it is a good example. It shows how we live unaware of our wholeness, our unlimited potential. Particularly in the way that latent energy lies within us. In life-threatening situations, we may have an opportunity to discover it in some way. The ancient yogis found this very limitation after having journeyed through overcoming the body and mind by practicing their previous yogas. Forging ahead into the limited energy normally available, they discovered and mastered energy-based yogas. Kundalini yoga is a prime example.

Striving Forth

"The ancient masters traveled their journey motivated by encountering the various levels of limitation inherent in humankind. By developing yogas to overcome the limitations of the body, mind, and energy levels, they continued the quest, and after mastering each one, they dared not cease until they had arrived at the journey's end. In order to complete their quest, they would, by necessity, encounter and transcend all manner of human limitations. This eventual transcendence is what is called enlightenment, or gnana."

"Yes, I see, Sir. This is why the Tamil Siddhas are often referred to as spiritual scientists! They experimented and made the discoveries with their own bodies, lives, and life experiences. This would explain why and how the Siddhas never separate any of the yoga paths into parts."

"Certainly," Pal replied. "You see this for yourself. Your time in the Kalpa house integrated many pieces into one necessary and flowing whole. The Kaya Kalpa cleansing, dark-room living, and tantra initiation all combined. A person is a multifaceted, polymorphous entity, the Siddhas have always stated. Further, each one will require a specific blending of the many paths in a very particular and individual way."

"Aha! I see. Yes, it is not like giving one path, like a meditation technique, to a group of people. While doing so may be useful, surely it has much limitation, Sir?"

"Of course. All are making a journey, and while the goal is one, each one is at their own particular point in their journey."

During a brief pause in our discussion, I reflected on my experience. Pal had been weaving together the many practices of healing work, mudra (energetic hand gestures), mantra (chanting of energetic sounds), meditation, kaya kalpa, and tantra to bring about my evolution. All along, he lovingly attended to my body to keep it healthy and strong. This blending of disciplines for each practitioner can be accomplished only by Siddha masters, because they have themselves traveled all of the paths. Having emerged victorious in their mastery of all of the yogas, they transmit this wisdom through the esoteric ritual of initiation. When they do so, they invariably share a most essential element that is best known as a key. Alone capable of unlocking the door of the practice, this key enables extremely potent and surprisingly fast results. A fine example occurred when I was staying in the Kalpa house and Pal gave me three or four hatha yoga *asanas*, or postures, to practice daily. He first revealed to me how the Siddhas utilize a secret when performing them. Never written down and passed only from guru to disciple, the secret affords wonderfully potent results. He had me practice the asanas for only a short time; when the benefits he expected came to me, he asked me to cease the practice.

Pal broke the silence and continued. "But they did not stop with finding the answers to limited energy. The ultimate limitation that begged their attention is also the most primal. What animates me? What has given life to me and sustained me? What makes me identify with the body and the world? What is the root force of all? These are boundaries that our ancestors encountered. The transcendence of these boundaries led the ancient ones to the basic Source of the universe: gnana. This path is called Vasi yoga.[4]

"By no means was the ancients' journey a simple or quick undertaking. Throughout the journey, they would have come up against every block, knot, and lock of the human body and psyche. In fact, every possible permutation of human existence would have been encountered in its entirety. No human problem, dilemma, situation, or limitation could have been bypassed. The enormity of this quest necessitated immeasurable courage and strength.

"As they moved through the virtually countless shades of humanity's veils, all of the spiritual and healing paths were revealed. Rituals, mantras, mudras, tantra, martial arts, meditations, pranayama, physical cleansing, and subtle cleansing, as well as countless other aids were discovered. When meeting any limitation, these ancient ones dove within themselves to discover the solution. Unlike any of us who followed, they lived in an incredibly novel situation. There was no one to consult and no map to follow, for they were the initial ones of humanity to embark on the grand journey within, this path to liberation.

"These yogis who completed this first journey of yoga did it in the far distant past. Long before our known history, in the

---

[4] Chapter 9 of this book provides ample detail about the Vasi yoga path.

very dawn of humanity, They began this most valuable quest. They began it by finding some grounding in Their lives through the fertility of nature. Once Their immediate physical needs were met, They looked beyond, searching first the natural surroundings, then the heavens, and finally within Themselves for the grand connection. This is the path They followed to arrive at the primal state of existence. These most ancient ones are the Tamil Siddhas."

"That is beautiful, Sir, and makes so much sense. Even from my little time evolving through different practices, I can see how some of it takes place for each of us."

"Yes, certainly we must each make our own journey. But, of course, humankind's first journey of yoga would have happened over an extended period and involved multiple people. For the individual, the journey, too, can take this route. If one has come into this life with a firm background in the earlier practices, then they can move quickly through these early practices. Likewise, another person may have a specific need in their life. It could be anything; a strong and healthy body, career success, and so forth. In this way, we cannot say that one path is higher or lower for a certain person. It is simply their need."

Ancient Pollination

When I came out of my reverie, I broke the silence. "You know, Sir, this reminds me of the BBC program *The Story of*

India, where the host reported the genetic findings about a village outside Madurai."

I went on to describe to Pal in detail how the genetic marker that was understood to be carried by the people who first migrated out of Africa long ago was found in a the residents of a small South Indian village. Himself a native of Madurai, he smiled his approval. Several years earlier, Pal had taken me to that sprawling metropolis to visit the grand Meenakshi temple, and then onward to the Mahasamadhi of Satti Swami. Later during that trip, he had taken me to Rameshwaram, a seaside town where the samadhi of Siddha Pantanjali, and the author of the *Yoga Sutras,* resides. The trip was a memorable and cherished time for me.

What I most enjoyed was the long drive with Pal. It was the first time that we had such an elongated, relaxed schedule. This afforded me the opportunity to ask him many questions that had long been simmering in my mind. I wanted to revisit our conversations about the Siddhas' travels during prehistory. Recorded in their twilight language, the ancient poetic verses and songs detail how the masters spread their wisdom to China, the Middle East, and South America. Pal kindly revealed, in a manner similar to that of his exposition about the Siddhas' history of yoga, various details on the subject.

There are many accounts of Siddha history that recount the masters traveling to distant lands and sharing Their wisdom about healing and spiritual attainments. The results of these travels can be seen in the similarities among the many forms of yoga, martial arts, healing arts, and medicine throughout ancient societies. Much like a flower that spreads its spores when rustled by the wind, the Siddhas traveled widely in the ancient world. Their intent was to give whatever wisdom could be accepted by the various societies they encountered. Historical records of these travels exist within the Siddha tradition. Passed down first by the oral tradition of songs, the poetic verses eventually found their way into Their cryptic writings.

Siddha Bogar is well known to have travelled to China at the express wish of his guru, Kalangi Nathar, who had spent much time there sharing his own healing and spiritual sciences with the Chinese. He sent his pupil Bogar to continue his mission. Siddha Bogar imparted healing wisdom about vital energy spots (Varma points) and thousands of herbal preparations.

Siddha Bogar wrote extensively about his time in China. In his work *Bogar Sapta Kandam*, he demonstrated a very strong way of speaking and interacting with others. In that work, he detailed what most would consider miracles bordering on fantasies. What I came to know of him, by reading his works and speaking with Pal, is that he was never concerned about the opinions of others. This man was an extreme rebel. After spending a considerable amount of time in China, Bogar found that his Indian appearance and language prevented the Chinese from fully accepting him. Eventually, he decided to overcome the limitations of being a foreigner. To that end, he transmigrated his vital body into the physical body of a deceased Chinese man. The physical body that he took had first to be cured of all illness, and so he used Siddha medicines, alchemy, and Kaya Kalpa to do so. This most secretive and profoundly potent system of the Siddhas purifies, nurtures, and revitalizes the constituent elements of the body, mind, and psyche. The aim is to restore health and youth and extend longevity.

There are many stories of Bogar's time in China. I have always been very fond of the following story:

Bogar was accompanied by three of his best disciples and his faithful dog on a long trip over mountainous terrain. At some point, he reached into a little pouch and produced five alchemical pills that he had made. He announced that they were his own Kaya Kalpa formulation that would grant immortality, and then he gave the first pill to his dog. The animal immediately collapsed. Next, he gave one to his closest disciple, Yu, who also fell over. He handed pills to his other two disciples, took one himself, and then immediately collapsed. The two disciples looked first at each other and then at the motionless bodies at their feet. Dismayed and fearful, they threw away their pills.

Lamenting the death of their master and companions, they descended the mountain to gather the supplies they would need in order to bury the bodies. When they returned to the mountain, all that they found was a note in Siddha Bogar's handwriting, which read as follows:

Blossoming of the Tradition

The Kaya Kalpa tablets are working. After awakening from my trance, I restored faithful Yu and the dog. You have missed your chance for immortality.

(Siddha Bogar, *Sapta Kandam 7000* [Chennai, India: Thamarai Noolagam, 2005])

His new body being better suited to move about in Chinese society, Bogar's teaching was now readily received. He was known as Bo-Yang and later as Lao Tzu. Siddha Bogar is thus the father of the greatly renowned philosophy of Taoism, and he continued to teach it in China for more than 200 years before he returned to India. Although these statements may seem grand or novel, the Tamil Siddhas recorded Bogar's exploits in verse and palm-leaf manuscripts that date back to prehistoric antiquity. The difficulty in proving this to others is that the verses are undecipherable to all but the Siddhas themselves.

Based on Lao Tzu's teaching of Taoism, which include his many writings such as the *Tao Te Ching*, the theory of the duality of matter and energy first appeared in China, in the fifth century BC, as the male yang and the female yin. The conformity of yin and yang to the Siddha teaching of Siva and Shakti is unmistakable. It is well known within both Siddha oral traditions and Siddha writings, that Siddha Agasthiyar propounded this theory well before the first Tamil sangam was founded in 9900 BC. Because no mention of the duality of matter exists in any Chinese treatise prior to Lao Tzu, it is understood to have been gifted by this great Siddha. In addition, alchemy as a science did not appear in China until 175 BC and was practiced as an art until outlawed by royal decree in 135 BC.

> *Consuming Elixir pill, I traveled eight sides,*
> *I saw the range of mountains, and,*
> *Saw the glittering plains of Gold mines.*
> *I saw mines abundant with copper ore,*
> *And saw the green mountain, and range of hills.*
> *I saw wonders in the land of the Chinese.*
> *I saw Mount Kailash and the reddish hills yonder.*
> *I saw the great Meru and Siddha Roma Rishi too.*
> *Acquainted with him, I learned all secrets;*
> *Then wishing to reveal the secrets of all arts,*
> *Consuming again another Elixir, I flew to China and settled there.*

(Siddha Bogar, *Sapta Kandam 7000*, [Chennai, India: Thamarai Noolagam, 2005], Verses 1243–1244)

After Siddha Bogar's initial teachings in China, another swami from South India arrived in China. The locals called him Bodhidharma. When he found that the monks in China were physically unfit and were falling into repetitive ritual practices, he abrasively challenged their entire system. Recently, while

Blossoming of the Tradition

watching an older National Geographic documentary about kung fu, I was pleasantly surprised to hear the monks at the Shao Lin monastery, the birthplace of kung fu, attribute their martial art to "a man from South India," whom they recognize as Bodhidharma.[5] To this very day, the monks there have dedicated the monastery building to him (although it was destroyed and then rebuilt sometime between 1647 and 1732) and revere his wisdom. Hailing from the land of the Tamils, who had practiced Varma as both a martial art and a divine healing method, Bodhidharma instructed the Chinese monks in what would become known as Qigong. Himself a master of Varma Adi, the martial art of the Siddhas, Bodhidharma first introduced martial arts to China. From Qigong, the Chinese monks would develop a fascinating array of martial arts, beginning with tai chi, which would later transform into kung fu. From this style, the many other forms of commonly known martial arts, such as karate and judo, would eventually come.

The decoding and full understanding of the cryptic writings of the Tamil Siddhas reveals an unfamiliar view of history and of humanity's common ancestry. That this common ancestry and its spreading of medicine, spiritual paths, martial arts, and alchemy is not accounted for in scholarly circles is no surprise.

---

[5] The narrator of the documentary recounted the legend of kung fu's origin, saying that 1,500 years ago Emperor Xiawen, a devout Buddhist, built a residential monastery in the remote mountains for Master Batuo, "who came from India."

All of the quotations by the Siddha masters in this book have been provided by Siddha Healer Pal, and he has described decoding the palm-leaf manuscripts as both extremely challenging and exhilarating. The difficulty in understanding Their twilight language rests in the many layers in which They couched the deepest meaning. For instance, a single verse about physical and mental balance also applies to spiritual realms. The claims laid forth in this chapter, whether about the history of humankind or that the Tamil Siddhas discovered and mastered all of the spiritual paths of the planet, may well be contradicted by other people. Historical scholars, students, teachers from the various schools of spiritual arts, or teachers of the various healing methods may be inclined to disagree and cite their own versions of history. That the deepest wisdom has spread throughout every part of the planet and has been closely guarded is reflected in the esoteric wings of all religions and societies.

The Sufis of Islam, the Gnostics of Christianity, and the Kabbalists of Judaism are prime examples of the Siddhas' insights being incorporated throughout the globe. This worldwide influence existed long before the religions themselves. The most profound, deep, and esoteric secrets of the universe have been and will always be shrouded in a cryptic manner. It is we who must evolve before being capable of approaching such immensity.[6] How

---

[6] A prime example of how and why the Siddhas have hidden their knowledge is revealed in "Chapter 13: The Water of Life."

each age must evolve is revealed such that humanity always has access to the most primal and divine knowledge. True wisdom is what I term as primal, because it incorporates all aspects of life. In this way, this book provides a holistic view of the various realms of the Tamil Siddha tradition. It even includes discussions of several hidden sciences and arts of the masters that had previously not been written about in detail. Even more relevant is that these topics are explained by a most authentic source, Siddha Healer Pal Pandian. Should some take issue with or disagree with what is presented in this book is of no consequence. My own life experience requires no outside confirmation and is, of itself, the prime authority necessary. As the ebony and simple people of South India still say when confronted with the paradoxes posed by the Siddha masters, "Only a tiger can lick another tiger."

The striking similarities of ancient civilizations have always fascinated me. That some common root was shared throughout the world was equally obvious, like pyramids around the globe being similar. Although scholars and scientists hold various theories, none includes the legends of the Tamil Siddhas. This is no surprise, because the Siddhas' accounts have always been held within their clan. In the end, it makes no difference to me by whom or how healing and spiritual arts were begun. What makes all the difference in the world, however, is the degree to which my own life experience is affected. That Healer Pal, through his influence, patience, and gracious nature, has come to care for me and for the transformation of my consciousness is more proof than a thousand scholastic degrees or archeological finds could ever hope to provide. The subjective experience holds more proof than do objective conclusions based on theories and external data.

Siddha Bogar Samadhi shrine

CHAPTER 10

Nectar of the Absolute

STEPPING BEYOND LIMITATIONS

The various factors in the journey to health can best be described as limitations. For Siddha Varma healing to be effective, these limitations must be addressed. There are two types of limiting factors. Some are external to us, such as medicines, food, occupation, and daily routine. Others are internal to us, such as our attitude toward life, level of determination with regard to well-being, and willingness to embrace change. Whenever someone seeks Siddha healing, I always discuss these limitations with him or her in detail. It is important that we gain a firm understanding of where we are currently before embarking on a journey. Often we like to consider our destination, our end desire, without being fully aware of our starting point in terms of identity. Who and where we are in relation to our goal is the limitation. However, this limitation is itself indispensable, because it contains the very energy that we need in order to transcend it and reach our destination.

In our modern approach to life, we are often hurried by the outside demands of work, school, family, friends, relationships, and even the preparation and eating of food. Overworked and overstressed, we have become conditioned to expect immediate gratification. This mechanical, insensitive manner of living has even infected our view of healing the body and mind. Given this, when a person expresses the desire to receive Siddha healing, all of these deranged lifestyle habits beg to be addressed. I often encounter people who inquire about Siddha Varma healing and expect immediate results—even though they have suffered for many years, and no other treatment has given relief. This is understandable, because our environment infuses us with this type of hurried, demanding approach to all aspects of our lives. For this reason, we always take time to discuss expectations with those who come to us at the healing center.

Of primary importance is that one have a strongly felt commitment to embracing health. This is no fleeting matter, because it requires something that we humans greatly resist: change. Not only must we change, but often we must embrace radical change. When someone is suffering from an acute or chronic disorder, an insidious adaptation has occurred: The person has come to identify with the disorder. This is a normal response, because the disorder, like an unwanted guest, has come to live in the person's house—the body and mind. This is only half the tale, however. In order to let go of an identity, we must simultaneously assume a new identity. Doing so involves a journey guided by a Varma healer. It is a journey of healing. To reach the desired goal, the journey's destination, the individual needs a strong sense of perseverance, patience (notably with oneself), and a sense of rebelliousness. For this purpose, to be a rebel implies going beyond what the person thinks that he or she knows and what society deems as possible, reliable, and scientific.

A certain type of approach, while well intentioned, is common in today's society. It is inherently faulty, because it reflects an over-aggressive, nonsensitive (left hemisphere) mind-set. This insensitive approach likes to treat acute and chronic diseases with strong medicines from the very beginning, the first sign of symptoms. The classic route traveled by modern medicine is characterized by this very manner. Again, this is no surprise, because society as a whole teaches us that, when we face a strong barrier, only equal or greater strength can overcome that barrier and provide the instant results that we crave. However, the wisest approach—and that of Siddha Varma healing—embraces the wisdom and patience of Nature:

Nothing in the world
is as soft and yielding as water.
Yet for dissolving the hard and inflexible,
nothing can surpass it.

> *The soft overcomes the hard;*
> *the gentle overcomes the rigid.*
> *Everyone knows this is true,*
> *but few can put it into practice.*

(Lao Tzu, *Tao Te Ching*, trans. Stephen Mitchell [London: Frances Lincoln, 1999])

The ordinary way we are conditioned to tackle any illness today is quite the opposite of this description. For instance, imagine a person who has a fever, which, of course, indicates infection and often is accompanied by inflammation. Although Healer Pal will recommend various solutions based on the individual case, the cure usually takes three to five days. Generally, for inflammation, our modern medical system will approach this same situation with steroids, a potent yet damaging agent. Thus, steroids can easily reduce the inflammation quickly but at a cost to the person's overall health. This manner of addressing a basic imbalance is not only rather shortsighted and aggressive but also extremely insensitive. This is a classic example of denying the basic laws of nature, specifically the "soft overcoming the hard."

Amritha Kalai

Not long after I had returned the time came for me to resume conducting healing sessions. Although I continued to utilize Systemic Vital Point Therapy as the starting point for treatment, the application of Amritha Kalai predominated the sessions. *Amritha* means nectar, and *Kalai* means specific, so Amritha Kalai is the universal Nectar in human form. While Systemic Vital Point Therapy accesses the Varma points through the physical body, Amritha Kalai is a unique form of Siddha healing that awakens the intelligence of the organizing principle of health. This organizing principle is the holistic aspect of Vasi in the individual and its cosmic reflection, which the Siddhas call *Thiruvasi*. The Siddhas revere Thiruvasi as the flawless cosmic blueprint of all creation, sustenance, and destruction. The rhythmically breathing Thiruvasi enfolds space and gives birth to all form and manifestation. Demanding much meditation and many years of practice, the potential it holds for healing is nothing short of supernormal in the hands of a master. Stretching into vast realms, it can be understood as having two levels of practice. I practiced the initial level throughout the year before the second level could unfold.

Amritha Kalai involves the highest dimensions of Siddha healing, touching the causal body and enabling the person to reclaim his or her connection with the transcendental aspect of existence. Perhaps the best way to describe Amritha Kalai is by defining what it is not. It is not a form of energy healing; energy healing works with the subtle body. Amritha Kalai's scope of influence is that which exists prior to and beyond the physical body, personality, mind, subtle body, and all else that has been born with us. Earlier, I described the causal body as the storehouse of Vasanas, the latent tendencies that give rise to our disposition, personality, and reactions to life. The causal body is also where all karmic impressions are held, where after death the next birth is prepared in accordance with the karma that has become ripe for experience. This preparation can occur only when the person, mind, and subtle body (energy body), has been completely eradicated. In this causal body, there is no individual except in an extremely subtle seed form. The next individual, as it were, comes into existence only when the sufficient karmic imprints have ripened. At that point, the search for a physical body in which to be born can begin. In order to effect healing in this causal body, the master must be of the highest order. The chosen students are initiated solely by the grace and healing spirit of the master.

There is a Nectar of life that comes from the Universal Whole, or Cosmic Whole. This is what Siddha Saint Ramalingam referred to when he said the following:

> *There is Amritha Kalai, nectar force, showering every day in the early morning. Without it, the livingness of the earth would be vanished.*
>
> (Pal Pandian, *Siddhas: Masters of the Basics* [Chennai, India: Pal Pandian, 2008])

This shower of Cosmic Nectar (Amritha), although always present, is most pronounced in the early morning, which is why that time is suggested for meditation. When we are in a state of unknowing, humility, silence, and beyond-body consciousness, there is a revelation of this Amritha as a divine presence.

This divine presence generates a rhythm. When it emerges from a depth of silence, we experience it as a heart-opening radiance, a reverberation, love, a grand openness. Siddha Saint Ramalingam called it "Absolute Grace, Effulgence." All ancient traditions have spoken about it, whether as the Holy Spirit in the Hermetic writings, the Tao in China, Kabbalah in Judaism, Bodhi Chitta in Buddhism, Vishwaroopam in Vaisnavism, and Chidamparam in Saivite. In ancient Jewish tradition, the Kabbalah is considered the *Inner Torah*, in which the nature of the divine is envisioned in two aspects: the transcendent (Siva in India) and the manifest (Sakthi). Furthermore, the Kabbalah speaks of *Sephirot*, the ten emanations of God that continually sustain the universe in existence. These ten forces are the parallel of both the microcosmic and macrocosmic dasa vayu of the Siddhas. In ancient China, this same insight was expressed in the word *Tao*, which in its original and most primal understanding roughly equates to "flow of the universe," the essence or pattern behind the natural world and which keeps the universe balanced and ordered. It too holds that all creation is an expression of that which is static or void, called *wu* (Siva), but which is experienced as dynamic, called yin and yang (Sakthi). Regardless of the words they use, all of these traditions point to the unseen power, force, or intelligence that engenders all life, all of creation, and its divine origin.

This sense of divine presence enfolds, cradles, and upholds all life. This is the divine intention (*Icha Sakthi*) to create in action (*Kriya Sakthi*). It is always functioning as the intermediary between the potential for creation and that which is created or manifested. It mediates the creative process and connects the created to its Source, *Gnana Sakthi*, the energy of pure wisdom. This is the effulgence that generates the forces of life and connects all things to Itself, acting within the wholeness of space to generate all specific forms. This is the divine dance, the primal Nectar, with its threefold process of Icha Sakthi, Kriya Sakthi, and Gnana Sakthi. Unlike the Big Bang theory of quantum physics, David Bohm's brave theory speaks of "membrane-like folds of space-time [that] form the universe. Space is literally enfolded, and form is generated." What brings this about is what the Siddhas long ago called Thiruvasi. Integrating these ideas into one's experience through sadhana (spiritual practice) opens the way for them to be utilized in Siddha healing sessions.

Immersing oneself into the first level of Amritha Kalai requires keen attention during the session, because during that time the healer attunes himself or herself to particular flows of life force. While the dasa vayu, nadis, and Varma points are included in this spectrum, a much more subtle realm is touched upon. The most succinct way to describe Amritha Kalai is that, on a most basic level, the entire array of life forces act in a dual mode, one of alternate convergence and expansion. Working with this level of vibrational energy is extremely subtle yet also incredibly inclusive and thereby effective.

For example, if a person suffers body pain due to a vata imbalance and, in turn, experiences mental and emotional distress (the causal factor for the physical manifestations), both the emotional wounds and the physical pain must be treated. Only in this way can true health be restored. Including all aspects of our being as a whole unit brings true results. Consider the following example of a middle-aged woman—a nurse by profession—who came to our healing center in the United States after having suffered from fibromyalgia for many years.

When we first met to discuss her situation, I asked if she had been dealing with depression or anxiety. She admitted that she had indeed been depressed and anxious and had been taking medications for the past fifteen years. In addition, because the depression medications gave her terrible side effects, she had tried numerous times to stop taking them. She attempted various approaches—from sheer will power to using alternative drugs to wean her off—but she always found herself unable to live without them. The systemic body pain of fibromyalgia varied from persistent aches to flare-ups of extreme distress. Even being touched lightly by another person could cause her unbearable pain. The fatigue that she felt drained her enthusiasm for her job, which she loved, and even the joy she felt with her family.

The modern medical system states that fibromyalgia resembles auto-immune disorders and may result from a gene malfunction, an injury, or some other unknown cause. Siddha healing has a different view of fibromyalgia and a different approach to healing for those suffering from it.

Long-held stress, whether called depression or anxiety and whether from a childhood trauma or accumulated over a long period, gathers in the mind. Eventually, the burden overflows from the mental and emotional realm of the unconscious and manifests or incarnates to the physical body. There it is held in the connective tissue and is felt as pain. This process occurs gradually and manifests as extreme pain, fatigue, and ongoing emotional distress. These are the symptoms of fibromyalgia.

The manifestation of this disorder, according to Siddha healing, is that the nervous system has become extremely deranged. Because the nervous system is the meeting place of the physical and subtle bodies, this issue must be addressed. Therefore, the treatment is to enable the subtle body to come back into alignment with the physical body. The pain that this woman felt, in fact all bodily pain, was due to an imbalance in the vata dosha. Based on this basic logic of the ancients, her healing journey began.

The initial approach taken in our healing sessions was to rebalance the vata dosha and thus bring greater balance to her mind. The application of the relevant Varma points lowered the vata so that it returned to its proper level and the appropriate locations in the body. In addition, stimulating brain-related junctures enlivened her body's natural sense of vitality, which was then reflected in greater mental balance. Slowly and with her physician's approval, she was able to wean herself off the depression medications. Within two months, she was no longer taking those medications.

Over time and by utilizing Systemic Vital Point Therapy, Adangal massage, and Amritha Kalai energy healing, the subtle and physical bodies came into harmony, and she was free of both body pain and mental distress. Facing her life from a newly grounded and balanced perspective, she was able to move through the loss of her job and find another fulfilling position in nursing, the work of helping others, which gave meaning to her life.

Should she continue to imbibe this quality—living without the mental and physical imbalances that she had previously accepted as her identity—to own it and allow it become a part of her and of her approach to life, it can become natural to her and to her daily routine. In this way, it can become her new identity, ensuring that the old identity of pain and anxiety will not return. Life will, of course, challenge her—as it does all of us—until she establishes her new identity and forms the habit of implementing it in all aspects of her experience. Doing so takes time, because now she must live through what was previously avoided and controlled via medication.

Underlying Matrix

In that example, the woman was finally freed of the physical and emotional pain that had plagued her for so long. With a newfound sense of being grounded in herself and in her life, she was able to flow into her cherished work. This is a beautiful example of how Siddha Varma healing provides a ripple effect that enables people to experience not only freedom from suffering but also greater levels of joy. The combination of all of the healing techniques that Pal had taught me enabled me to flow into the healing sessions with a unique degree of efficacy. The sessions also were extremely enjoyable for me. Imbibing the nectar flow inherent in the human body, which stands as prior to physical and energetic properties, afforded me the opportunity to explore the most subtle dimensions of creation.

If this explanation seems too esoteric, you need look no further than your own body. At this very moment, your body is performing countless miracles, none of which we are conscious or fully understand. Food is being broken down into nutrients and waste, air is continually being sucked into the body and then expelled, blood and oxygen are circulating at tremendous speed and with tremendous force, lymph glands and hormones are playing their parts, muscles are contracting and relaxing, and countless other miracles are taking place. All of these do not necessitate our being conscious of them. We need not direct them. They do not even require our knowledge of them. Even our most prized possession—belief—is not only unnecessary but entirely irrelevant.

Below these physical functions of the body lie more subtle primary functions. For each organ and physiological purpose, an energy resides within us. An example is that, in order to live, we must breathe the surrounding air. We often say that air is responsible for life. If this is so, why does a dead person not breathe air and live instead? The obvious answer is that there is a force within the lungs and which operates with intelligence, the prana vata. This is one of the dasa vayu, the one that influences body tissue and fluids. All such functioning of the body relies not on our will or knowledge but rather on one inherent, involuntary dynamic that functions within us.

The term *involuntary mechanism* expresses the concept that the motion of subtle fluid and tissue in the human system is driven by inherent forces rather than by voluntary processes or external agencies. These inherent forces underlie and organize form in order to express the original intention. This is the blueprint of a living being. This blueprint is a quantum-level ordering matrix that is epigenetic, meaning that it precedes genetics and underlies embryological formation and further differentiation. This was described in chapter 4 of this book as the dasa vayu that separate from the Vasi and give rise to physical growth, movement, and the eventual interaction of the being with the external world. More succinctly stated by Pal in answer to a question from me, "Varma [healing] is stronger than karma."

Because karma is not something that we Westerners are conditioned to understand, appreciate, or believe, I propose the following concrete example of an Amritha Kalai treatment session to which a physician of Indian descent sent his elderly mother.

Herself a physician during her working years, she suffered from a disorder that baffled doctors: She had lost all sense of taste and smell. The lack of taste and smell affected her mood, outlook, and food intake. Her family was greatly concerned, because she was aged and now beginning to deteriorate not only physically but also emotionally. Her physicians had tried every medicine available. Out of desperation, her son sent her to the Siddha Varma healing center.

After the first several healing sessions, when I asked whether she was sleeping well, she replied that she'd had a strange dream. It had happened the night after her previous healing session. In the dream, her mother was scolding her. At some point later in the dream, she saw a snake and was not happy about it. The dream showed that her ancestors were having some difficulty and therefore were influencing her, and the presence of the snake indicated that the disorder was due to karmic influences. During a course of healing, the realm of dreams, or reveries, reveals the aspects of the unconscious that beg to be addressed. Archetypes, known as deities in the Eastern tradition, which represent the collective psyche of humanity, often show themselves and point the way for the healing to flow, because they represent the collective traumas of our consciousness.

This should not be a surprise, for we have previously explored the vastness of the unconscious. The collective nature of humankind's psyche resembles what today is called genetics and in Siddha healing is called family, or ancestral, karma. We also know, from chapter 6 of this book, about Siddha Tantra, that the deities of India personify these energy patterns of humanity's psyche. Had the elderly woman been in India, we would have asked her to attend puja (ritual of worship) at Goddess Durga's temple. This activity is recommended because Goddess Durga represents the wrathful aspect of our unconscious realm and would provide the great benefit of nullifying the woman's karmic debt. Puja is like surfing karmic waves instead of having them wash over us and knocking us down.

Because she was in the United States, Pal suggested that we take a different approach to her healing. Each morning when she awoke, she was to immediately take a shower while wearing the very same clothes she had slept in. Afterward, she was to put the clothes in the washer immediately. She was to follow this routine for fifteen days. It sounds crazy, right? Nevertheless, until the unconscious aspects of her psyche were addressed, healing would not take place; her senses of taste and smell would continue to evade her.

After the first two healing sessions, her family happily reported that she was beginning to be more positive and playful and less moody. After four weeks of treatment and adherence to the morning routine, four of the six tastes had returned. Then the time came for her and her husband to return to India. After three months in India, all of her tastes had returned. For the past three years, she has had no further difficulty. This is an example of Amritha Kalai affecting the level of the causal body, mitigating karmic imprints, and restoring health. It is by the graceful showering of Amritha, or Nectar, that such deeply rooted issues can be resolved.

Nuances of Amritha Kalai

There is a second level, or dimension, of Amritha Kalai. For that level, the healer engages the flow of Cosmic energy, the Universal Grace showering aspect. From the healer's involvement in the session, once the person drops all selfish, ignorant identification, the Vasi in their body reverberates as the Thiruvasi of Lord Natarajar, Siva. This is the creative principle of the Universal Nectar, and from here it settles in the heart of the Absolute.

The physicist David Bohm, when speaking of a holographic paradigm, stated that "a hologram is a unified field in which the information of the whole is contained in each and every part." We have already explored the three bodies: the physical body, the subtle body, and the causal body, which are also known as body, mind, and spirit. There is a fourth body, which is called *Maha Karana*, the Universal causal body. Through this body, or field, our three bodies are formed, manifested. Having gained an individualized sense, we experience the veiling aspect of creation, *Pancha Krithiyam*. It is in this profoundly core field that

Amritha Kalai healing operates. It does so by kindling the link between a person's causal body and the Maha Karana and then directing the creative energy to the subtle body and physical body. This second level of Amritha Kalai includes many subtle dimensions, and we healers journey with each individual to touch some portion of its spectrum.

By simply touching a few places on an individual's body, the healer must attune with these energies, feel the dasa vayu movements, and release the imbalance in specific Varma points. The highest level of a healer's mastery? The healer should be able to heal without touching the person. Through his or her eyes (*Nokku*) or pointing a finger at the person from a distance, the Amritha Kalai healing takes place. As for what is necessary, Pal has said, "For this, one should be in deep meditation to drop one's sense of individual identification, or one should have the loving surrender to the Absolute."

> *The silent sages destroying the threefold bond are established where their selves are destroyed. This is the dance of the Lord of the assembly, whose very form is Grace.*
>
> (Unmai Vilakkam, "Exposition of Truth," In Pal Pandian, *Siddhas: Masters of the Basics* [Chennai, India: Pal Pandian, 2008])

CHAPTER 11

The Web of Life

Because the Siddhas have never separated their paths, my own journey has reflected this same integration. Pal skillfully wove my personal spiritual journey with the social, or healing, aspect and incorporated the ordinary responsibilities of life, creating a milieu in which I was bound to continually confront all unconscious impressions. The tantric practice continued to flow. With such a full, constructive schedule, I had little time to think or wrestle with philosophical considerations. Because of this, the vision quest opened the deeper recesses of the mind's hidden fragmented nature. This led me further into the shadow realms, usually in the form of continued visions of, visitations by, and encounters with deities. Some of the shadows revealed the hidden fears; others bestowed blessings. The tantric journey, even amid the busy schedule of career, healing sessions, family life, and writing, continued to move quickly. In this book, I have related only a few of the mystical experiences. There is one, however, that occurred on a very auspicious date. On the evening of Pal's birthday, once again before I could actually fall asleep, I found myself at the top of an enormous mountain.

There are two caves at the top of the mountain, and, having reached the summit, I rest at the mouth of one of the caves. I sit on the ground, cross-legged and facing the cave's opening, surrounded by bronze and stone statues of various Indian deities. They are very large, at least ten feet in height, and they amaze me. I cannot imagine how they got here. Glancing over my shoulder at the abyss below, I notice clouds hugging the waist of the mountain. It seems that I am sitting at the top of the world. Returning my gaze to the statues, I have the peculiar feeling of being in a garden of divine worship and blessing, each deity frozen in its particular form with His or Her distinct hand mudras and ornaments. Just to my left stands the most gigantic statue of them all, a bronze, dancing Lord Siva. I am struck by an unmistakable resonance between us. Gazing up, I am somehow aware of unspoken communication, and I can hardly believe the intensity of the closeness as the waves of silent speech flow back and forth between us. My eyes are now guided back to the cave's opening. As I ponder both the cave and the inner expanse of the mountain, I realize with complete certainty that the mountain contains countless caverns and rooms. Images of them flash before my eyes. They vary in size, shape, lighting and, most notably, the number of people contained within. Two things become clear to me. The first is that I have indeed traveled to the summit, from inside the mountain, and am familiar with the endless rooms. Second—and this seems to bring me a significant amount of joy—is my distinct understanding that anyone could visit me here and be comfortable. I am silently instructed to enter the second cave to my left.

The main difference between the two caves is that this one is extended past its mouth by a large wooden structure of ancient design. The walls and roof are made of tightly bundled sticks that allow for a small amount of light to seep through, and the floor is constructed of beautiful, narrow, wooden planks. Measuring perhaps ten meters in length, the opening resembles a mouth that has given birth by yawning, and its child is the seamless blue sky that stands just below the heavens of infinite space. After inspecting the structure, I see, sitting on my right, my dear teacher Pal resting on the floor cross-legged with his eyes closed. I dare not greet or disturb him, because he is obviously lost in deep Samadhi (merging with the Source). Of all that passed before, in this moment I am most certain of one fact: Pal is facilitating this entire event. I become aware that someone is approaching from behind me, and I turn around to see a man emerge from the cave, from inside the mountain.

A rather short swami, or monk, garbed in orange, with head shaven, he exudes the paradoxically comforting qualities of the most profound humility and the most immense power. Feelings of extreme comfort and openness naturally arise from within me, and our greetings to each other are the most intimate one could possibly conceive. We sit on the floor opposite Pal, and the swami begins to ask me questions. When he asks about the time I spent at the other cave opening and my experience there,

I reply that the dancing Siva spoke with me. I spy two friends of mine in front of that same cave, and I ask if the first one, who is of Indian origin, is my brother.

His reply is a simple "No."

My other friend from Lebanon comes into view, and I repeat my query. Again, the swami says, "No." The sun shines through the walls and roof, giving the scene a luminous glow so that the beauty and serenity of the scene thrill my entire being. Reaching within his robe, the swami then pulls out a large, shiny nail, hands it to me, and silently asks me to follow him.

He walks gracefully back and forth across the width of the structure, inspecting every single particle of the floor. I obediently follow in his footsteps, while wondering what he could possibly be searching for with such intensity. Suddenly, very near the end of the hall and only a few feet from the mouth of the cave, he locates the exact spot that he has sought. We sit facing each other, and then he hands me a small hammer. I follow his unspoken command to place the nail on the very spot he had so intently sought and then tap it once, very lightly, with the hammer. Immediately, a small portion of the floor opens. To my surprise, I see a small, silver object sticking straight up from the opening. My shock and relative inattention to detail are obvious, because I think that it is a surgical scalpel and am concerned that someone could step on it! The swami's amusement is obvious when he laughs at my naive assumption and asks me to look more closely. Upon examination, I see that the object is not a scalpel but rather a small spear (Vel) of Lord Murugan and that it is covered in ancient sandalwood paste. When I recognize the Vel, I feel the word "Skanda" loudly pronounced in the surrounding air, my head, and throughout my body.

The light at the opening of the hall is bright here, and the wind blows the thin yet invigorating air in swirling motions around us. It is surely a cold air that is caressing us. However, although I know that I should feel its bite, my only sensations are of being massaged by its movement and lifted from within by its crisp, pure nature. When the swami asks me to read what is inscribed on the Vel, I pull it out. I scrape off the encrusted sandalwood paste and see intricate Tamil writings. My eyes shift to the portion that contains a numerical sequence, and I relay to him the numbers: 3, 1, 1. "Ah" is his only reply for the moment. Again, he reaches into his orange robes, and this time he produces a tiny yellow book. As he carefully turns the pages of the book, looking intently for the exact page that refers to the numbers on the Vel, I gaze at the endless sky.

Several pairs of eagles are soaring in front of us, and they screech their joy both at being freed from the chains of gravity and in respectful salutation to the swami. Soon he finds the page for which he was looking and fixes his deeply fascinating eyes on me. He relates to me in a soft, incredibly loving tone what was written in that page: "Be happy in your job and in your life; relax—it will all be fine."

Then, looking back within the book, he shows me the title at the top of the page: Valli. This word now reverberates throughout the space and my entire being.

Rivulets of the Absolute

From this same page, he reads to me again: "You will know yourself as both part man and part god and bring healing to many people."

I am struck speechless by his assertions. We sit together looking out at the vast expanse of sky above, yet intimately aware of the entire ball of planet Earth and all of her inhabitants below.

Dancing Siva-Lord Natarajar

When I opened my eyes after that mystical experience, I sat on the bed feeling, seeing, and sensing a glowing golden aura.

Throbbing silence filled the room. After some time, I uncharacteristically called Pal in the middle of the night. I felt that I should share with him my joy for the birthday gift he had given me.

"The mountain is Arunachala. The swami is Lord Siva, who has come to shower blessings on you," he said.

I was speechless. Well, at least briefly.

Then, all at once, questions bubbled up out of me. "What is the meaning of the Vel, the spear? Who is Valli, Sir? And why would the name 'Skanda' come to me?"

"As you know, Lord Murugan is the son of Lord Siva and goes by many names, Subramani, Karthagai, and one is Skanda."

He continued, "Each name depicts a particular flavor or fragrance of the God. Skanda means the fragrance of flowers, of the earth. It also means aggregate, or bound together. This means a synergistic wholeness. For you, in this instance, it carries the opposite of the word *scattered*."

"And what of Valli, Sir?" I queried.

"Skanda, Lord Murugan, has two consorts. The first is Devayanai, and she came from the celestial realm and so is pious and pure. The second one is Valli. She is also beautiful, but she is earthy, because she is human, from a tribal village, and so carries the specific traits of playfulness and mystery and is dark-skinned. For his part, Lord Murugan played mischievous games with her to win her affection."

"And what is the difference, Sir? What is the purpose of doing and bringing this particular name to me?" I asked Pal.

"Ah. You see, Lord Murugan does not keep his divinity for himself, sitting in heavenly realms. He likes to express it here on earth, hence the name 'Skanda,' which means 'bound,' 'aggregate,' and is the fragrance of the earth. This is why he has a consort of the earth, one who beautifully shows these qualities. They are, once again, telling you that this is your path. You must stay grounded in the ordinary routines of daily life and interact with people in the same way."

Continuing to pester him, I asked, "The Vel, Sir, it really surprised me to see it, since I have only been aware of it by seeing a few pictures of Lord Murugan. Usually it is gold, but this one was silver. What could any of this mean?"

His reply was surprising to me: "Gold has to be refined. Its purity must be brought out through purification methods. However, silver is already pure. We can say that its color is white. The aggregate of all colors is white. It is a beautiful sign and symbolizes the gift of self-inquiry to you."

I can no longer recall how I expressed my gratitude for the journey, his blessings, and the kind and tender manner in which Pal cared for me. I was aware then and continue to be aware that any words I could choose would fall far short of expressing my feelings.

The message that I should flow with my daily routine as the path by which to express the inner changes was, indeed, repeated through my encounters and dreams. Within this is the very message of tantra itself: to cherish the magic of day-to-day life in all of its simplicity! There is something hidden in each task and each encounter. Our very essence lies entangled in all that we touch and do. *However, this is not in any way to be considered or taken as a practice.* Rather, it is a reflection of our inner quality, and that is an enormous difference. This inner quality is the distillation of consciousness that drips into our being and flows from the devoted, determined path of tantra.

THE FEMININE PSYCHE

At the level of the Self, we are neither male nor female; we are beyond.
—Pal Pandian

The focus up to this point has been on the shadow work of tantra; the other mode of tantra, that of the contra-sexual aspect, has been given little attention. As mentioned in chapter 7 of this book, the two channels do not occur separately, but, rather, they actually intertwine throughout the journey. Taking a closer look into this journey, there is an inherent limitation: words themselves. The message of tantra, the Siddhas, and the Siddhas' wisdom is expressed in this book solely from my own experience with as little theory interspersed as possible. The theoretical passages that are included come from the most authoritative source possible: Pal Pandian. With this limitation in mind, I can speak with absolute assurance from the male view but then must provide Pal's words to me about how a female tantric approaches her own masculine-feminine integration.

> *When I perceive the Beloved in my heart, there is no form; it is only the fullness of Love.*
>
> (Darya Khan, In Pal Pandian, *Siddhas: Masters of the Basics* [Chennai: Pal Pandian, 2008])

The process by which a boy becomes a man is straightforward: he must break away from the all-embracing maternal world. This is the most crucial turning point in his life. It is also necessary for his ability to go out into the world, because it addresses his spatial orientation. These are fundamental features of a masculine psyche. His inner world? Well, that is another matter. It demands that he cross the tortuous maze of his masculine psyche and return to where he broke away from.

From the moment he identifies with the masculine gender, his feminine psyche constellates within him. He learns what it is to be a boy in two ways. First, he accepts all that it means to be a boy and rejects all that seems the opposite. This requires the second way, that of differentiating, separating, and analyzing. These are the foundation of the left hemisphere of the brain.

Growing up is all about building one's own psyche. Whatever gender the boy identifies with, that is his functional, conscious psyche. Of course, all that is rejected—the feminine psyche—is pushed further into the shadows within. God forbid that he should ever experience any manner of his feminine nature! If he does, he shrinks back or overemphasizes his masculinity. One example is turning aggressive when he feels a loss of control. This is how men in most societies live.

The vicious reaction to half of his own inherent nature reveals a disturbing truth about him: He is afraid of his feminine psyche, one half of himself. As a man, he strongly believes that that mingling with his inner feminine psyche will make him lose his masculinity. How does he compensate? Relationships. He feels that he can safely experience all of his feminine needs through relationships. In this way, he feels in control of managing his masculine image.

However, this process has simply caused him to become one gender and to separate from, or reject, the other gender. The result? He has forgotten what it is to be whole, to be beyond gender. Should he eventually tire of the repetitive game of life and crave to be whole, he must follow a spiritual path to meet his inner feminine psyche, his forgotten aspect of self. When the day on which he feels the lack of wholeness dawns, his search can begin. His journey into tantra can commence.

In tantric discipline, the enigmatic feminine calls the man back within himself in numerous ways. She calls him by exerting

Her fascinating presence in several disguises. She is temptress and virgin; She is child and adult. She invites him into the mystery of Her inner world, the terrible and beautiful depths of the eternal feminine, by way of a gradual learning experience called *Sri Vidya Upasana*. In my own quest, Sri Vidya Upasana took the form of Sri Chakra Upasana.

This archetypal feminine Sri Vidya includes the understanding of the ancient magic of earth, the potency of herbs, the rhythm of fertility, the charisma of sexuality, the love of motherly affection, and the spontaneity of learning. In Her negative aspect, She is the white witch of C.S. Lewis's *Narnia* books, who turns animals into stone. Cold and uncaring, the witch personifies the devouring aspect of the feminine, the aspect of which every man is afraid. If a man is to have an evolutionary relationship with his inner feminine psyche, he must acknowledge Her dark side. Even though we no longer burn witches, our unaccepted fear of the feminine still denies us access to Her natural wisdom and understanding.

> *The feminine psyche carries both illusion and creativity.*
> —Pal Pandian

She is simultaneously both: Mother Nature and our inner nature. Humankind's collective denial of Her influence and potency has ravaged both the earth and our natural, unified self.

The wonder of the feminine psyche is part of the mystery of creativity.

—Pal Pandian

To be open to our creative potential is to be open to the unconscious, the domain of the Goddess. Man is always afraid of being swallowed back into the womb of the unconscious. Only by acknowledging this fear can he enjoy the shield of Perseus, with which the demigod could look at the Gorgon's snake-covered head without being turned to stone. By facing his fear of the feminine, man enjoys a deepened experiential journey through his feminine psyche. Siddha Tantra guides a man through a wide spectrum of goddesses, such as Valai (Bala), Tripura Sundari, Kamalatmika, Raja Rajeshwari, Shyamala, Kali, and Manomani. Yet every aspirant need not journey through all levels. The guru chooses the type of worship for the aspirant. There is nothing hierarchical or linear in Siddha Tantra.

Goddess Valai is a young girl whom all Siddhas adore. Just as empty vessels can hold fresh water, detachment from habitual patterns provides new space for spiritual learning. That is how Valai symbolizes inner learning. She symbolizes the dawn.

Goddess Tripura Sundari, the teenaged girl, symbolizes the spirit of fertility. She is the goddess of the three states of waking, dreaming, and sleeping. These are also referred to as the *three cities* or the *three kingdoms*. Being aware in all three states in an unbroken fashion is a clear sign of elevated consciousness. Without her blessing, one cannot maintain unbroken, singular awareness throughout all three states.

Goddess Manomani, the grandmother, symbolizes compassion in the role of guiding spirit. This is an impersonal mode.

> *A goddess can open a man to the music of his soul.*
> —Pal Pandian

She allows the meaning of the "music of his soul" to manifest in his life. Meaningfulness comes not from the outer world but from the inner recesses of the archetypes, the unconscious, the realm of the gods and goddesses. Traditional spiritual paths have spoken that the deities reveal our inherent life purpose, or Dharma.

Modern society's material culture has forgotten the eternal truth of the role played by gods and goddesses. If we are cut off from our inner selves, life soon turns empty, and no matter how much outer abundance we accumulate, this hollowness remains. For any man, his inner feminine psyche can connect him to his inner being, from which meaning can flow into his daily life. The discipline of tantra guides an aspirant through making this connection. Once he is on the path, She brings into his life the fruits of detachment, learning, leadership, and compassionate service to fellow beings. She thus reconnects him to the source of life, the Self. This reconnection makes him whole again. She shows him his core and reveals his inner purpose, the inherent meaning hidden within *everything*!

The Inner Masculine

In contrast to the boy's stepping into manhood by breaking away from the maternal world, the woman never psychologically leaves the arms of the Great Mother. A girl's initiation into womanhood is her first menstrual period, which draws her into the cycle of fertility, the great cycle of nature. The woman remains inwardly connected to the Source as she brings life into the world. The nature of the feminine psyche is inclusive, in contrast to the masculine psyche, which is analytical and functions through separation and exclusivity. The function of the woman's inner masculine psyche is to provide the focus that is lacking in the feminine psyche's otherwise diffused consciousness. A female aspirant of the Siddha path who does not have the support of a positive and harmonious relationship with her inner masculine cannot differentiate the content of her unconscious. She is unable to discriminate which unconscious dynamics belong to her and which belong to another. Her inner masculine is necessary in order to create definitive psychological boundaries that result in well-defined containment of her consciousness.

The feminine psyche includes an instinctual sense of the relatedness of everything, while the masculine psyche draws a line and separates. A woman's inner masculine psyche provides the knife that cuts and excludes. The act of exclusion is an integral part of defining boundaries. This function of the masculine psyche appears contrary to the feminine psyche's function of embracing and including. Therefore, a woman must find a way of defining boundaries without violating her instinctual feelings of wholeness.

> *Know the male, yet keep to the female: receive the world in your arms. If you receive the world, the Tao will never leave you, and you will be like a little child.*
>
> (Lao Tzu, *Tao Te Ching,* trans. Stephen Mitchell [London: Frances Lincoln, 1999])

A woman's inner masculine gives clarity and grounding, which creates her sacred inner space. This space is essential for her inner work as well as her spatial orientation in the outer world. How else can she channelize, or enact her deep inspiration? Pal's own tantric teacher used to say to him, "The spear of Lord Murugan symbolizes this aspect."

Lord Murugan is the deity that a female aspirant should worship from the beginning of her tantric spiritual journey, because He represents the Universal Male. Later, other deities may emerge and guide her journey. However, if Lord Murugan settles as her personal deity, He then reveals to her all of the modes of experiences symbolized by the other gods. He shows her the alpha and omega! Without the clarity and channelization of His spear, the woman's inner journey may be easily polluted by projections and problems. Allowing unnecessary intrusion by others creates a gaping vulnerability. An inner space is invaluable. The woman should value her deepest needs and thus avoid becoming a doormat for her family, friends, and colleagues.

The focus, clarity, perseverance, and channelization provided by her inner masculine psyche enables her to balance her outer softness. While the nature of the feminine psyche is to be inner and hidden, the masculine psyche belongs to the conscious, outer world. A unified bond with her inner masculine psyche allows her to manifest what is within her and function creatively in the outer world.

However, the masculine psyche also boasts a strong shadow side. Although it enables a woman to successfully function in the outer world, it can cut her off from her inner self. Sadly, many women are paying this price in today's masculine-dominated culture. They are driven by masculine power rather than a masculine psyche that supports them in expressing feminine values.

> *The inner space of a woman in union with the constructive masculine psyche is symbolized by Lord Natarajar, the Dancing Siva.*
> —Pal Pandian

While the feminine psyche connects a man with the inner meaning of life, the masculine psyche enables a woman to show her inner meaning in her outer life. A woman remains inward-facing, focused on the Source, and the masculine psyche acts as mediator between this inward nature and her outer life. It connects her outer life to the natural center of her being. The supportive aspect of the masculine psyche helps her to bring her inner wholeness to her consciousness. This is a great revelation, not only for herself but also for her environment.

The Emergent Union

> *Our inner consort is a powerful reality.*
> —Pal Pandian

Living deep in the unconscious of all constellates the counterpart gender, begging for light, recognition, reconciliation, and finally marriage of the two psychic counterparts. Most people experience this as an image projected onto the stage of personal relationships. The spiritual inner journey reveals how our real love affair is essentially within ourselves. In our dreams, we often get to taste this love—the passion of meeting or the eroticism of a lover's embrace. These intimate dreams are not reflections of repressed sexuality or unlived romance. They are, in fact, inner encounters toward union within oneself.

As the journey deepens, one realizes more and more. Insights come by pure grace. The urge to evolve occurs not by the will of the ego but by the flowing from the Self. Love and acceptance take us to the stage of divine union, where opposites integrate and a deep unity is made conscious. The awareness of a hidden unity is not the fruit of a single moment of self-realization but of a continuing process of integration that often persists over years.

As opposites go on to constellate within us, we continue to discover deeper aspects of ourselves in a new light. By integrating the conflicts of our personal shadows, we find ourselves encountering the collective, archetypal world where the conflicts of humankind lay buried. The wounded feminine, a product of our patriarchal culture, is an archetype that most are forced to confront. Her anger and pain, once accepted and understood, can transform the seeker; otherwise, the seeker remains caught in deep resentment.

Without the ability to confront the deeply hidden, terrifying collective unconscious of humanity, all attempts, although noble, remain tragically incomplete. Under the guidance of a Siddha, transformation takes place within both the personal world and the archetypal world. By transforming ourselves, we make this small but lasting contribution to the collective. At the end of this endless journey, we discover that the goal was none other than our own essential nature.

> *All things have their backs to the female and stand facing the male. When male and female combine, all things achieve harmony.*

(Lao Tzu, *Tao Te Ching,* trans. Stephen Mitchell [London: Frances Lincoln, 1999])

Integrating the twin aspects of one's psyche is to become whole. It is the true meaning of *marriage*. To wed the polar opposites of creation within our being is the only means of attaining psychological health. This step must be taken before enlightenment can dawn. After this marriage, the opposite gender is no longer viewed or experienced in the common way. The marriage is a curious thing to live through. Absent are the enormous layers of neurosis, the deranged impressions of the planet that divide all of humanity into separate forces. This is repeatedly played out in the arena of relationships in the mode of emotional/physical predator and prey. The two aspects, the two genders, ache to join with, commune with, and dissolve into each other. Doing so, they leave behind the isolated experience of existing as one half of a being. The circus known as the dilemma of seeking in another that which inherently hides within has folded its tents and left town forever.

The dormant mature dame is stirred to awake;
Whence He with Her in amity knit—Rise and fly!
Proclaiming that you have seen your True Self—Rise and fly!

("Tiruvunthiar," Verse 14, In Pal Pandian, *Siddhas: Masters of the Basics* [Chennai, India: Pal Pandian, 2008])

Dreaming of Navatri

It is appropriate that the discussion of the male and female paths in tantra is followed by a brief exploration of union. While uncovering the darker one, shadow work and integration of the contra-sexual aspects are important to all who walk the path of tantra, an overview of how the gods and goddesses interact with us is equally appropriate.

It had been almost two years since I had last seen Pal and nearly four since I had left the Kaya Kalpa house. In this book, I have related some but not the vast majority of my encounters with the Beyond. Before returning to India in late 2014, I had ceased giving healing sessions, because the corporate job demanded much of me prior to an extended holiday. Also, because I would be spending Thanksgiving and Christmas in India, I took the opportunity to spend time with family.

During these months leading up to my departure for India, the festival of *Navatri* (*nava* meaning nine, and *atri* meaning night) was being celebrated all across India. Navatri pays homage to the

Goddess in all of her forms. For nine nights and ten days, Indians adopt a festive mood, gather with family, fast, pray, and—especially—attend rituals at the temples of the divine feminine. They do so in order to invoke Her and gain Her blessings.

During that year's Navatri, an especially vivid and particularly grace-imbued dream came to me. The dream lasted the entire night, and I could not leave the experience even when I awoke. It followed me as I went through my morning routine, keeping itself fully in my awareness. The dream is recounted below, followed by Pal's reply to my email:

I am walking down a hotel hallway to go to a business meeting for the pharmaceutical company by which I am employed. With me is a young companion of perhaps twenty-five years old. The hallway is lined with guards who are dressed in riot gear, heads covered in black helmets, and faces obscured by heavily tinted shields. As we approach the meeting room, the guards suddenly seize my friend, and she responds, uncharacteristically, by struggling mightily, screaming, and making a rather outlandish scene. When the guards have her under control, one of the guards looks at me and states that she is a government spy who has been trying to undermine me. While being restrained and carried away, she looks directly to me and begins laughing hysterically. By then, I am happy to see her go.

The dream seems to reset, and then I am again walking down the hotel hallway toward the business meeting. This time, however, I am accompanied by a woman who, although more mature in age than my previous companion, is absolutely beautiful. More importantly, her undeniable physical attractiveness is totally overshadowed by a lustrous inner beauty that is completely spellbinding. It is as if her inner self effortlessly exudes a golden hue, which, in turn, emits not only comforting warmth but also an aroma of heavenly bliss. When we reach the guards, I expect them to duplicate their previous action with my new companion, but, to my pleasant surprise, they remain standing at attention and allow us to pass.

After the meeting, the two of us go to my home, and we spend some time in the garden. The surrounding trees, flowers, grass, and birds are alive and engaging with us in such a harmonious fashion that there are no defined boundaries between us. We play with nature in this fashion for some time, and even the wind, sky, and the tiniest insects sense our presence and communicate with us intelligently, lovingly, and respectfully. I am unsurprised by the flow. The entire time that she and I interact and gaze at each other, I continue to be amazed by the infinite depth of her beauty. She is the most feminine, mature being I have ever encountered, and our bond is unmistakable. We embrace. In that moment, a flood of unspoken communication flows between us, and again I sense the flow of the golden-hued substance of which she is formed. After we have embraced for some time, her body becomes passive and extremely soft. By this sign, we both know that the time for her to leave has arrived, because she must attend to other matters in some distant corner of the universe.

After this exhilarating encounter, I find myself back at the hotel and approaching my business colleagues, who are on a break from a different meeting, in the lobby. I mention to a close friend that I have met the most beautiful, extraordinary woman. Eyeing me with some suspicion, she calmly states that she has heard of this woman. Cautiously, she informs me that the woman is perhaps not completely benign. There is more, much more, to her, my friend tells me. Puzzled by her words, I want to find out what she means. Using my phone, I search the Internet for the mysterious woman's name. I find many pictures of her, and, when I open one, I see that she looks just as beautiful in it as she did in person. As I gaze at the picture for a few moments, however, her face slowly transforms and shockingly takes on the form of a monster. Confused, I lose awareness of my surroundings as the shock of the woman's transformation sends me swirling.

Eventually, the disorientation fades, and I become aware of where I am, in a large, circular room. The walls are painted white, and the sun shines in through various openings at the distant top, near the high ceiling. Looking about myself while attempting to become grounded in the new setting, I observe many other men, women, and children, none of whom are familiar to me. Scanning farther, I see the same black-clothed, helmeted guards standing apart from the rest of us. A sense of dread creeps in, because they are facing us and are lined up in military fashion, each carrying a stick used for beating and controlling crowds. Although the situation seems ominous, I am unprepared for what happens next. Dispersing to the exterior walls, each guard opens a previously unseen door. The most hideous, sadistic creatures that I could have ever imagined enter the room, and the guards leave.

These are no vampires of romantic lore. They are highly deformed monsters, hairless, with bulging spines, conical skulls, and black streaks contrasting with their grayish-white skin. Their completely black eyes are only a bit less frightening than their enormous fangs, long, clawlike hands, and unimaginably foul odor. Moving with preternatural swiftness, they seem incapable of standing erect, and they instead scurry about the walls, floor, and ceiling as if impervious to the effects of gravity. Their intent is obvious—to devour everyone who is present. I watch in horror as the people in the outer circle are attacked. They scream horrifically as they are torn apart, limbs gushing blood and organs spilling forth. The ecstasy of the monsters is evident as they rush to drink the blood, becoming further intoxicated and so even more cruel. Utter panic sets in, and everyone rushes about, looking for an escape. There is none to be found. I gaze upward at the sun-splashed ceiling, hoping that it might provide refuge. Disappointment quickly sets in as the gravity-defying beasts move through the sunlight without suffering any adverse effect. Shrinking away from the people just in front of me as they are set upon by the enormous demons, I realize that there is no hope of escaping. The horrific sounds of snapping bones and tearing flesh fill my ears. Body parts are flung about, striking me with force, and blood soaks my clothes. The stench of the beasts, death, and the iron-rich red liquid fills my nostrils and disgusts me. Death is imminent, and the hopelessness of my situation has become apparent.

My surroundings shift again. Now I am standing just outside the room of horrors. Looking about, I notice the infrastructure of a city. Highways, bridges, and buildings surround me, but they are long deserted. I appear to be the only inhabitant at present. Nevertheless, I feel the urge to move away from the carnage that has just occurred. I see a modern city in the far distant horizon and know it to be the only place of refuge. Between myself and my destination, however, are countless slum cities. Amazement surfaces, for it seems that I must travel through entire countries to reach my home. The immediate route I must take is a river that flows just in front of me. I hesitate when I see that the river is filled with innumerable body parts. Heads, legs, arms, torsos, and organs all rest at the bottom of the river. Pausing for only a moment, I suck in as much air as possible and steel myself for the journey ahead. I wade into the river, and float on the surface as best as possible in order to avoid the dismembered bodies, allowing the current to carry me downstream. As careful as I am, still the occasional body part brushes against me. I shudder in disgust.

When I reach the end of the river, I pull myself up onto an abandoned street. As soon as I stand erect, I notice an approaching band of tribal men, all naked from the waist up and carrying primitive bows and arrows. Surrounded, I watch as they get closer to me and yell at me to stand still. Their leader steps up to me and informs me that they will quickly make the decision whether to kill me or allow me to join their band. After much shouting, I am relieved to be handed their weapon of choice and told to follow them. Our band invades a neighboring tribe's city with the intent to raid their supplies. I am instructed to follow just behind the chieftain. We quickly subdue the inhabitants, whose clumsy stone axes are no match for our arrows. We enter a primitive structure that holds our rivals' supply of food and weapons. As our chieftain gathers the spoils of the raid and passes them on to others in our band for inspection, I roam. Surprising me, a camera rises from the floor and scans the entire room. Feeling that we are being watched, I pick up an abandoned stone axe and casually destroy the camera. A gang of uniformed men appear from underground. Because the uniformed men are holding rifles, our entire tribe ceases activity and drops our weapons. Defeated, we sulk off and leave behind the spoils of the raid. Because the tribe has been humbled, I feel free to take my leave and continue on my journey.

Walking through vast and countless slum cities, I begin to lose track of time and distance. I feel certain that I have been walking for a number of days, but the only thought I have is disbelief at how poorly and primitively the people are living. Recognizing that the majority of people live here rather than in the city, I feel both saddened by their plight and heartened by their ingenuity. Each slum I walk through has its own culture and unique innovation. Inspecting each society's ability to make do with whatever resources it happens to have, I soon notice that I am approaching my destination.

A young, dark-skinned girl, perhaps four or five years old, approaches me. She is extremely confident and well-spoken. She asks if I met the vampires, and I reply that I most certainly did.

"Yes," she states, "they are real."

Just as I am about to inquire about what they are and their meaning, a woman stands up and, with great fear, speaks to me. "Her mother is a famous and very powerful prostitute. She will be very unhappy if she finds you speaking with her daughter."

I gaze at the young girl, who is smiling back at me, and then I decide to heed the woman's advice. The young girl and I say our goodbyes, and I resume my walk.

Because the slums were on a lower level, I now climb a long staircase. When I reach the top of the staircase, I stand at a locked gate. Guards on the other side question me and inspect my clothing. Apparently satisfied, they allow me enter the city, which is bathed in glorious sunlight. Clean streets, electric power, and fresh air rush to greet me. Despite the change in surroundings, my attention is focused solely on how I never knew so much existed just beyond our normal world and how none of us is aware of the vast realms, poverty, and diversity that exist just beyond our borders.

Dear Steve,

Navatri Blessings and Greetings.

The dream is vivid and beautiful in all its moments. Yes, Navatri, as you know, is about the Divine Mother and all her many faces. The nine nights of Navatri are devoted to invoking, worshipping, and admiring every aspect of the Goddess in all Her forms. By doing so, we allow ourselves to accept, and we involve ourselves in understanding that the Goddess manifests in many, many forms, most of which we normally would not expect to encounter.

Your dream is an ideal representation of this. The entire journey you traveled depicts various encounters with the Divine Feminine.

The childlike, the beautiful yet hidden darkness, the pure darkness, the demonic, the wise, the kind, etc. All are forms of the Divine Mother.

The Goddess does not manifest only as light, brightness, or purity. She is also the dark, the demonic, and the lowly form, such as the prostitute. If you recount your dream to yourself again, you may see it in a new light.

This is the journey of Navatri that occurs in both the world and the microcosm—the journey into the unconscious or hidden realms, what we are unaware of (poverty), and the conscious journey through it with the guidance of Higher force, Sakthi, the Goddess.

Surely your personal journey flowering is gracious to see.

Thank you for sharing this. Today is the last day of Navatri, victorious day, Vijaydasami, as the Goddess destroyed the evil. BLESSINGS AND GREETINGS TO YOU.

ARUNACHALA SIVA,
Pal
HOLY HILL

All of this, both "good" and "evil," is the Mother, the Goddess. As the cosmic substance, She has given rise to all creation both light and dark, auspicious and inauspicious. These are the attributes assigned to the dynamic aspect of the divine. Yet just like a mother does, She loves all of her children. Throughout history, humanity has been rather obsessed with trying to separate ourselves from what we do not like and chase what we think is good or worthy. We usually do so in a compulsive way, which in turn leads to endless conflicts on both a personal and planetary scale. However, the spiritual journey is one of integration. In tantra, integration is achieved by drawing out of the human psyche all of the unconscious patterns, splits, repressions, and fears that lie dormant there. The most primal of all splits is the acceptance of one gender and the rejection of the other gender within our consciousness. Their reconciliation and eventual union, or marriage, is a necessary and vital step in the journey. In the dream, She led me through encounters with Her varying forms to shake up preconceived notions of good and evil. The encounters forced me to confront ingrained ideas of avoiding some things and seeking other things. They taught me the lesson that all such ways of interacting with life must be left behind. When the time came that I could return to India, I took with me the deepening tantric experiences and all that I had learned from the Amritha Kalai healing sessions. I was eager and hopeful that Pal would find me fit to go deeper into both tantra and Amritha Kalai.

CHAPTER 12

Vasi: The Unique Path of the Siddhas

When I arrived in India for my next visit, I had some idea, for the first time ever, of what might occur and what Pal might reveal in greater detail. However, my assumptions were only partially correct. Pal has never ceased to exceed my expectations. The depths of Siddha wisdom stretch far beyond the mind's ability to conjure or conceptualize. Yet, the most basic tenet of the Siddhas is one that Healer Pal embodies most powerfully: compassion. This is no secret. He himself has stated that the reason he wrote a book on the Siddhas and has continued his healing mission is his witnessing of many young children suffering intractable diseases and injuries. I had first read his book years earlier, and then one afternoon, while we were sitting together in Dwarka Mayi, Pal spoke to me about such a case.

"There was a nine-year-old boy, a brilliant student, first in his class. One night, only a month and a half earlier, while he was sleeping, the fan, which had a loose bolt, fell and hit him on the head. The boy suffered a skull fracture and bleeding from the nose and ear. He was quickly taken to the hospital. They repaired the fracture and stopped the bleeding. However, he was left with paralysis on one side of his mouth, and his right eye he could not close at all.

"Hearing of us, they brought the boy to Dwarka Mayi. I applied a few Varma points and then had Amrita do an energy healing session. But he would not close his eyes. He does not like to since the accident, his mother said, and he will not sleep at night. His subconscious mind still registered that anything can happen, and the thought 'Why did I not move or block it from hitting me?' still rested in his unconscious mind.

"Slowly, with his mother's help, we managed to get him to lie down, relax, and eventually to close his eyes and fall asleep. While in this state during the session, he unconsciously jerked both of his arms in front of his face and then began to cry softly, all while in the unconscious state. A release! When he awoke, he was capable of easily closing his right eye three-quarters of the way. They will continue coming for more treatments."

"'Sir,' I asked, 'would not many things have been layered on top of this one event that lies dormant in the boy's subconscious?"

"Yes, indeed. In the future, even if a loving woman comes to him and wants to soothe him, he will refuse her. Anyone coming to him to help him relax and flow, he will reject them. Even after many years, when I consider no longer giving sessions, these are the types of reasons *that compel me to continue healing. Here was this brilliant, sweet boy whose life was a beautiful example to others, and then he became too shy to speak to anyone. They made fun of him. He could not speak clearly, could not do simple things like sleep. He saw himself as awkward and just nine years old. What is a person going to do with their time on this earth with such things as this around us? This is such a powerful sword that we have. We can really help people. When I work with such people, I have never considered it as a task. I am thankful to Them [the Siddha masters] who have shared this.'"*

For several reasons, I have relayed this conversation exactly as it occurred. The first is the simple way in which Pal relates with others. He is never prone to use spiritual jargon, and his effortless humility and love for humanity exudes from his presence much like the gently flowing smoke that rises from a burning incense stick. Indeed, Dwarka Mayi is a haven for the weak, sick, and suffering and is suffused with the palpable vibration of healing grace. When I am fortunate enough to visit India, the time that I spend with him in Dwarka Mayi gives me the greatest joy, bathing my soul in the golden sea of the grandest love and wisdom.

Second, the boy's situation beautifully encapsulates much of what has been expounded in the earlier chapters of this book and thus succinctly ties them together. All of us suffer innumerable types of internal and external traumas. These traumas alter our life flow, and these wounds rest in the unconscious realms. One after the other and layer upon layer, impressions gather in the warehouse of the unseen. From there, they alter our life experience. In the boy's case, we can see how a physical blow would have long-lasting physical and psychological ramifications. As he progressed through his life, his inability to accept love and compassion would have forever stunted his emotional growth. His entire intent for being born, his life's purpose, had been altered. Our modern medicinal practices certainly have their place, especially in treating physical trauma. In his case, they may have saved his life following the accident. However, the impact of the fan created more than just an injury to his physical body. In order for him to regain well-being, more than just the physical needed to be taken into account, simply because we are more than physical entities. After the wound had been tended, he was left with scars, both physical and emotional. The trauma would live in his subconscious and affect him for his entire life unless it was addressed in a way that would enable it to be released. It is in these unseen dimensions that life's events accumulate, stagnate, and then influence us in ways that do not serve us well. In order to be truly healthy, or whole, we require our entire being to be healed. The restoration of the body, mind, and spirit to their original intent provides balance and grounding in our primal constitution. With such restoration, we are released and thus free to fulfill the intention of our unique life's expression, all in

Vasi: The Unique Path of the Siddhas

harmony with the greater design, flowing with Nature and Her boundless beauty. *This is Siddha Varma healing.*

After Pal had related to me the story of the young boy, we sat together in silence for some time. Only a few days earlier, he had initiated me into the final, or highest, level of Amritha Kalai healing.

"There will be no more classes or instruction now," he told me. "You please follow your healing spirit, and someday in the future, your own lineage can come forth."

Unable to find suitable words, I placed my hands in Namaste and simply thanked him. I reflected on all of the years that had passed before and the countless hours I had spent learning and practicing at his healing center. The road had been very long: Systemic Vital Point Therapy, pulse diagnosis, Adangal, dasa vayu, and all of the various energies and forces, especially Vasi. I spent years of practicing energy healing techniques that I did not include in the earlier chapters of this book. And just a few days earlier, I had been initiated into the final level of Amritha Kalai and the several dimensions that lie within it. From the very first year, I never asked Pal if there were other levels of Siddha healing. I simply arrived in India each year happy to receive whatever Pal was willing to give me. Maybe that seems odd to others, but for me it was just natural. Our time together also included spiritual initiations and physical cleansing. Over time, he also revealed to me many of the esoteric arts of the ancient

Siddhas. During this very trip, Pal had spoken to me more clearly and in greater detail about tantra, alchemy, and Vasi yogam, the yoga of the Siddha masters.

Vasi Yogam

> *If one keenly observes the place and the exact moment at which the prana is consumed by the apana, he does not grieve.*

(Yoga Vasistha, In Sage Valmiki, *The Supreme Yoga*, trans. Swami Venkatesananda [Delhi: Chitern Yoga Trust, 2003])

Although Vasi plays a particular role in Siddha healing, the Siddha masters learned of its secrets long ago in their search for spiritual perfection. This seemed a bit confusing to me when Pal first told me, so I asked him, "Sir, Vasi is used in the higher dimensions of Siddha healing, but I don't understand how it is also a yoga. How did the Siddhas learn of its different uses?"

"The Siddhas were jnanis, perfected masters who had come to know all the workings of creation. Many lived in solitude in remote caves. And the ones who lived in society, as farmers, merchants, and so forth, would not reveal themselves. They did not need anything, for They had already attained the All. But through Their yoga, They came to know all the secrets of the cosmos and how it exists in miniature form in the human body. It is from this understanding that They came to know how to heal all diseases and restore true health and well-being. Out of compassion for humanity, They encoded these secrets to share with the people. This is Their gift to the world. This is what Siddha healing really is. But the masters used Vasi yoga to attain enlightenment, so this is how They came to learn of all the dimensions of Vasi. This is the true Siddha yoga."

The deepest aspects of Siddha Varma healing, internal alchemy, and spiritual realization all rest upon the divine interplay of Vasi, so Pal reserved it until I had matured. Paradoxically, it is the most basic and essential of all in the physical dimension. Yet its birth and origin lie in the Beyond. In our ordinary approaches to life and learning, we are accustomed to starting with the basics and then moving on to the complex. From this approach, the mind is conditioned to revel in complexity and revile the simple as inessential, crude, and primitive. Unfortunately, the mind has no access to and is utterly useless in the far lands of the spirit and its liberation. In divine apprenticeship, all notions of complexity, learning, and ordinary understanding must become prey to the tiger of wisdom. Indeed, when he initiated me into Vasi yogam (*yoga* in Sanskrit), Pal cautioned me to tread carefully even though it appears to be an exceedingly basic practice.

"Never let yourself think of it as a simple practice," he advised, "for the obvious is the most elusive."

The Fountainhead

For several years I had been practicing what Pal calls *Vasi induction*, which I later learned are techniques, of which there are several levels, to prepare one for Vasi yoga.

"But how does this whole process differ from what I have learned about Vasi when doing healing work, Sir?" I asked.

"Of course, you know that the energy we take from outside is of an acquired (temporal) nature, whether through breathing, eating, or drinking. What is important to understand is that this need to take energy from outside ourselves occurs only because we have first spent our inner and primal nature by externalizing with the outside world, so we have to replenish it. This process begins when we are born and is necessary in order to relate with the world. But now you also know that this same process depletes our life force, Vasi. While the baby is in the womb, it is the umbilical connection with the mother that provides all nourishment. The mother and baby breathe in rhythm through this connection. In this mono-receptive state, the baby carries its own karmic seeds yet without emotions, desires, or intellect. This is because there is no need for acquired energy. While growing within our mother, it is Vasi which sustains life. The flow of life force is not spent identifying with the outside world. This is signified by the fact that the baby's life force flows from the navel down to the base of the body, the perineum, up the spine, and then rests at the crown of the skull. Not being required to relate to the external world means that our life force does not need to be expressed via the frontal path and dissipated through the face."

"Oh, yes. I see. So this is what changes the flow from the back to the front, once we are born," I said.

"Yes," Pal replied. "Upon birth, the baby experiences its first contact with air and starts to breathe. *This first breath is our first acquired energy.* This first breath then mingles with the original, or primordial, pulsation, which has been enlivening the infant throughout its womb state. The cutting of the umbilical cord, coupled with the baby's act of crying, forces the energetic flow that previously snaked up the spine to reverse its flow. Once the cord is cut, the energy now spurts upward from the belly button through the front of the body and out of the face. The infant's externalization, a requirement in order to relate with the world, has begun. Over time, the child will become spatially oriented to the world by its senses of seeing, hearing, tasting, and so forth. As the baby grows, acquired temporal conditioning also takes place. Conversely, the Vasi gradually wanes. This is when the primal pulse of Vasi releases from itself the ten vital forces or airs, the dasa vayu."

"Only then do the ten vital forces, the dasa vayu, come, Sir?"

"That's correct. They separate from the Vasi so they can empower all the energies necessary for movement and interaction with the environment. Each force takes on a specific function. This is known as *kalai*, or *kala* in Sanskrit. The force known as kundalini provides the movement of each of the ten vital forces. They travel their respective routes in the body via subtle channels called nadis, of which 72,000 exist."

In addition to the forces for living being released from the womb of Vasi, the directional change of energy from the back of the body to the front of the body is another notable occurrence during birth. In Siddha tradition, the back channel is called the solar channel (*Surya kalai*), the path of the sun, and the front channel is called the lunar channel (*Chandra kalai*), the path of the moon. While resting in the womb of its mother, the baby has no need to identify with anything of the external world. The fragmentation of consciousness occurs only upon the spurting of the energy upward and out into the world. Just as the cosmic moon receives its light from the sun, this temporal condition, or limited consciousness, is what makes a person's identity fragmented rather than integrated. The sun of unified consciousness has been left behind for an exclusive approach—a fragmented, lunar approach—to interacting with the external world. The victorious reversal of this flow leads one to authentic spiritual enlightenment.

> *My mother groan'd! my father wept.*
> *Into the dangerous world I leapt:*
> *Helpless, naked, piping loud:*
> *Like a fiend hid in a cloud.*
>
> *Struggling in my father's hands,*
> *Striving against my swaddling bands,*
> *Bound and weary I thought best*
> *To sulk upon my mother's breast.*

(William Blake, *The Essential Blake*, selected by Stanley Kunitz [New York: HarperCollins, 1987])

BROKEN IDENTITY

When we leap into the world from the womb, our fragmented, limited, and non-integrated consciousness appears as a spectrum of colors. We have left the primordial intent, which is the pure subjective aspect or individuality. In the Siddha system, the sun is the symbol of this pure subjectivity. Through our breath and mental gymnastics, we slowly but surely dissipate our divinely inspired life force.

The inward breath draws twelve units, eight used to sustain the body and four returning to the reservoir of Vasi. Then, upon expiration, a minimum of four units of breath is released. Yet even while inactive, we have used sixteen units—four more than we are ever capable of taking in. This demand is placed upon us by the habitual nature of our externalization of consciousness. In turn, we rely solely upon what we can take in from the external world just to maintain this insidious depletion of life, which is born from our notions of fragmentation. Unknown to us, however, the sun of singular consciousness and the moon in her fullness lie hidden within us. Until we take up the quest, we are doomed to continue living in the ordinary, common mode of everyone else. We are stuck in the middle, not knowing our true Source. We exist in the twilight of humanity, that period between sun and moon and between moon and sun.

Reverberation

"The practices of Vasi induction and Vasi yoga are, of course, secret. So how do I explain them in the book, Sir?" I asked Pal.

"Yes, like all our dimensions, they are only for the initiated. But you can speak about how they have been mentioned in the songs of all the eighteen Siddhas and today flourish only through the present-day lineage of wandering Siddhas and those living in the caves of remote mountains. Vasi yoga is not a form of pranayama. While it does speak of the dimensions of breath, its true aim is recognition of the subtle perception. It is the pulsations hidden within one's breath. It is also not to be confused with the kriya yoga of Yogananada, for that path is based upon forcible breathing techniques. Nor is it to be confused with what is called the Siddha yoga of Muktanada, for what he called Siddha yoga is nothing but the Kashmir Saivite philosophy and its dimension of *Shaktipat*. The Tamil Siddhas declare that all external methods of breath control are to be left behind, because they are of limited value. Vasi yoga is the art of attuning oneself to the respiration that occurs *internally*. Over time, the Vasi yogi will show no signs of external breathing. Although the slowing and, at times, cessation of breath can occur with various forms of pranayama or meditation, the practice of Vasi yoga is a vastly different path. Vasi yoga is the swiftest and surest sadhana for achieving spiritual realization. Its secondary benefits are to instill vigor and youthfulness. Requiring tremendous determination and patience, what actually occurs is the return of the ten vital forces back to their womb, their origin of Vasi. The result is the return of the immaculate life force to its pre-birth fullness and the pulsation of primal wisdom. It is the eventual goal of radical, complete enlightenment. This is the aim of Vasi yoga. To this end, one must remove the 'three coverings' of the three Gunas, six tastes, and five Bhutas."

Transcending the three coverings which bind the individual to the physical mortal dimension places the individual beyond the limits of the physical universe and in the realm of the Siddha Masters. By doing so, one is freed from all constraints of past and future and all forms of causation. Pal speaks directly about the supreme nature of Vasi yoga, the eventual goal of all forms of yoga known to humanity, in his book, *Siddhas: Masters of the Basics*:

> *Vasi yoga is the most supreme science of spiritual alchemy, having as its goal nothing short of total liberation from all karmic encumbrances[7] of material existence. Vasi yoga is the system of attaining the "Immortal body." This alchemical path transforms temporal mundane existence into spiritual and immortal being. The practice demands high discipline, fierce determination, but most imperative is a genuine initiation from the Master, which is not easy to come by these days.*

I am aware of the rarity of such masters, because Pal once related to me the search that he undertook, in his youth, for such a One. His determined spirit to find a master willing to initiate him into Vasi yoga eventually came to fruition but not before a long, exhaustive quest. This mystery-shrouded yoga begins with the reversal of the moon, bringing it in conjunction with its sun. Unlike any manner of pranayama, Vasi cannot be said to be any form of breath control or regulation, for hidden within one's breathing is a pulsation. Hidden within one's form is that which gives life and

---

[7] Karma is often misunderstood as something to be acquired (good karma) and avoided (bad karma). However, enlightenment is the complete transcendence of all duality and causation; thus all notions of karma are permanently dissolved, as both good and bad karma are equally binding.

sustains existence. The conversion of one's personality to one's individuality is called "joining the moon with one's sun," as Pal has stated. This conversion happens in Vasi yoga by an initiation of the marriage, or communion, of the moon and the sun.

The word *aspiration* is defined as "a strong desire to achieve something high or great."[8] This is an outcome of the pure intent of Vasi yoga. This intent reaches its culmination and transforms into pure aspiration, called *fire* by the Siddhas. At that point, the moon has communed with her source of light. The yogi is within the Fire that eternally burns inside the sun. This entire journey takes place on the posterior side of the practitioner's body, for there lies the *agni nadi*, the fire channel. The Fire is set ablaze, is fueled by the inner prana, and grows in a process that is called Rivering the Fire, or *Neruparu* in Siddha terminology. As the intense aspiration moves up the back side of the practitioner's body, it seeks the cooling aspect in the region of the head. There lies the moon in her fullness, inviting the return of her sun. The criterion for the communion of sun and moon is the opening of the *suzhi munai* in the forehead. That opening is followed by the descent of the moon along her path, which is the reversal of the route following during birth. This is another meaning of the words "If you want to be reborn, first you must die," which Pal spoke to me during the time in the Kalpa house.

---

[8] *Merriam-Webster's Collegiate Dictionary*, 11th ed., s.v. "aspiration"

The marriage, or communion, that occurs crystallizes the individuality in the practitioner's head region. Following the arrival of the sun's fire, this individuality begins to melt and drip the nectar called Amritha. The dripping of Amritha is the primordial state falling from the skull via the *Amritha nadi*, or Nectar channel, of the practitioner. Finally, this Nectar of the gods seeks to rest in the right side of the practitioner's chest, the location known as the spiritual heart. This process is internal alchemy.

Metaphorically, the Siddhas refer to this process as *Kaal Thalai Maruthal*. Literally translated, this name means "opening the head as two and reversing the leg as one's head and the head as one's leg." The merging in the spiritual heart, on the right side of the chest, is called *Thakara Vidya*. A practitioner in whom this merging has occurred has reached the highest state of spiritual enlightenment, known as *Jivan Mukti*, or liberation while still in the body. It is the state of sahaja samadhi and is the most extremely rare state, beyond even the state of Turiya, the transcendental state.

> *That in whom reside all beings and who resides in all beings, who is the giver of grace to all, the Supreme soul of the universe, the limitless being—"I am That."*
>
> ("Amritbindu Upanishad," In Pal Pandian, *Siddhas: Masters of the Basics* [Chennai, India: Pal Pandian, 2008])

The Mother of Vital Forces

Life spurts first as body consciousness and subsequently as world consciousness. We relate to the world by the releasing and separation of the dasa vayu. Vasi is the mother of these vital forces. Therefore, the primordial pulsation of Vasi and its yoga hold the key that unlocks the door to immortality. Having attached our consciousness to the world and its endlessly whirling dramas, we forget about our primordial energy. We come to depend upon the temporal for our survival. Steeped in illusion, we repeat our days and nights in a compulsive search—this restless, mechanical searching that we have come to call life.

Yet we can achieve that which we incessantly crave only by the reversal of the very path we have already traveled. The Siddhas used symbolic language to describe Their journey in order to maintain its purity. Kept exclusively within Their lineage, Vasi yoga remains the most potent and sure path to liberation.

> *Never let yourself think of it as a simple practice, for the obvious is the most elusive.*
> —Pal Pandian

Those words, conveyed to me by Pal upon my initiation into Vasi yoga, sum up the divine gifts of the ancient Siddhas.

Over the years, I have discovered that any attempt to explain even the basic tenets—whether of Siddha Varma healing, tantra, or Vasi yoga—encounter a startling barrier: simplicity. Invariably, the ones I have conversed with end up simply staring blankly back at me as if I have just uttered nonsensical words of an alien language. I am sworn to secrecy, but if I were to explain the initial step of Vasi yoga, its shocking simple, direct method probably would be laughed at by others. Of course, it is impotent unless the practitioner is initiated by a Siddha master. Only through initiation are the wisdom, power, and blessing of the lineage bestowed.

The utter simplicity of Vasi yoga is reflective of Truth, which stands as its own support, needing no confirmation or explanation from outside Itself. Reflecting our essential nature by pointing directly to the primal state of being transcends all notions of the duality of existence and nonexistence. Complexity has no place here. Intricacy and all of its accumulated weight of never-ending theories, doubts, and viewpoints evaporate in a direct confrontation with the rising sun of the experience of our most essential nature. Devoid of complexity, the Siddhas' wisdom is the perfect mirror of Their humble abidance in the primordial and ever-present, most natural state. Thus, the following is said:

> *When a superior man hears of the Tao,*
> *he immediately begins to embody it.*
> *When an average man hears of the Tao,*
> *he half believes it, half doubts it.*
> *When a foolish man hears of the Tao,*
> *he laughs out loud.*
> *If he didn't laugh,*
> *it wouldn't be the Tao.*

(Lao Tzu, *Tao Te Ching*, trans. Stephen Mitchell [London: Frances Lincoln, 1999])

CHAPTER 13

The Water of Life

Uttering for success in Pranayama
Consume first the Elixir of Lord Siva.
If you practice Pranayama ignoring the Elixir Kalpa,
Be it even until the world ceases to be,
Oh! Your life will escape from you,
You will fail.

(Siddha Agasthiyar, "Antha Ranga Disksha Vidhi,"
Verse 351, In Pal Pandian, *Siddhas: Masters of the Basics*
[Chennai, India: Pal Pandian, 2008])

Primal Matter

Long before modern science, the defining of chemical agents, the periodic table, and what we today call chemistry, ancient civilizations pursued the secrets of nature in a more inclusive, holistic way. The tradition of alchemy is perhaps the most well-known yet misunderstood ancient science. With its objectives of transmuting base metals into gold, finding the fabled *philosopher's stone*, and developing an *elixir of life* that would give youth and immortality seems more like a Hollywood movie than any form of science. Over time, alchemy was essentially outlawed due to religious fears, scientific skepticism, and its lack of pragmatic results. I had only heard of it faintly and thought it was confined to the attempts to create gold. That goal seemed not only an unworthy goal but impossible to achieve; therefore, I, like most people, just assumed that alchemy was nothing more than superstition and greed from the Dark Ages. However, treading the path of the ancient Tamil Siddhas through the secretive, mysterious, and strangely shocking South Indian culture has given me an entirely different understanding of such prejudices.

Throughout history, alchemists' prime search has been the fabled philosopher's stone, long considered a substance that bestows rejuvenation and possibly immortality. It has also been thought to bring spiritual enlightenment as the conclusion of the Great Work. Although commonly understood to simply be the transformation of iron, bronze, brass, and copper into gold, there is an esoteric meaning of the alchemy. Its true aim is the transmutation of the individual's limited human consciousness into the "gold" of enlightenment. Another meaning is the transmutation of the "base metal" of the body into the "gold" of immortality. This transmutation is accomplished by inducing Amritha, the elixir of life, to flow within oneself. Thus, it is a form of external alchemy, because it consists of taking external substances into oneself. Internal alchemy includes the yogic practices that induce the Amritha to first drip and then flow within, leading to enlightenment. The external forms of alchemy hold great attraction in the belief that they speed up the practitioner's spiritual efforts.

> *The Alchemical operation consisted essentially in separating the prima materia, the so-called chaos, into the active principle, the soul, and the passive principle, the body, which were then reunited in the personified form in the conjunction or "chemical marriage" . . . the ritual cohabitation of Sol [sun/masculine] and Luna [moon/feminine].*
>
> (Carl Jung, *Mysterium Conjunctionis,* Vol. 14 of *Collected Works of C.G. Jung,* ed. and trans. Gerhard Adler and R.F.C. Hull [Princeton, NJ: Princeton University Press, 1970])

In Western alchemy, the philosopher's stone has been known by various names, including the *white stone by the river*, the *Holy Grail*, the *Bread of Life*, the *Fountain of Youth*, *Manna from Heaven*, the *sword in the stone*, and the content of the *Ark of the Covenant*. Most often, it has been referred to as *prima materia*, or first matter.

Rivulets of the Absolute

Alchemy and its search for the philosopher's stone was common to all cultures, whether ancient Egyptian, Greek, Arabic, or European. Included among the ranks of alchemists were Robert Boyle, the founder of modern chemistry, and Isaac Newton, the father of modern physics. The foundation of alchemy was that, through some mysterious working with the philosopher's stone, a water or elixir could be derived. This *water of life* is referenced in the religions of Islam, Judaism, and Christianity.

> *But whoever drinks the water I give them will never thirst. Indeed, the water I give them will become in them a spring of water welling up into eternal life.*
>
> —Jesus Christ (John 4:14 [New International Version])

Long before Western cultures began their legendary searches for immortality and enlightenment from the primal substance of creation, the Siddhas of South India had both perfected and guarded these secrets. That alchemy has been kept secret by the Siddhas is the overriding reason for the West's search being almost completely unsuccessful. Some of the most essential components needed in order to identify and transmute the philosopher's stone stretch far beyond secrecy. Only by the unmistakable blessing of the divine is one allowed to enter such sacred halls of wisdom. The great Rasa Siddhas, who are alchemical Masters, have always considered the transmutation of metals into gold as mere child's play. That transmutation is only the beginning of one's training. The true aim of Siddha alchemy is the elongation of life span and the raising of one's consciousness. The extension of healthy living is useful in enabling one to work out all of his or her remaining karmic debts and avoid enduring rebirth again and again.

> *Whoever has ears, let them hear what*
> *the Spirit says to the churches.*
> *To the one who is victorious,*
> *I will give some of the hidden manna.*
> *I will also give that person a white stone with a new name*
> *written on it, known only to the one who receives it.*

(Revelations 2:17 [New International Version])

Called *Andakkal* by the Siddhas, the philosopher's stone and its resultant distilled elixir have also been referred to as *Amritha Kalasam* (the vase of ambrosia), *Pranava Peetam* (the altar of the primal nine), and the *un-deletable bowl*. The preparation that allows one to attain *Vaan Porul*, or heavenly bliss, through perfection in yoga, results in union with the divine. This philosopher's stone is seeded by nature and is the residue of the primal creative energy. It is the Primal Creator, the causative substance for all other substances to be created. The Siddhas also use the word *Andam* to describe the philosopher's stone, because one meaning of the word is Universe, which implies all of existence. Andam is none other than the Primordial matter itself in its *as is* state and is known by Them to have descended to Earth.[9] Siddha Agasthiyar mentioned this in his cryptic twilight verses:

> *Siva, immersed in Samadhi, lies buried under the earth.*

(Pal Pandian, *Siddhas: Masters of the Basics* [Chennai, India: Pal Pandian, 2008])

THE ESSENCE OF ETERNITY

The Siddha art of Kaya Kalpa has already been mentioned in this book, and its purpose is usually described as rejuvenating the body, preventing disease, and increasing longevity. Unique within the Siddha clan is the understanding that a body free of disease helps the mind to be clear and calm. In turn, a clear, calm mind greatly aids the aspirant in diving deeply into spiritual practices and so produces stronger and quicker results. Although the Ayurvedic system has its own method, called *rasyana*, it is in no way similar to the Siddhas' Kaya Kalpa. Rasyana consists mainly of a purification process. The entirety of rasyana is contained in the first step of Kaya Kalpa, whose later steps include a powerful path for restoring and maintaining physical youth for extremely long periods—at times even granting immortality. Having unlocked the secrets of the philosopher's stone in ancient

---

[9] The scientists at the European Organization for Nuclear Research (CERN) who search for the God particle are perhaps looking in the wrong direction.

times, the Siddhas have used its distilled elixir, or water of life, for this culmination of Kaya Kalpa. Extremely potent medicines can also be derived from the components that result from the alchemical process of the elixir, and so the elixir also is called *Muppu* (universal medicine or elixir).

Even within the Siddha clan, Kaya Kalpa being taken to this extreme level of attainment is a very rare occurrence, because in doing so the practitioner must rely solely on divine instructions. One must cross enormous barriers and overcome challenges at every step along the way. Without the precise knowledge and blessings, the journey leads to death rather than longevity. Extreme rules of conduct, diet, and lifestyle also are necessary. Without such comprehensive knowledge and divine guidance, there is no chance of success. This is a prime reason that alchemy failed, almost without exception, in the Western cultures.

Another reason that success eluded those outside the Siddha clan is that the elixir is only half of the process. Because this water of life is taken from outside one's self, it is external alchemy. In order to achieve the goal, one also must be deeply involved in internal alchemy. These internal methods are esoteric practices that prepare the body, mind, and spirit to accept the radical changes that are to occur. Without this preparation and the resulting high state of consciousness, there is no hope of alchemical transformation even with the elixir.

I had read about the philosopher's stone in Pal's book *Siddhas: Masters of the Basics* and had long wanted to question him about it. What I most wanted to know is whether he himself was in possession of such a thing. My timidity at broaching the subject lay in the fact that it all just seemed too impossible to believe. Even if such a stone did exist and Pal had found it, I doubted that he would ever reveal such a thing to anyone. Although he had inducted me into Kaya Kalpa with the aim of preventing diseases and increasing longevity, I remained in the very early stages of purification. This was due to the continued necessity of my working in a corporate environment. By maintaining a lifestyle that demanded an analytical approach, the rejuvenation of my body was being postponed.

A Golden Glimpse

One day, despite my reservations and without any questioning on my part, Pal surprised me by beckoning me into a private room. He withdrew a small vial from a pouch and then emptied its yellow liquid into a small metal bowl. Immediately, the strangest scent filled the room. Horse urine? Garlic and leather smashed together? I had no idea what this smell was, but one thing was perfectly clear: I recognized it. Smells instantly recall complete memories. Such a memory invaded my consciousness. It was familiar, but I could not, try as I might, place it.

When I said as much to him, he laughed and replied, "Yes. Everyone will know this smell. It is basic to each and every one. This is because it is the primal matter."

Stunned, I just stared back at him. I knew what I was looking at, but I couldn't grasp its enormity. He further indulged me by allowing me to ask any questions I wished.

Periya Swami, a great Rasa Siddha, introduced Pal to alchemy. Having wandered all over the world to unlock the secrets of the philosopher's stone, Periya Swami eventually returned to India. It was then that his exhaustive search bore fruit. In truth, finding the fabled stone is a monumental task in itself. Even an enlightened Sage is not capable of identifying the stone unless the divine grace wills them to do so. Containing both demonic poison and the ambrosia that bestows eternal life, the elixir rests in a sacred container called Amritha Kalasam, which can be translated as the bowl of Nectar or the vase of ambrosia. Having many questions about the elixir in front of me, I first asked Pal how it is used by Siddhas to attain immortality.

"Being in contact with Western alchemists, I have found several things they are doing there," he revealed. "Actually, the laboratory alchemists seem to be more correct in their search, whereas the spiritual alchemists tend to be distracted. They both speak highly of Paracelsus, but I am not sure that he had knowledge of internal alchemy. He may not have achieved the enlightened, immortal state. We cannot be sure. However, there were great Sufi saints of the Muslim world, like Al-Razi and Jabirb Hayyan, who knew the internal secrets, as they were Sages."

"What are these internal alchemical methods, Sir, and why are they so vital?" I asked.

"First, there is a vast code of restrictions. It is not easy to use the memory of the body to create new cells in this way. All the Vasi is binding to create new life. This takes a very long time.

"There are ten deaths that one must go through," he continued, the "*dasa diskshas*. All the Siddhas who followed this speak of the extreme struggles involved—it is the worst period one can imagine. Leprosy and so many other diseases must come while one lives underground beneath a temple and bathes with only the water that drips down. The austerities that must be practiced are many, and these ten deaths that must be experienced are no small matter."

Pressing on, I asked him about the internal practices.

"Internally, you must do yoga and must not interfere with Nature's Dharma for you. If you try to change it, it will betray you. This is why those who have been blessed with the path of finding the philosopher's stone rarely take the elixir."

In other words, it seems that, rarely, one may be given the grace to produce the elixir; being given the blessing to imbibe the elixir is even rarer. Imbibing the elixir without having received a divine signal would result in death. This potency, the necessity for divine instructions, and the extremely complicated internal esoteric work are the reasons that the Siddhas have reserved this knowledge for those of the highest consciousness. Sharing these secrets without such reservations would be disastrous.

> *You will not fall in death,*
> *No shadow of you,*
> *Nor shadow against lamps light,*
> *Nor shadow mirrored on still waters,*
> *If these quantum qualities emerge in one's form,*
> *The body's externalized covering peel off one by one—*
> *You radiate like the golden sun himself.*

(Siddha Sundaranandar, "Siva Yoga Gnana," Verse 31, In Pal Pandian, *Siddhas: Masters of the Basics* [Chennai, India: Pal Pandian, 2008])

The secrecy and cryptic language of the Siddhas has been repeatedly spoken of in this book, and the philosopher's stone is a classic example. Writing in Their twilight language, the Siddha masters ensured that only the initiated would be able to understand what they were saying about the stone. Those outside their clan who try to decipher Their language will always fail. This failure is widely known today as *Shivambu,* or self-urine therapy. When I learned of this practice, I was not only skeptical of its usefulness but also bewildered as to how anyone first came to do such a thing. Drinking one's own urine? As it turns out, those who started this practice were attempting to understand the Siddhas' writings that pertain to the elixir of life.

The Siddha masters cleverly wrote that a young girl's *amuri*, for which the common definition is "urine," is to be drunk, because it is the virgin state of primal matter, or the *Alchemical Puja of Goddess Valai*. Of course, what the masters were referring to was the distillation that gives the ambrosia, the yellow, strongly scented liquid that was sitting in front of me. It took several minutes for me to stop laughing. To this very day, based on a literal translation of Siddha writing of which they are not capable of understanding, people are drinking urine! "Only a tiger can lick another tiger." Indeed. Is it not evident from experience that when people take any religious writings literally and then attempt to act on them the results are, at best, mixed and, at worst, horribly inauspicious?

The attraction of living forever in an exalted state of enlightenment is tempered greatly by the severe austerities that one must undergo to reach that state. All of the person's unfulfilled karma comes forth in the form of disease. All of the body's dead cells, such as nails, hair, teeth, and the seven-layered bodily skin loosen. This is a heavy price to pay for metamorphosis. Thus, all habitual patterns, or cellular memories, dissolve and are replaced by the enlivening light spirit.

The Water of Life

When will the shadow of me vanish?
When will my embodied body be without its
dissipative composition?
When will a sword will pass unhindered through my body?
When will my core self engulf my body?
In that moment, as a self-generated pill, My whole being.

(Siddha Yugimuni, "Mathi Venba 100," Verse 8, In Pal Pandian, *Siddhas: Masters of the Basics* [Chennai, India: Pal Pandian, 2008])

Pal was showing me the yellow liquid from the philosopher's stone, but there is an additional substance derived from the stone, a white liquid. These yellow and white liquids are distilled according to a highly secret procedure. Furthermore, the ratio and sequence of how to imbibe these two liquids is known only by the guru. The ancient texts state that the process takes about fourteen years. During that time, the dasa diskshas, the ten deaths and the ten rejuvenations, occur. Without precise, divinely bestowed instructions, the end will always be failure in the form of horrible death.

The strong-smelling liquid that lay in front of me was none other than the *First Substance*, the prima materia or primal matter from which everyone and everything comes. When Pal first withdrew it from the pouch, he had lit incense and placed the vial of ambrosia in front of an altar. Performing a puja and worshipping this substance is only appropriate, for this substance is the *First Matter*, the elixir sought by so many for so long, and thus also God.

> *What can stabilize the body?*
> *It is the gracious Kalpam! Kalpam!*
> *If you consume that primal Kalpam,*
> *It is the fruit from the fire of meditation.*
> *Now where has death gone?*
> *It has merged into the absolute intelligence.*
> *Where has gone the I, the ego?*
> *It turned to ashes in the fire of Nandhi, the Bull of Siva.*
>
> *When it is burnt in the fire of Siva's Bull,*
> *Those poisons that make one grey and wrinkled also crumble,*
> *In the inner cosmos where breath subsides,*
> *In the now emerging flame*
> *at the verge, Suzhi Munai,*
> *If you boil your body in this flame,*
> *The habitual impurities of body burn.*
> *If those impurities are burned,*
> *You are carried to the Hall of Gnosis.*

(Siddha Ramadevar, "Siva Yogam," Verses 57–58, In Pal Pandian, *Siddhas: Masters of the Basics* [Chennai, India: Pal Pandian, 2008])

CHAPTER 14

The Bitter Truth

An obvious question has yet to be asked, much less answered, in this book. It is a question that few of us ever ask ourselves and yet a most basic one. While some people involve themselves in what we call a spiritual quest, all of us are actually searching every moment of our lives. It does not take an undue amount of observation to see that each morning upon waking we seek one thing after another: the first cup of coffee, the first meal of the day, planning for our work, family life, social life, and so on. Every moment of the day, we are looking to fulfill what we consider our needs in order to live. Even from birth we instinctively search out our mother's breast. This is the beginning of how we move through life. We are all searching. From this point of view, there is no difference whatsoever between one who seeks spiritual union, or yoga, and one who seeks material fulfillment. This leads us to a most simple and obvious question: Why do any of us seek a spiritual path? Oddly enough, the understanding of the reason for and the manner of our incessant searching lies hidden in the domain of dreams. Of course, we dream each time we sleep, leaving the physical body and inhabiting another form. Learning to become aware and conscious during this shift holds vast potential for spiritual development. Of equal importance is the fact that the daily experience of sleeping and waking occurs within the bookends of birth and death. This may seem obvious, but there lies within it an overlooked parallel of tremendous value.

"The Siddhas say that we should laugh at our experiences while awake but take our dreaming experiences seriously," Pal has told me.

That the realm of dreams holds the key to the unfolding of our subconscious I discovered only when I began to follow the path of tantra. As I traveled to various dimensions, I felt the dawn of an awareness that I had left my physical body behind and now inhabited a more subtle form, or subtle body. Thus, I gradually became more familiar with abiding in the subtle body. Each sojourn or visitation from what Pal calls *the Beyond*, the domain of the gods and goddesses, far exceeded a typical lesson. They effected the very refinements of my consciousness that the spiritual path is intended to produce. Many of them manifested themselves in the dreaming phase of the simple routine of nightly sleep.

While sleeping, each of us has the common experience of dreaming, regardless of whether we remember the dream when we wake. Because dreaming is so commonplace, the significance of the experience is usually overlooked. Nevertheless, until we stop and deeply consider the dream state, we will remain ignorant of an enormous portion of our living experience, not to mention our essential nature. Personally, I can understand why most people are disinclined to bother with such things. Dreams do not pay the bills, work our jobs, or take care of our children; therefore, they are considered useless. Phrases like "she's a dreamer" or "daydreaming his life away" are common. Not until I discovered some easily overlooked aspects of dreams did I become more curious about the dreams we have each night.

For instance, I may have eaten a wonderful, satisfying meal before going to bed. However, if I dream about being hungry, I obviously do not feel a state of fullness. What is sure, however, is that the food I ate just before bed is of no use to me in the dream state. Only dream food can satiate dream hunger. While we are asleep, the dream experiences are as real as the waking experiences, as shown by dream hunger being fulfilled only by dream food.

Let us continue with that example in which I dream about being hungry.

I walk into a dream restaurant, order, and wait for my meal to arrive. I look about and see that there are other people, tables and chairs, the street outside the restaurant, other buildings, and an entire city that I just walked through on my way here. All of these are completely real to me. For proof of the reality of the dream, we need look no further than the hunger pangs and the fact that they cannot be satisfied by anything other than the dream meal I am about to be served. Of course, I must wait for the cook to prepare the meal and the server to bring it to me, and that takes time. The city, the buildings, and the time spent waiting for the meal all prove that, in my dream state, there is both a time element and a space element.

The buildings and city all took time to be constructed and occupy space. We construct and move about in, or more accurately, are *moved* about in by compulsion, the dream worlds in order to act out various experiences. Whether we are being chased by a monster, driving a car recklessly, or enjoying a lover's embrace, each of us finds ourselves in environments in which we are forced to participate. The simple fact of the matter is that unfulfilled desires compel us to participate in both the dream world and the waking world. The desire to satisfy hunger by eating food, regardless of which state we are in at the time, is a basic example.

The vast realm of unconscious impressions forces us to act out or live out a seemingly endless variety of experiences. Waking each morning and falling asleep each evening, we inhabit worlds that we create unconsciously. Of course, the elements of time and space are different in the dream state than in the waking state. Furthermore, everyone who inhabits our dreams, everyone with whom we interact on all levels, springs forth from within our own consciousness. The environments, cities, mountains, people, and experiences that we encounter each night exist solely within us. While we interact with these, we inhabit a particular form, or body. Our dreaming state and the dream body that we inhabit are not chosen by us. We are forced, or pulled, into sleeping and dreaming each evening. Entering the dream state is in no way a choice but rather an immediate shift from identifying with the physical body to identifying with the dream body. Pal explained it to me quite clearly:

> *Ordinarily people do not go into the sleeping or dreaming states. Those states come to them and overtake them. It is like trying to go to sleep. When we try to, it does not happen. Sleep comes to us; it overtakes us against our will.*

All one need do is attempt to exert control over this process by being aware while falling asleep, losing consciousness of the physical body, and then inhabiting a dream body. Ordinary individuals do not have the ability to maintain a singular awareness while in the waking state, dream state, and deep dreamless sleep state. Such ability is solely the living experience of an enlightened Sage.

Chapter 3 of this book details the three bodies: physical body, subtle body, and causal body. During dreams, we inhabit the subtle body, or dream body. After crawling into bed each evening, we effortlessly move from the physical body to the subtle body and then have various experiences, each as real as the next. The only difference is that the waking state seems to be longer, and the dream state seems to be shorter. Many are quick to argue that the waking state is real and the dream state unreal, based on the fact that the world that we experience when we are awake has existed for a long time and existed even while we were dreaming. This interpretation is, however, based on a false assumption. While we are dreaming, we are aware of that world and no other. In that dream world, we suffer or enjoy only those experiences that exist in that world.

Considering only our waking state to be real and dismissing all other states of our living experience denies an enormous part of ourselves. This denial springs from our fragmented, nonintegrated existence. Major Chadwick (Sadhu Arunachala) was a former British Army officer who became a devotee of Bhagavan Ramana Maharshi. His doubts concerning whether only the waking state is real came from his typically scientific outlook, which he had acquired by being raised in the Western manner of confining reality to a narrow set of parameters. He had difficulty releasing his doubts about the various states of consciousness until he faced their reality directly:

"We are such stuff As dreams are made of, and our short life Is rounded by a sleep."

Shakespeare really did know what he was talking about, and it was not just poetic effervescence. Maharshi used to say exactly the same.

I suppose I questioned Bhagavan more often on this subject than any others, though some doubts always remained for me. He had always warned that, as soon as one doubt is cleared, another will spring up in its place, and there is no end to doubts.

"But Bhagavan," I would repeat, "dreams are disconnected, while the waking experience goes on from where it left off and is admitted by all to be more or less continuous."

"Do you say this in your dreams?" Bhagavan would ask. "They seemed perfectly consistent and real to you then. It is only now, in your waking state, that you question the reality of the experience. This is not logical."

However I tried to twist my questions, the answer I received was always the same: "Put your doubts when in the dream state itself. You do not question the waking state when you are awake—you accept it. You accept it in the same way you accept your dreams. Go beyond both states and all three states, including deep sleep. Study them from that point of view. You now study one limitation from the point of view of another limitation. Could anything be more absurd? Go beyond all limitation, then come here with your doubts."

But in spite of this, doubt still remained. I somehow felt at the time of dreaming there was something unreal in it, not always of course, but just glimpses now and then.

> "Doesn't that ever happen to you in your waking state, too?" Bhagavan queried. "Don't you sometimes feel that the world you live in and the thing that is happening is unreal?" Still, in spite of all this, doubt persisted.
>
> But one morning I went to Bhagavan and, much to his amusement, handed him a paper on which the following was written:
>
> "Bhagavan remembers that I expressed some doubts about the resemblance between dreams and waking experience. Early in the morning most of these doubts were cleared by the following dream, which seemed particularly objective and real: I was arguing philosophy with someone and pointed out that all experience was only subjective, that there was nothing outside the mind. The other person demurred, pointing out how solid everything was and how real the experience seemed, and it could not be just personal imagination.
>
> "I replied, 'No, it is nothing but a dream. Dream and waking experience are exactly the same.'
>
> "'You say that now,' he replied, 'but you would never say a thing like that in your dream.'
>
> "And then I woke up."
>
> (Alan Chadwick [Sadhu Arunachala], *The Call Divine*, March 1954)

We can properly and accurately question and investigate the degree of reality that we experience while dreaming only *while* we are dreaming. Forming opinions and doubts about the reality of dreams by positing questions while we are awake is as ridiculous—and equally impossible—as doubting the reality of our waking life while we are dreaming. Simply put, all doubts about the dream state arise in us only while we are awake. While dreaming of a love encounter or a nightmare, we experience the respective feelings of love or fear and are incapable of assessing them with doubts about their reality. In the moment we inhabit, waking or dreaming, our life's experience is real for us. No other reality seems to exist.

Throughout the years, I have noticed that individuals who are unfamiliar with Eastern systems vehemently oppose the basic logic that a dream is as real, in the moment of the experience, as a waking experience. Furthermore, these same people resolutely cling to the notion that only the waking state is real and that experiences while dreaming, as well as during deep dreamless sleep, are not only unreal but also meaningless. This perspective is indicative of two basic patterns. First, and most obvious, is that these people have never investigated any alternative to popularly held beliefs. Second, and most relevant, is that their lack of inquiry *into their own experience* proves that they are very attached to their waking experiences. Yet each night they spend time in another world. Because a large portion of our lives is spent in a state other than the waking state, is it not shortsighted to believe what others tell us without ourselves looking for answers?

Our entire lives are spent alternating between the states of waking and sleeping. The very reason that this is so vital to grasp is that this alternation, this duality, mirrors the great alternation of birth and death. The understanding of this similarity brings us back to the question of why some people begin a spiritual search. Actually, another question is far more relevant. What is the *purpose* of any spiritual search?

Is This It?

There is little doubt that all of us who begin some type of spiritual search do so from a feeling of dissatisfaction. The normal activities of life seem to lack substance and are often accompanied by pain. We look about us and find no solace in the ordinary ways of living. The hollowness inside us aches and yearns for fulfillment. We begin by looking for a solution to these nagging questions and problems. Thinking that we can transcend all difficulties, we then take up various spiritual pursuits in order to free ourselves of these dilemmas.

Anyone who is on a spiritual path and possesses any degree of humility and sincerity should be capable of one most essential admission: the acknowledgment that he or she is unaware of the eventual goal of the journey. Would we make a journey on a particular road if we were already standing at the destination? Of course not. Healer Pal speaks directly to this when he says,

"When we are unaware of the nature of Truth, how can we be aware of how to reach it?"

> *Ponder not; think of nothing; see yourself not in the foreground. What you behold, let it be that.*
>
> (Saint Manavasagam Kadanthar, "Thiru Arut Payan," Verse 8, In Pal Pandian, *Siddhas: Masters of the Basics* [Chennai, India: Pal Pandian, 2008])

There is however, a more hidden factor, which only the rare seeker ever reaches. It can be summed up in a single word: Why? Why do we embark on this quest? What is the actual purpose of undertaking a spiritual path?

This question is lacking in us while we practice spiritual pursuits. Yet without it being clearly answered and kept in mind, we all risk being sidetracked into lethargy, indifference, or the assumption that we have completed the journey. Like a compass that points the way to our destination, clear awareness of the purpose is necessary to continue on our chosen path. The alternating states of waking and sleeping reflect the grandest fluctuation of the duality of life and death, which demonstrates our actual purpose. To be most succinct, the only reason that anyone has begun or ever will begin a sincere spiritual quest is that most certain experience that we have in common: death.

To become intimately acquainted with death is the sole purpose, the actual goal, of all spiritual quests. *This is the bitter truth.* The truth is bitter and indigestible, because the ultimate goal is not finding our bliss, improving our lives, manifesting our desires, being free from our problems and limitations, or any such things. These are simply diversions from the ultimate goal, the purpose. All of us are born and die. Likewise, all of us wake and are pulled into sleep.

> *That which we term death is just like sleep*
> *That which we term birth is just like awakening.*

—Siddha Thiruvalluvar, "Thiru Kurall 339," Verse 339, In Pal Pandian, *Siddhas: Masters of the Basics* [Chennai, India: Pal Pandian, 2008])

Although I had been seeking spiritually for years before meeting Pal, the notion of why rarely, if ever, had occurred to me. Even after being taught by him for some years, this question remained unaddressed. However, after he initiated me into the spiritual realm of the Siddha path of tantra, he spoke to me, in no uncertain terms, about its purpose:

"The purpose is to become acquainted with death. We must move through the fear of it. For this, we should become adept at consciously leaving identification with the body. Whenever we de-identify with our physical body, the mind identifies with the subtle body. So, normally, people are not aware at the time of their death and so are pulled from the physical body and, according to their karma, stay in the earthly realm. But when we are leaving the mortal frame, we have to de-identify with all the bodies, the physical, the subtle body, and so forth, because we should be in a de-identified state with regard to all the bodies. When alive, people are identified with their physical body. In meditation, they are identified with their subtle body, and when dreaming, they are identified with their dream body. The mind always likes to identify with a body, and so, when death comes, they will immediately identify with their subtle body and then be stuck in the earthly realm. We should learn to live without identification with any of these bodies. That is why the Siddhas say, 'Have a dead man's eyes, and Walk like a corpse.' It is only in this way that, in the moment of death, we will not identify with any body. We already know our true Center."

What he and the other Siddhas mean is that we should move through life unattached to the ever-changing, ephemeral nature of manifestation and instead remain grounded in our Center. When I heard these words for the first time, my response was the usual sense of excitement and enthusiasm that is characteristic of my approach to spirituality. As the years passed and I became more familiar with what is actually involved in learning to live without identification with any of the bodies, my simplistic attitude changed. The reason for this shift in attitude came from my understanding more deeply what is required. Life can easily distract us and pull us into the dramas and colors of her many forms. Without the continually graceful grounding of the guru, the bitter truth of our life's quest can be easily forgotten.

The Spin of Oblivion

In the same way that we are pulled from our waking identification with the physical body and pushed into identifying with the dream body, death exerts its will over us. This pull occurs because the mind likes to identify with some form, some substance, some body. This is the mind's nature, and it will continue to pull us until it is utterly transcended, until we attain enlightenment. Just as the shop window of our conscious mind effortlessly and endlessly changes its displays, we are incessantly pulled into identification with the various bodies. The mind's inherent tendency to identify with the vast storehouse of humanity's individual and collective impressions propels this ongoing drama. This mode of constant identification, springing from our attachments, latent tendencies, and desires, prevents us from reaching that most natural state of simply *being*, the state of being without identification with any form.

> *There is really no difference between the ignorant and the knower of truth except that the latter is free from the conditioned mind. . . . He whose mind is free and unattached*

does not get involved once again in this samsara [cycle of birth and death].

(Yoga Vasistha, In Sage Valmiki, *The Supreme Yoga*, trans. Swami Venkatesananda [Delhi: Chitern Yoga Trust, 2003])

Only by living in our natural state do we eliminate all conflicts, dilemmas, and forms of agitation. Being free from any possibility of doubt, anxiety, limitation, or other notion of stress is possible only when the identification with all form has been eradicated. Achieving this is no simple task and is not accomplished by a sudden flash of insight or what the new-age movement markets as "enlightenment." I know well the immediacy with which the mind identifies with form, as demonstrated in the following experience that I had.

Lying on a table in India while receiving an Amritha Kalai healing session, I immediately begin to relax and submerge within myself. In a flash, I find myself hovering above the beach at the lake in front of my house back in the United States. Acutely aware that I am inhabiting the subtle body, I think to myself, "I wonder how the water will feel in this state, since the weather is so cold." I dive into the lake and find the sensation of the lake's liquidity and coldness present yet incapable of touching me. I then rise up to again hover above the water. The desire to enter my vacant house arises within me. I quickly ascend further into the night sky and observe the many stars and planets before proceeding to fulfill my wish and fly through the roof of my home. I look about the empty rooms, but then a new desire arises within me. I immediately fly into the night sky and mix among the heavenly bodies. I travel to and quickly explore the stars, planets, and galaxies that previously had seemed distant. Having experienced the sensation of traveling vast distances without any noticeable time passing, I return to my neighborhood and once again hover above the lake, observing the natural setting of water and trees.

"What the hell am I doing here?" I think. "My body is back in India, lying on the table. Enough of this playing about. I want to return to my beloved Arunachala."

Immediately, I am back in India, suspended in midair in front of the holy mountain, the sunlight blazing. Gazing at Arunachala, I have a single thought: "I want to enter the mountain." Without any effort, lapse of time, or thought I am taken through various worlds and experiences inside Arunachala. Afterward, I am aware of lying on a vast expanse of still water. The only other aspect of creation is the seamless blue sky that stretches above me. Nothing else exists.

The significance of my experience during the healing session is how quickly and unconsciously the mind can attach itself to a body. I found myself immediately transported back to my home environment in the United States without any effort or conscious awareness. It was simply the most familiar environment.

Furthermore, I cannot stress how quickly this occurred—no time passed. Even while it was happening, I was shocked when I realized where I was and what I was doing. When I remembered that I was actually in India, the very place I work so hard in order to visit, I felt foolish for wasting my time elsewhere. However, even when I did finally return to India, at the end of the experience, I had no interest in returning to my physical body.

Equally important is where I was in my personal journey when I had this experience. Having trod the path of Siddha Tantra for three years, I had already made wondrous progress but certainly not because of any virtue that I possessed. Determination, faith, and as much cheerful patience as I could muster were all I have ever had to offer. Despite my many shortcomings, the guru and Siddha lineage had showered me with profound grace. I wish I could explain or share that grace with others, but it has never made sense to me since I did not earn or deserve it. Rather, it was simply a gift. Because of this good fortune, what would normally take ten to fifteen years for a person to accomplish had passed amazingly quickly. Throughout that time, I had uncovered and encountered much of the unconscious. During that very visit in India, I had traveled to Palani Hill. The trip to Palani is especially significant for tantrics, because at the top of the mountain is the temple of Lord Murugan, or Skanda.

After the trip to the temple of Lord Murugan, several significant changes took place within me. I had been quite ill for several days and made the ascent while suffering a high fever. During the descent, however, I realized that not only were the fever, fatigue, and bodily pain absent, but I felt an incredible degree of vigor coupled with an unmistakable sense of lightness and clarity. During the evening that followed my darshan (divine sight) of Lord Murugan, the marriage of the feminine and masculine aspects of consciousness occurred. It is said that one who visits this temple in sincerity and piety receive his or her heart's true desire.

Locked in a Dream

This merging of the dual aspects of consciousness is a rare occurrence and what Carl Jung defined as being whole. However, it is not enlightenment, because as Pal told me, "At the level of the Self, we are neither male nor female; we are beyond." The reason that I have detailed these particulars of my personal journey is twofold. The first is to dispel any notions of the goal of spiritual practice being achieved via a particular experience or insight. This very idea is passed around in new-age circles. Second, the experience of traveling in the subtle body during the healing session happened *after* this marriage has taken place. Even though the masculine and feminine polarities within me had been reconciled, the mind still habitually identified with a form, a body.

The marriage of the masculine and feminine celebrates the end of a long, meandering sojourn. What appears as a phase is in fact an intricate journey. Essentially, the journey continues until all traces of personal and collective impressions are extinguished. Self-realization is the complete transcendence of all aspects of duality and limitation. It is the eradication of all traces of identification. In the absence of self-realization, almost everyone experiences one of two possible results upon death. In either result, the individual is pulled, as if going to sleep, into the subtle body and remains in the earthly realm. Being stuck here is really the appropriate understanding.

The first possibility is that the person is not aware that they have died. Much like the character played by Bruce Willis in the movie *The Sixth Sense,* the person may have suffered a sudden or unexpected death, which prevents him or her from moving out of the earthly experience. For example, a person who is much attached to work and dies in the office may simply continue to work at their desk. Incapable of "digesting" the death experience, those who die without having achieved self-realization remain bound to the earthly realm. What has actually occurred is that the person is in the subtle body but thinks that he or she is still in the physical body. This example shows the importance of the dream state and regular meditation. We should become familiar with leaving the physical and dwelling in the subtle body, and dreaming offers us this chance each night.

Nonetheless, the dead person in the example is experiencing something akin to a stupor state in that he or she continues to think that they are existing in the physical body. How does this occur? In the exact same fashion that *we create a body and world each night in our dreams.* The dead person simply proceeds with the same mind activity as before death. This can go on for many, many years. It ends when the dead person either encounters the shocking truth that he or she is indeed dead (as in the movie) or finds saturation in this stupor state. Another possibility is that someone comes to inform and guide the dead person beyond the existence of being stuck. This most often involves a shocking experience that the person has indeed died, as in the movie. When this occurs, the person can finally, usually after hundreds of years, dispense with the subtle body, gain rest within the causal body, and then proceed with the personal journey.

A second result is experienced by the majority of people who die: they choose to remain in the earthly realm. These people know that they have died but continue to crave a physical body and its experiences. This craving compels them to stay and seek to enjoy and experience their unfulfilled desires. Normally, we refer to these dead people as ghosts. Whichever of their desires is strongest determines where they are, and they attempt to satisfy that desire, that attachment, whether it be food, drink, relatives, a city, or a house, etc. Quite often, they attempt to attach to another person in order to experience the physical stimulation that they crave. Usually, this other person is a family member. Pal once related a story about this to me:

A young man worked an office job and visited his parents often. Although his father greatly enjoyed drinking alcohol, doing so every day, the son was always indifferent to alcohol. Yet, when he was with his father, he would have a cocktail, but his father would have many each day. When not with his father, the son rarely drank. And then his father died. Over time, the young man began to drink each day when he got home from work. However, after some time, that one drink every day turned into three drinks, then four, and so on. Eventually, his mother visited him. After observing his new routine, she said to him, "You're just like your father!"

The father's unfulfilled habit drove him to stay in the earthly realm after death and seek to continue indulging in his desire for alcohol. To do so, he attached to his son and thus influenced his life routine. We would say that the son had an entity attached to him. Frankly, this is not uncommon.

One who dies after having lived a fulfilling, complete existence is a rarity. A prime example, however, is the gentle, old grandmother who lies on her deathbed with the sole wish to see her granddaughter. As soon as her granddaughter arrives and she sees her one last time, the grandmother gracefully slips away and leaves the mortal frame. Very few die with no attachments, no unfulfilled desires or needs, but those who do pass without a strong need to identify can proceed with their journey, resting in the causal body, the storehouse of karma. Although this experience is a rarity and a blessing, it is not enlightenment or transcendence. These people are still on the personal journey and will undergo future births.

Falling to the "Great Sleep"

The ancient cultures had knowledge of what the soul encountered after bodily death. Relying on their intuitive wisdom and nature, they placed prime importance on mystical experiences and revelations. Unlike our modern society, which relies solely on scientific data that is observable and calculable, they trusted the wise beings among them. To this day, ancient religions revere ancestors during a specific, auspicious time each year. They do so in order to help those who may be staying in the earthly realm to be released and allowed to continue with the journey. Their burial ceremonies reflect this same understanding. The bardo technique of Buddhism is a prime example of how the saints gather to help a soul to leave the earth and continue the journey. Members of the very early Christian church also would have had this wisdom, which explains why Christians today sprinkle water on certain chakras of the deceased, use particular incense, and say specific prayers.

Of course, over time, the practices have become mechanical rituals and so have lost their potency.

For the overwhelming majority of people, there is a vicious cycle of birth and unconscious death. An analogous experience is played out for us each night when we fall asleep and each morning when we wake. If we are not capable of being fully aware of ourselves as we move from the waking state to the dream state to the deep, dreamless sleep and then back to the waking state, we have little hope of being aware when the "great sleep" of death comes to take us. This bitter truth is played out in a vicious cycle. Ending this cycle is not just the ultimate purpose of any spiritual practice. It is the *only* purpose.

> *O Rama, one should, with a body free from illness and mind free from distress, pursue Self-knowledge so that he is not born again here.*
>
> (Yoga Vasistha, In Sage Valmiki, *The Supreme Yoga,* trans. Swami Venkatesananda [Delhi: Chitern Yoga Trust, 2003])

The Path of the Awakened

Much like an enormous maze that contains many paths yet only one path that leads to its exit, the goal of spirituality has a single victorious outcome. The Siddhas say that to be conscious in the three states of waking, dreaming, and deep, dreamless sleep is the only way to transcend death. This transcendental state is the authentic enlightenment. In the East, this is known as Turiya, or the fourth state.

> *That state in which the mind is freed from its characteristic movement of thought and in which there is only the experience of peace, is known as "deep sleep in wakefulness." When this same state of "deep sleep in wakefulness" matures, it is known as Turiya, or the fourth state.*
>
> (Yoga Vasistha, In Sage Valmiki, *The Supreme Yoga*, trans. Swami Venkatesananda [Delhi: Chitern Yoga Trust, 2003])

Being fully aware of one's self through all three of the states and so being de-identified with them is the only path that leads one out of the maze, or cycle, of continued birth and death. Not to mention the ghostly post-death realm that most are forced to encounter again and again.

In tantra, the three states of waking, dreaming, and deep sleep are referred to as the three curtains, veils, cities, or kingdoms. Whatever name they are called by, they are ruled over by a deity, a goddess. In Siddha Tantra, She is Tripura Sundari. It is She who grants transcendence. Because She rules over the states of waking, dreaming, and deep sleep, She can enable one to be conscious during these states in a singular, unbroken awareness. This is Her blessing on the devotee. One so blessed becomes fully aware of one's self in the waking state, and this awareness carries into the dreaming and deep, dreamless sleep states. Never losing one's true Center, never being pulled into the unconsciousness of the three states, can be accomplished only by having the transcendental awareness, or Turiya, that underlies and rules all three states.

The bitter truth is that life and its pleasures last for a short time. Yet our existence stretches both before and after the physical sojourn. Whether rejoicing in the birth of a baby or mourning the death of a grandparent, all of our focus is concentrated on whatever experiences we can accumulate with the physical body. Yet, throughout our entire lives and all of our experiences, the inevitability of death chases us.

> *Stealthily the cat of senility catches the mouse of youth. . . . Birth and childhood lead to youth, youth leads to old age, and old age ends in death—and all these are repeatedly experienced by the ignorant.*
>
> (Yoga Vasistha, In Sage Valmiki, *The Supreme Yoga,* trans. Swami Venkatesananda [Delhi: Chitern Yoga Trust, 2003])

Stretching back to my youth, it always seemed that Nature had dealt me a cruel hand. All I had wanted was to roast a marshmallow. Instead, I found myself confronted by the existential crisis of the certainty of death. Lifting Her cosmic dress, She had allowed me the faintest glimpse of Her most private parts: the enormity of the inevitable decay and death of all things. This hit me hard at the time. It stunned me into a feeling of insignificance and smallness. Because I had been incapable of digesting Her shocking lesson, I continued to stumble through life, haunted by my fleeting encounter with the bitter, indigestible truth. Yet the seed that had been planted would eventually sprout into a yearning for wisdom. Finally, the guru would aid me in digesting the inescapable. The treatise *Yoga Vasistha* is the finest example of Siddha Jnana, which is the Siddhas' wisdom expressed as the non-dual Truth.

> *One should work in this world as much as is needed to earn an honest living. One should eat in order to sustain the life force. One should sustain one's life force only for the sake of acquiring Self-knowledge. One should inquire into and know that which frees him from sorrow [cycle of birth and death].*
>
> (Yoga Vasistha, In Sage Valmiki, *The Supreme Yoga*, trans. Swami Venkatesananda [Delhi: Chitern Yoga Trust, 2003])

The Bitter Truth

This most bitter, indigestible truth is nothing more than becoming intimately familiar with death, to "Have a dead man's eyes and Walk like a corpse," as Pal said. This is the only purpose for which any of us embark on a spiritual path. If we convince ourselves that by meditating or taking yoga classes we can achieve our desires in life or exist as the sages and masters, we only delude and bind ourselves further. Ending the cycle of birth and death is the only worthy goal to achieve in our short time here. Although the notion that we experience innumerable births and deaths may seem alien to a Western mind whose conditioning is otherwise, ignorance is no defense in the cosmic court. In some way, however, the idea that we are not subject to repeated lives is true, because as Pal has said, "We live once, and that is forever."

Facing the truth of ourselves and our lives is bitter because we are enmeshed in countless dreams of how we wish to be, and so we construct ongoing worlds in which to wander. Each day, we move through notions of "I shall have that," "Oh, I should be more like this," "Soon I will have this, and then I will be like that," and so on. Ignorant of our eternal nature, we attempt to cage ourselves in lives confined by the bars of limited notions, both our own and others'. Then we wonder why we are unable to achieve permanent peace and contentment. Only when we have become disgusted with the accepted approaches to birth, life, and death will we be interested in seeing ourselves as we truly are and so face the bitterness of awakening. Pal has explained it beautifully:

> *Life is a great circle. Loosening the identifications and the identifier himself is the way to participate in this great circle. This daring loosening allows us to flow, to become the whole circle. To hold on at any point on this circle is to forget our original unborn nature, as there is no place we begin and nowhere we end.*

Appendix

SIDDHA TRADITION AT PRESENT

The world of Siddha healing can be said to have two basic dimensions: Siddha Varma and the much more widespread and well known, Siddha medicine. Although Siddha Varma has been detailed in the earlier chapters of this book, one remaining thing must be related so that authentic Varma healing can become better known in the future. Pal has informed me of this, based on his observance of many teachers in South India who openly give instruction in Varma healing. While this is not entirely appropriate, the scope of such teachers' knowledge confines their ability to the most basic level of Varma healing—the manual method of Kaibaham Seibaham, or what we in Pal's lineage have given the name Systemic Vital Point Therapy. These modern-day teachers, who we can only presume possess good intentions, have no access to the higher, more potent Varma healing—Adangal, spiritual energy, and certainly not Amritha Kalai, which is unique to Pal's lineage. These esoteric and supreme arts are the sole practice of the Siddha masters and their direct lineage.

The aspect of Siddha healing that has been shared openly and spread widely is medicinal wisdom, in a similar fashion to the later yet better known Indian medicinal discipline of Ayurveda.[10] The difference between them is that the medicine of the Siddhas became fragmented, or less consolidated, while the practice of Ayurveda has remained cohesive. The reasons for Siddha medicine's fragmentation are mainly the secretive nature of the ancient masters, the antiquity of Siddha medicine, and the later social and religious prejudices toward the Siddha clan. Although the Siddha and Ayurvedic medicinal systems share common foundations, there are great differences between them. An in-depth comparison of the two is beyond the scope of this book. However, should one seek Siddha healing today, whether in India or in the West, it is best to first have a firm understanding of the past, which clarifies how Siddha medicine has progressed to its present condition.

Siddha medicine has been passed down for thousands of years through two sources: the guru lineage and the family lineage.

---

[10] The government of India has stated that Ayurveda is 6,000 years old and that Siddha medicine is at least 14,000 years old. However, this estimated age of Siddha applies only to the medicinal art of the Tamil Siddhas and not to Them or Their tradition.

These two both belong to the category of traditional healers, have their own beauty and, like all things, possess inherent limitations.

Guru Lineage

The Tamil Siddha masters began by exploring the body and mind, looking for its limitations of sickness, weakness of frame, and death itself. Through the healing power of yogic practices, lifestyle, diet, and nature's plants, minerals, and animal derivatives, They developed a system of both medicine and healing. They shared the discoveries with Their most trusted disciples, first through the oral tradition and later to be transcribed in veiled language in poetic verse on palm-leaf manuscripts. In this way the guru lineage has persisted with incredible purity to the present day.

A tradition grows ancient as it flows through the generations that carry on the contributions of each guru to His or Her disciples. The styles and methods, personal insights, and discoveries of each guru are handed down through the lineage. Several lineages flourish within a tradition, each with its own characteristic style based on the region, environment, and the accomplishments and knowledge of each successive master. This simple, organic way of passing on knowledge is sufficient to tend to its local area. Even today in the Siddha system, we can see how each lineage has its own secrets for approaching disease and its own treatment style. The medicines used, line of treatment, and knowledge can vary from one lineage to the next. This indigenous method is the guru lineage's strength, because as a whole the lineage contains the entirety of that type of Siddha medicinal wisdom. However, this very strength is also the system's inherent limitation.

The limitation is that there is no cohesive system of Siddha medicine. In contrast, standardization of diagnosis and line of treatment can be seen easily in modern medicine. For example, if a person has a lung infection and seeks treatment, whether he or she is in New York, New Delhi, or Tokyo does not matter. A physician in any of those places will follow the established, definitive protocol for diagnosis and treatment. In other words, the patient receives identical—or nearly identical—care regardless of location. This is the major component missing from the traditional healers of Siddha medicine, whether they have been trained by a guru or by a family lineage.

Family Lineage

In its own way, family lineage has served Siddha medicine well through the ages. This is notable, because the guru lineage is, by its nature, restricted in number. Over time, certain native healers decided not to become gurus but instead to become householders, get married, have children, and live in society. Such an individual would have been a great healer and then passed the knowledge and skill on to a son or daughter, who would in turn do the same. This family lineage of Siddha medicine is similar to the way in which artisans, craftsmen, and the like throughout history passed their professions on to their heirs.

Sharing with the guru lineage the inherent limitation of a lack of standardization, the family lineage has an additional limitation. Although the inception of a family lineage has been founded by a wise, dedicated healer, there is no way to guarantee that this type of naturally inspired healing could continue through the generations without interruption. In each generation, a son or daughter would be expected or even required to follow in the healer parent's footsteps—whether or not the child wants to do so. Therefore, divine inspiration may not exist. The lack of this most essential component would be detrimental to the passing on of the family's healing art.

The deep, most divinely given manner of healing, Varma healing, is also lacking in the family lineage. Although a few descendants of family lineages may practice Varma, they possess only limited knowledge of it. As such, they are capable of addressing only a few specific ailments. The highest levels of esoteric healing, such as Adangal and Amritha Kalai, are completely unavailable to such healers. Those levels of healing are the sole possession of the extremely few gurus of the most supreme nature.

Academic Setting

The recent introduction of Siddha medicine into the academic world began in the last fifty years as the Indian government began endeavors to mainstream Siddha medicine. To that end, there are three public universities and five private universities of Siddha medicine in the state of Tamil Nadu and one in the state of Kerala. These universities are focused on the medicinal realm of the Siddhas. While there is a separate department for Varma, it is taught by academics so no real theory is given. Instead, the teachers simply instruct the students in a few Varma applications for specific disorders. The academic model was established to enable Siddha medicine to spread more widely, which is an obvious benefit for humanity. Another beautiful outcome is the eventual standardization of diagnosis and treatment protocols. This modernization of care will allow more people access to this most ancient of medicinal wisdom. However, some challenges must be overcome before the medicine of the Sages can be fully folded into a modern environment.

The challenges in mainstreaming Siddha medicine into a modern academic setting begin with the way in which the universities have approached both the staffing of professors and the development of course curriculum. When the time came to seek out professors of the various subjects, the challenge of finding the most qualified and experienced healers was felt immediately.

Appendix

When the universities searched the ranks of family lineages, the healers' narrow expertise and lack of higher education may have been viewed with unjust prejudice. For those few Sages of the guru lineage, this unintentional prejudice was magnified many times. Living and healing in the flow of existence, a true Siddha healer is beyond the need to conceptualize any knowledge and has no desire for fame, fortune, or any other worldly ambitions. The one attachment of such a healer is, invariably, the purity of Siddha medicine and healing (and, of course, profound love for his or her own guru). True Siddha healers' healing prowess and wisdom is vast, transcending what truly can be taught in book or classroom environments. All the while, the face presented to the world and to those who seek a true Siddha healer is one of extreme simplicity. At times the manner is rather abrasive, and it is generally unimpressive to the common-minded. They cannot be bargained with, in any fashion, to compromise their medicinal and healing efficacy.

When the universities began looking for professors, they surely were familiar with the stories of several Siddha healers. Those stories included tales of miraculous healing of countless diseases, among them the most incurable. When they were face to face with these same men and women of the Tamil Siddha tradition, however, their shock at them being such simple, common people was obvious. Based on the legends, they had expected to see supermen, but they were dismayed by these uneducated individuals. Faced with the conundrum of staffing a modern academic university program with this type of people, they took what at the time seemed a safer route and instead chose professors of a more mainstream background.

The main limitation of bringing authentic Siddha medicine into a university setting is that the professors themselves have limited practical experience. Thus, they can offer their students only theory that is both bereft of experience and devoid of the divine aspiration that flows from the guru lineage's ancient roots. Further compounding this dry approach is the manner in which the subjects are taught. Beginning their studies by taking the same classes and using the same textbooks—covering anatomy, physiology, and disease pathology—as do the allopathic students, the students are given an overly intellectual framework.[11] Finally, when the students move on to Siddha textbooks, several hurdles remain.

Having begun their learning immersed in the theories of mainstream medicine and its narrow understanding of human anatomy and disease, the students lack some basic knowledge of the Siddhas. With their initial exposure to the human body based

---

[11] This lack of holistic understanding is a key shortcoming of the university approach. A holistic view is the basis of the Siddhas' medicinal and healing systems; this most basic, essential component is lacking in allopathy. Instead focused solely on disease, the system of allopathy has no true, or holistic, understanding of what it means to be healthy and free of disease in body and mind.

solely on its physical components, they have the idea of a person being bound by physical laws, which is severely limiting. When they are exposed to the anatomical concepts of the Siddhas, with the chakras as a prime example, they learn them on a purely intellectual level. Because the professors and the authors of the textbooks have no authentic experience of the subtle body and its energy flows, they are incapable of passing on to the students anything more than mere theory. In an allopathic anatomy lesson, students easily can be told about the femur bone and then can touch their own femur for proof of its existence. In contrast, in a Siddha anatomy lesson, the professor can explain the base chakra, or Mooladharam, but all that he or she can offer the students are words from the textbook and his or her own theories. Is it not evident that one viewpoint will predominate over the other?

The other limitation that has arisen from this academic design is that, when the professors retire, the candidates to fill their spots are their former students. In this way, the mode of instruction and curriculum has remained unchanged during the past twenty-five years. This model has created much misunderstanding between academics and native healers. Further compounding the situation is that the universities, with their ready access to the government's ear, have been convincing in their argument that only graduates of their programs should be allowed the title "Siddha doctor" or even "Siddha healer"! Tragically, today those very repositories of infinite wisdom and grace whose lineages have preserved Siddha healing for millennia, the healing Siddha masters Themselves, are confined to the title of "*herbal practitioner.*" The problem is academia's view of and approach to native Siddha healers. The universities have had no reverence for the wisdom and depth of experience of native Siddha healers.

The Solution

Healer Pal and Steve

A Siddha Varma Healing workshop conducted by
Healer Pal for a group of government Siddha doctors at
Madurai, India. Author delivers a brief speech.

Thankfully, the gap between traditional practitioners and academic practitioners has begun to narrow. We are beginning to see many academically trained Siddha doctors seek out and meet Siddha healers. They wish to further their learning about the traditional manner of the Siddha masters. To this end, we extend our profound gratitude for the additional work they have accomplished, particularly that of which the traditional healers were incapable: the standardization of the system and clinical trials. The result is that Siddha medical practices will be able to be spread throughout the world.

The limitations listed above still exist, but there are occasional exceptions. Siddha healer Pal Pandian conducts workshop seminars for doctors from Siddha academic institutions. Universities regularly invite him as a guest to lecture to both students and professors. In this way, he contributes to bridging the unnecessary gap between native healers and academically trained doctors. From his interactions with academia, Pal has experienced firsthand the shortcomings of the classroom approach. The example about professors' and students' knowledge of the chakras that bind the physical and subtle bodies being limited to what they have read in a textbook is a good one.

Thankfully, with the existence of healers like Pal, aspiring students are in good hands. In a simple manner and ten minutes' time, he can take them to their own direct experience of the root chakra at the base of their body, the Mooladharam. Although Siddha medicine and healing is an almost lost art and has diffused over time, rare gems such as Pal still exist. The gap between the ancient and the future can be bridged by these sorts of healers, who hopefully can be encouraged to take the initiative to share with academically trained Siddha doctors the experiential aspect of Siddha healing.

The extremely rare jewel is a Siddha healer who has dedicated his or her entire life to seeking out and studying under many gurus, assimilating all of their wisdom and then continuing onward to the fusion of the vast spectrum of healing wisdom. The results are the most comprehensive, sensitive, and profoundly effective knowledge of medicine and healing. Such is Healer Pal, whose life direction and example gives birth to the healing wisdom of the ancient masters being made available today.

Healer Pal and His Lineage

Having spent his entire adulthood in the selfless service of humanity, Pal, through his 20 years healing experience found a common energetic thread, which is present in the Vital points (Varma points), Adangal movements and massage (Kalari movements), and Amritha Kalai. He integrated these three in a system, which he names Vasi Therapy (Vasi Healing). His students both in India and abroad are firmly rooted in Vasi Therapy (Vasi Healing). Healer Pal's Dharma has come to flow along a different route. Having discontinued his medicinal practice he is now involved in two other modes.

He conducts retreats for the general public which expound the ways of well-being in day-to-day life based on the insights of the Siddha system. The retreats intend to spread awareness among the general public about the various Siddha dimensions. The second mode is more exclusive, intended for aspirants seeking a path to enlightenment under the Siddhas' guidance, specific to Pal's lineage. This tradition is not intellectual but organic in nature (energy based instead of theory dependent). Its prime intent is not realization alone but manifesting and embodying the essence of Mother Nature, thereby living in the state of natural Consciousness. The second mode is offered to those seekers who choose to devote and dedicate themselves to this path and its purpose.

Although I certainly have my own deep experience of Siddha Healer Pal's powerful spiritual instruction, the following simple, direct words from his book, *Siddhas: Masters of the Basics* are far more potent:

> *The revelations of the Siddhas are impersonal and ultimately aim at non-egoistic livingness. They describe us as just different combinations of the same Cosmic force coming through the planets and stars. The ego, our sense of personal identity, is mere fiction, an illusion that does not exist. We all have the same basic nature, both superficially and in depth, and go through the same basic life experiences, good and bad, solely for the purposeful growth of our consciousness. No soul*

> *gets any special treatment, good or bad. In this way, our differences come merely from being at various stages of the one process and not because we are in Truth truly different or separate, better or worse, than one another.*

His devoted students in India reside in Tiruvannamalai, Madurai, and Chennai. As for the international students, in addition to myself, three other individuals carry on his lineage and have received BSS diplomas from the Indian government in the instruction of Varma and Yoga:

- Samer Sayyed, a man with a soaring healing spirit, who has become a cherished friend, was mentioned in chapter 5 of this book. He can be found alternating between Lebanon, India, and Europe.

Samer

www.vasitherapy.com

Appendix

- Caroline Jensen holds the delightful capacity of a healing spirit that contains Pal Pandian's essence. She lives in Denmark, where she cares compassionately for all who seek the solace of her tender essence.

www.caroline-jensen.com　　Caroline

- Borbala Kasza resides in Hungary. Flowing from her natural compassion and gentle heart, she cares for those who suffer in body, mind, and spirit.

kasza.borbala@yahoo.com　　Borbala

A Final Note

The term *Siddha* refers to one who has attained perfection in both the spiritual and worldly realms, and it is often ascribed to those who perform siddhis, such as walking on water, turning water into wine, and so forth. As such, many of the later traditions refer to Siddhas because, in truth, such Beings belong to no society or religion. Their lives are grounded solely in Existence. We have explored the beginnings of this tradition in South India, with the Tamil Siddhas, and this primal lineage is the subject of this book. In order to avoid any confusion, a brief clarification is imperative.

Some may have heard of "Siddha yoga,'" which is a movement started by Swami Muktananda in India. However, the swami and his foundation are in no way affiliated with the Tamil Siddha tradition. Nor are Swami Muktananda's methods, traditions, or aims in any way related to the Siddhas' spiritual and healing lineage. Furthermore, what they call "Siddha yoga" is in no way Vasi yoga, the yoga of the Tamil Siddha masters.

Another potential misconception concerns Yogi Babaji, of kriya yoga heritage. Paramahansa Yogananda may have taken kriya yoga to the West and popularized Babaji, the yogi who resides in the Himalayas. Later, Yogi Ramiah, who hails from Tamil Nadu, also began teaching kriya yoga in the West, claiming that Babaji was part of his own lineage. However, like Swami Muktananda's

Appendix

"Siddha yoga," Yogi Babaji's kriya yoga is in no way affiliated with the Tamil Siddha lineage or tradition, nor are its methods at all connected with what has been conveyed in this book. Yogi Ramiah has made the further claim that Babaji was a disciple of his own guru, none other than Siddha Bogar. However, there are absolutely no references in the ancient Siddha manuscripts to this having been the case. Siddha Healer Pal has stated that there is no evidence of Babaji, or Nagarajan (his birth name), having been with Siddha Bogar or any of the other Tamil Siddhas.

In the future, many will claim to be of the Siddha tradition. Some may even claim to be Siddhas themselves. They will be mildly delusional, at best. No Siddha master has ever claimed to be anything other than a humble devotee of the Divine or would ever permit others to refer to him or her as such. Those who allow such liberties show themselves as bereft of the most basic elements of the Siddha masters. They can offer only their own limited views and prejudices.

For those who are fortunate enough to have such an encounter, the first meeting with a Siddha is always a shocking experience. Should the further blessing descend into their lives that they are taken into Their secret realms, there is no turning back to the ordinary. However, to seek Them with the idea of gaining something will always end in failure. To find Them, we must be willing to risk everything that we think we have and all that we imagine ourselves to be. In the end and in truth, it is They who will find those who are willing to be stripped naked of both the collective and the individual. The payment extracted for such relationship is nothing less than one's mortality.

> *He that has earned the Grace of the Guru shall undoubtedly be saved and never forsaken, just as the prey that has fallen into the tiger's jaws will never be allowed to escape.*

(Bhagavan Sri Ramana Maharshi, *Nan Yar* [Who Am I? The Teachings of Bhagavan Sri Ramana Maharshi], trans. T.M.P. Mahadevan [Tiruvannamalai, India: Sri Ramanasramam, n.d.])

Glossary

Adangal	Varma points, or reservoirs, where subsided energy resides
agni	fire
agni nadi	Fire pathway or channel
aham sphurana	Exuberance of being-ness
Ahamkara	The Individuating principle, the Power of identification
ambrosia	Nectar of Life
Amritha	Ambrosia, the Nectar of Life
Amritha Kalai	The Siddha Varma realm of nectar energy
Amritha nadi	The nectar pathway or channel
Andam	Cosmos, Universe; another name for the philosopher's stone
apana	One of the five major vital airs: downward-moving vital air
archetype	Primal or ancestral imprint
Arunachala	Holy mountain in Tamil Nadu, India
Asan	A master of Varma science

asanas	Body postures for integration of the body and mind; body postures used in hatha yoga
ashram	Indian hermitage
atma	soul
Atman	Self, the core of an individual's personality
Ayurveda	The science of life, a form of holistic alternative medicine traditional to India
Babaji	The founder of kriya yoga
Bala	See Valai
Bala Marga	A member of the ancient Siddha lineage founded by Lord Murugan
bhasma	Incinerated form of medicinal preparation
Bhraman	God, Self, Consciousness, The Absolute, The Ultimate
Bhutas	The five primordial elements of which the universe consists
Brahmin	In India, the highest caste, or social class
causal body	The bliss sheath, the repository of the Vasanas
chakra	Plexus, energy center
Chandra kalai	Path of the moon in the body, the frontal line of the energy channel in the human body
chi	Energy
darshan	Divine sight or experience
dasa vayu	The ten vital airs, or forces
Devayanai	The first consort of Lord Murugan
Dharma	Inherent order of existence; an individual's duty fulfilled by observance of custom or law
dosha	A biological humor
doshas	The three biological humors
Dravidians	The ancestral people of Southern India

Dwarka Mayi	Former residence of Shirdi Sai Baba; Siddha Healer Pal Pandian's healing center, which is named after that place
elixir	Ambrosia
giri valam	See pradakshina
gnana (jnana)	Enlightenment, wisdom, realization
Gnana (Jnani)	One who has achieved gnana
gnanendriyas	Sensory organs, organs of knowing
Goddess	The divine form of the feminine
Gunas	Qualities, or attributes, that arise from the Primordial Two
guru	Spiritual teacher; the literal meaning is "dispeller of darkness"
Hiranyagarbha	The universal womb, the cosmic dreamer
internal alchemy	Spiritual practices aimed at achieving enlightenment
Ishwara	God, cosmic deep sleeper
Jivan Mukti	Freedom from the circle of life, the highest state of spiritual enlightenment
Kaibaham Seibaham	A manual method of applying healing, it is also called Systemic Vital Point Therapy
kalaam	Rippling energy that has a specific effect
kalai	Specific
Kalpa house	A place where the rejuvenation process is conducted
Kamalatmika	An Indian tantric Goddess
kapha	The earth dosha, one of the three doshas, or biological humors
karma	Law of action and reaction; the binding force of action

karmendriyas	Organs of action, or grasping
Kaya Kalpa	A Siddha procedure for achieving physical rejuvenation and longevity
Kona Nilai	Angular link of Varma points
kosam	Body
kriya	Action
Kriya Sakthi	The power of activity
kundalini	Spiritual energy; the unrealized potential energy, the coiled energy, at the base of the body
left-hand/right-hand paths of tantra	The two styles of North Indian tantra
Lord Murugan	In Indian mythology, the younger son of Lord Siva
Maha Karana	The Universal causal body
Mahasamadhi	The demise of the body of a realized person
Mahabhutas	The primal elements of manifestation, of which there are five
Maha Prana	The primal creative energy, cosmic energy
Manomani	The Goddess of pristine mind in grandmother form
mantra	Syllables that bring stillness to the mind
maru kalam	The complementary nature of Varma points
mathirai	A measurement of pressure
mudra	Symbolic hand gesture; a hand gesture to channel energy in the practice of yoga
Muppu	universal medicine, or elixir
nadi	Energy channel in the body
Namaste	An Indian form of greeting
Navatri	A nine-night Indian Festival that pays homage to the goddesses

Nectar	Essence
Neruparu	River of fire
Nokku	Sight
pitta	The fire dosha, one of the three doshas, or biological humors
pradakshina	Circumambulation
prakrithi	In Siddha healing, the predominant constitution of a person's physical and mental makeup; the literal meaning is "firstborn"
Prakrithi	Cosmic substance, Primal substance; Sakthi Tattwa, the feminine aspect of the Primordial Two
prana	Life force, or functional physiological energy, one of the ten vital airs
pranayama	A form of yoga that is focused on the expansion of prana by breath regulation and breath exercises
pranic body	Also called the vital air sheath, consisting of the dasa vayu
Primordial Two	Siva and Sakthi
puja / pooja	Ritual worship
Purusha	Primal Spirit, Cosmic Spirit; Siva Tattwa, the masculine aspect of the Primordial Two
Raja Rajeshwari	An Indian goddess
rajas	Dynamic principle, attribute of nature
Rasa Siddha	A group of Siddhas that deal with alchemical science
rasyana	The path of Rasa, an Ayurvedic purification process
sadhana	Siddha spiritual practice
samadhi	Merging with Source
sangam	An ancient Tamil academy; Union

sattwa	Pure or ideally balanced; illumination as equilibrium
Sakthi Tattwa	the feminine aspect of the Primordial Two
Shakti	A goddess; the Universal power of consciousness
Sri Chakra	Symbolic composition or representation of the Universal power (Sakthi)
Skanda	Lord Murugan
Shyamala	One of the five goddesses of Siddha Tantra
Siddha	A person who abides in the natural state of consciousness
Siddha Varma healing	An ancient Siddha healing science based on the primal vitality residing in the human form
Siddha Vasi yoga	The core spiritual practice of Tamil Siddhas of Tamil nadu, primal pulsation (not pranayama)
Siddhahood	The art of living the perfected state
siddhi	divine ability, or supernatural Siddha power
Siva (Shiva)	God; pure consciousness
Siva Kalai	The poised state of rippling energy, the primordial pulsation of all life
Sivam	The Absolute, Consciousness, Self, God
Sri Vidya	Spiritual path for attaining realization by experiencing the archetypal feminine of the Universe
subtle body	One of the inner bodies, composed of the subtle aspect of the vital air sheath, the mental sheath, and the intellectual sheath
Surya kalai	Path of solar energy in the body, the back line of the energy channel in the human body
Suzhi Munai	The vortex at the end of the central channel in the body, the true agni chakra

Swabhava	A Siddha tantra aspirant's inherent character, or primal nature
swami	Holy man
Systemic Vital Point Therapy	Pal Pandian's English translation of the term Kaibaham Seibaham
tamas	The restraining quality of the three attributes in nature
Tamil	Language spoken by the people who live in Tamil Nadu, India
Tamil Siddhas	Ancient sages of Tamil Nadum India
tattwa	Principle of Cosmic evolution
Thiravukol	The realm of cosmic energy
thodu	Touch
Thodu Varma	One of the ninety-six secondary Varma points
tridosha	The three doshas as a collective
Tripura Sundari	A tantric Indian goddess in teenaged form
Turiya	The fourth state of consciousness, the transcendental state
Upasana	In Siddha Tantra, the worship of a prescribed personal deity
Valai	The goddess of learning, in child form
Valli	One of the two consorts of Lord Murugan, the earthly consort
Varma point	An energy junction in the human body (there are one-hundred-eight)
Varma Sastra	A Varma manuscript on the science of Varma healing
Vasanas	Subconscious patterns
Vasi	See Siva Kalai
Vasi yoga	See Siddha Vasi yoga

vata	The air dosha, one of the three doshas, or biological humors
Veda	Ancient spiritual knowledge revealed by the Aryan community
Vijaydasami	The tenth day of the Navaratri festival
Virat	The cosmic waker, who is omnipotent
viyadhi	Disease, disorder
Yantra	A geometrical symbol representing Sakthi; a geometric pattern of flow in Adangal
Yoga Sutras	A treatise, about ancient yoga
Yoga Vasistha	A Sanskrit manuscript of Sage Vasistha's teachings to Lord Rama
Yoga	A spiritual practice that gives exclusive importance to the faculty of dispassion; the literal meaning is "union"

Bibliography

Adams, Robert. "The Cow Lakshmi." In Narain, *Face to Face with Sri Ramana Maharshi*, 358–359.

Agasthiyar (Siddha Agasthiyar). "Antha Ranga Disksha Vidhi." In Pandian, *Siddhas: Masters of the Basics*.

"Amritbindu Upanishad," In Pandian, *Siddhas: Masters of the Basics*.

Bhagavan Ramana: The Friend of All. Tiruvannamali, India: Sri Ramanasramam, 2008.

Blake, William. *The Essential Blake*. Selected by Stanley Kunitz. New York: HarperCollins, 1987.

Bogar (Siddha Bogar). *Sapta Kandam 7000*. Chennai, India: Thamarai Noolagam, 2005.

Chadwick, Alan (Sadhu Arunachala). *The Call Divine*. March 1954.

Jung, Carl G. *Mysterium Coniunctionis*, Vol. 14 of *Collected Works of C.G. Jung*. Edited and Translated by Gerhard Adler and R.F.C. Hull. Princeton, NJ: Princeton University Press, 1970.

Kadanthar, Manavasagam (Saint Manavasagam Kadanthar). "Thiru Arut Payan." In Pandian, *Siddhas: Masters of the Basics.*

Keers, Wolter A. "Wolter A. Keers Was a Dutch Teacher and Writer Who Lectured on Yoga and Advaita in Europe." In Narain, *Face to Face with Sri Ramana Maharshi*, 196–200.

Khan, Darya. In Pandian, *Siddhas: Masters of the Basics.*

Maharshi, Bhagavan Sri Ramana. *Nan Yar* [Who Am I? The Teachings of Bhagavan Sri Ramana Maharshi]. Translated by T.M.P. Mahadevan. Tiruvannamalai, India: Sri Ramanasramam, n.d. Last accessed December 1, 2015, http://www.sriramanamaharshi.org/resource_centre/publications/who-am-i-books/.

Menon, M.M. "M.M. Menon Was from Palghat Kerala." In Narain, *Face to Face with Sri Ramana Maharshi*, 274.

Mudaliar, Natesa. (Sadhu Natanananda) "Sadhu Natanananda (Natesa Mudaliar) Was a Scholar Who Authored Many Books on Sri Ramana." In Narain, *Face to Face with Sri Ramana Maharshi*, 129–133.

Nagamma, Suri. *Letters from Sri Ramanasramam.* 5th ed. Tiruvannamalai, India: Sri Ramanasramam, 2006.

Narain, Laxmi. *Face to Face with Sri Ramana Maharshi.* Hyderabad, India: Sri Ramana Kendram, 2005.

Pandian, Pal. *Siddhas: Masters of the Basics.* Chennai, India: Pal Pandian, 2008.

Ramadevar (Siddha Ramadevar). "Siva Yogam." In Pandian, *Siddhas: Masters of the Basics.*

Rumi, Molana Jalal-e-Din Mohammad Molavi. *Rumi's Love Poems.* Edited by Maria-Magdalena Blidarus. Scribd website, last accessed December 1, 2015, http://www.scribd.com/doc/35453168/Rumi-Love-Poems#scribd.

Sattaimuni (Siddha Sattaimuni). In Pandian, *Siddhas: Masters of the Basics*.

Siddhar, Pampatti. "Songs of Pampatti Siddhar." In Pandian, *Siddhas: Masters of the Basics*.

Siddhar, Yugimuni. "Yugi Chintamani." In Pandian, *Siddhas: Masters of the Basics*.

Sundaranandar (Siddha Sundaranandar). "Siva Yoga Gnana." In Pandian, *Siddhas: Masters of the Basics*.

Thirumular (Siddha Thirumular). "Thirumanthiram." In Pandian, *Siddhas: Masters of the Basics*.

Thiruvalluvar (Siddha Thiruvalluvar). "Thiru Kural 339." In Pandian, *Siddhas: Masters of the Basics*.

Thoreau, Henry David. "Walking." *Atlantic Monthly* June 1862.

"Tiruvunthiar," Verse 14. In Pandian, *Siddhas: Masters of the Basics*.

Tzu, Lao. *Tao Te Ching*. Translated by Stephen Mitchell. London: Frances Lincoln, 1999.

Vakkiyar, Siva (Siddha Siva Vakkiyar). "Siva Vakkiyar Padakgal." In Pandian, *Siddhas: Masters of the Basics*.

Valmiki (Sage Valmiki). *The Supreme Yoga*. Translated by Swami Venkatesananda. Delhi: Chitern Yoga Trust, 2003.

Vasistha (Yoga Vasistha). In Valmiki, *The Supreme Yoga*.

Vilakkam, Unmai. "Exposition of Truth." In Pandian, *Siddhas: Masters of the Basics*.

Wordsworth, William. "The World Is Too Much with Us.
In *Great Short Poems*, edited by Paul Negri. Mineola, NY: Dover, 2000.

Yugimuni (Siddha Yugimuni). "Mathi Venba 100," Verse 8. In Pandian, *Siddhas: Masters of the Basics*.

Acknowledgements

The list of people to acknowledge and thank is very short. The reason is rather simple. Until the book was largely complete, I was asked to tell no one of its undertaking. It remained a secret love affair.

To my Teacher, Siddha Healer Pal Pandian, I wish to place my most profound gratitude before him. Having told me years prior that I would write on the *Tamil Siddhas,* he waited patiently for me to mature. Once I was sufficient in ripeness, he reminded me of his wish. The loving guidance incessantly flowed from him until I was able to find some ability to communicate in written form. His graceful wisdom he boundlessly shares with me like father to child. It is the source of all the words within. His Divine spirit remains my sole refuge. *Appakku Pillai Adakkam.*

The only other one who had knowledge of this work is Pal's life partner Amrita, and to her I am immensely grateful. She is not a woman to mince words. I like this type of person very much, as it matches my own nature. This manner of interacting with me was essential, for I am no author. Her influence allowed the writings to become readable. Entire chapters were to be discarded. My natural tendency to ramble? She let me know what to do with that.

Once the time came to find an editor, the search led me to Stuart Horwitz, Founder and Principal of Book Architecture. He had his work cut out for him as the manuscript was still in a very rough format. Not only editing was required. Instead, Stuart patiently set about teaching me how to organize the material into a format that began to resemble a book that could be enjoyed. Truthfully, Stuart had to teach me how to write and find a voice where all the material would make sense. His guidance and organizing skills led me through every phase needed to easily navigate the maze of proofreading, editing, interior design, and publishing. For his encouragement, patience, and expertise, I am eternally grateful.

When the copyediting phase came about, it was Stuart who recommended Louann Pope. The work she was given would have been a headache for any editor simply based upon the nature of the material involved, however, I suspect my stubbornness complicated her job significantly. Coupled with a very short time frame within which to complete it all, she was given a difficult task, yet her diligence and attitude in working with me helped to move the process along with perfect timing. I wish to extend my sincerest thanks to her and hold her work in the highest regard. Always professional and courteous with me, her zeal for impeccable editing is a testament to both herself and editors everywhere.

The design, layout, cover, visuals, proofreading and overall experience of the book has been expertly crafted by the team at 1106 Design. Recommended by Stuart, it did not take long for me to understand his deep faith in them. Ronda, Michele and the whole team literally walked me through each and every phase with the kindest patience and loving attention to detail I could have ever imagined. This they performed despite my naive assumptions and occasional demands that, in retrospect, were practically unreasonable. Their kindness, expertise and uplifting guidance allowed for the writing to manifest as the book.

About the Author

Siddha Healer Pal Pandian and Steve

Steve is a longtime student of Siddha Healer Pal Pandian. He is the founder of the first Siddha Varma Healing Center in America and has been awarded a BSS degree by the government of India in Varma and Yoga instruction. A devotee of Bhagavan

Sri Ramana Maharshi, Shirdi Sai Baba, the Tamil Siddhas, and the holy hill Arunachala, he makes regular visits to Tiruvannamalai, India, where his time is spent with his guru, Healer Pal. He currently resides in Florida, USA, where he attends to those who suffer from physical and emotional disorders with Pal's spiritual healing methods known as Vasi Healing. Steve also gives lectures and seminars on the Siddha dimensions of healing, tantra, and the yoga of Siddha alchemy.

    Steve can be reached at:
        siddhavasihealing.com
        steve@siddhavasihealing.com
        Facebook—Siddha Vasi Healing
        A list of Healer Pal's students and their contact information can be found at: healingsiddhas.com

For those sincerely interested in Siddha spiritual instruction:
        aswatha2008@gmail.com

www.ingramcontent.com/pod-product-compliance
Lightning Source LLC
Chambersburg PA
CBHW021114300426.
44113CB00006B/145